Metaphysics
as
Rhetoric

SUNY SERIES IN MIDDLE EASTERN STUDIES
Shahrough Akhavi, editor

Metaphysics as Rhetoric

Alfarabi's *Summary of Plato's "Laws"*

JOSHUA PARENS

STATE UNIVERSITY
OF NEW YORK PRESS

Published by
State University of New York Press, Albany

Printed in the United States of America

For information, address State University of New York Press, State University Plaza, Albany, NY 12246

Production by Bernadine Dawes • Marketing by Dana Yanulavich

Library of Congress Cataloging-in-Publication Data

Parens, Joshua, 1961-
Metaphysics as rhetoric : Alfarabi's Summary of Plato's "Laws" / Joshua Parens.
p. cm. – (SUNY series in Middle Eastern studies)
Includes bibliographical references and index.
ISBN 0-7914-2573-8 (HC : alk. paper). – ISBN 0-7914-2574-6 (PB : alk. paper)
1. Plato. Laws. 2. Plato–Contributions in political science. 3. Fārābī. Talkhīṣ Nawāmīs Aflāṭūn. 4. Fārābī–Contributions in political science. I. Title. II. Series.
JC71.P264P37 1995
321'.07–dc20 94-49027
CIP

10 9 8 7 6 5 4 3 2 1

To Ralph Lerner

CONTENTS

PREFACE

Postmodernists claim that Western thought has struggled throughout its history to ground human action on reason.[1] Ever since Plato, philosophers have dreamed of the rule of philosophy or reason. Above all, philosophers imagined they could replace the myths of their various societies with a demonstrative account of the whole, and that on this metaphysical foundation, they could raise a rational society with rational laws. The Enlightenment at its most ambitious seemed to harbor the hope of eliminating religion, belief, or commitment from political life and replacing it with a rational, secular foundation. Plato, however, was never so ambitious. His lack of ambition derived from a healthy respect for both the claims of religion and the limits of politics. This respect in turn enabled him to take the claims of belief or commitment more seriously than Enlightenment thinkers did. The limitations of the Enlightenment attack on religious belief seem to have given rise to the postmodernist revival of commitment, if not religious belief. Because Plato's approach to the relation of religion and politics lacks these limitations, the postmodernist attempt to extend their critique of (modern) rationalism to Plato is misguided.

Postmodernists accuse Plato of initiating the history of Western metaphysics. According to Heidegger—one of the leading sources of postmodernism—first there was Plato's *idea* as metaphysical ground, then Aristotle's *energeia*, . . . and, finally, Nietzsche's will.[2] Heidegger claims to have at least initiated an overcoming of this history. Unlike Hegel, who portrays it as an ascent toward absolute knowledge of Being, Heidegger portrays it as a descent toward an ever-increasing forgetfulness of Being, a forgetfulness that poses a great threat to human being. According to Heidegger, however, precisely in such times of increased danger the resources for salvation can be found.

My purpose is not to refute Heidegger's presentation of the whole history of metaphysics. Indeed, I believe there is some truth to the claim that we have become forgetful of Being. Rather, I wish to show that Plato was not the founder of metaphysics that Heidegger claims he was and that his analysis of action escapes the postmodernist critique.

In this study, I turn to a tenth-century Muslim philosopher, Alfarabi, because the view of Plato he presents is altogether different from the view of Plato that Heidegger inherited from the Western Christian tradition. For example, in his *Philosophy of Plato,* Alfarabi describes a Plato who has nothing to say about the Ideas. Above all, Alfarabi's Plato engages in an inquiry into political phenomena without metaphysical presuppositions. One could even say, speaking anachronistically, that his approach to politics is phenomenological. In this respect, he shares more with Heidegger than he does with the metaphysical tradition that Heidegger claims Plato founded.

Before moving forward with a description of Alfarabi's Plato and his ironic similarities to Heidegger, it is necessary to clarify what Heidegger means by metaphysics and how he views himself as departing from its history. Its primary meaning is the inquiry into being *qua* being–what Scholasticism referred to as *metaphysica generalis.* Although Heidegger claims to be overcoming the metaphysical tradition, he does not claim that he is overcoming the question of being *qua* being. On the contrary, when he refers in his earlier writings–for instance, his magnum opus, *Being and Time*–to "fundamental ontology" he has in mind precisely this question;[3] in his later writings, he abandons this terminology because it seems to have misled readers into thinking that he was still part of the history of metaphysics or, in other words, still looking for the ground or cause of all things. Instead, he uses phrases such as "the question of Being."[4]

Rather than criticize the tradition for asking the question of Being, Heidegger criticizes it for the answers it has given and how it arrives at these answers. From the very beginning, its methods and answers have led to a forgetfulness of Being rather than to a continuing openness to the question of Being. The most profound indicator of this forgetfulness is what he describes as the confusion of Being with beings.[5] In his *Kant and the Problem of Metaphysics,* Heidegger describes one of the manifestations of this confusion. The question of Being had from the very beginnings of ancient philosophy, even prior to Plato and Aristotle, been a dual question. It concerned "knowledge of beings as beings" and also "knowledge of the most remarkable region of beings." Eventually, in Scholasticism, the question of being *qua* being or *metaphysica generalis* came to be overshadowed by the question of the most remarkable region of beings or *metaphysica specialis* (which traditionally encompassed psychology and cosmology but referred, above all, to theology).

To my knowledge, the most obvious manifestation of the ascendant role of *metaphysica specialis* in Scholasticism was the centrality of the search for the definitive proof of God's existence in thinkers from Anselm to Thomas. By the time Kant entered into the history of metaphysics, *metaphysica specialis* would come to be viewed as the "authentic metaphysics."[6]

The most significant result of this predominance of *metaphysica specialis* was that Being came to be understood as a being, even if the highest being. For Heidegger, however, Being is not a being–not even God. Because the medieval Christian tradition viewed the eternal God as the highest manifestation of Being, however, for it Being came to be identified with the permanent, the unchanging, or with "presence" (*parousia*). Heidegger calls for a new approach to the meaning of Being. Traditional *metaphysica generalis* was defined and delimited by its ascendant partner, *metaphysica specialis.* Because Heidegger denies the ascendant role and even the validity of traditional *metaphysica specialis,* his approach to the Being question must be wholly different from traditional *metaphysica generalis.* Rather than orient his questioning toward God (whom, of course, Nietzsche has pronounced dead), Heidegger hopes to reorient it toward the questioner, human being.[7] Traditionally, human being (and Being) was understood vis-à-vis the eternity of God. Consequently, the essence of human being was thought to be divine contemplation or theory. Heidegger reorients his questioning about Being toward human finitude; Being is understood, above all, vis-à-vis human action.[8] To draw out the effects of this reorientation I turn to the following contrast Heidegger draws between modern metaphysics and his own view: For modern metaphysical thinkers such as Kant and Descartes, such unchanging theoretical constructs as geometric space and an eternal temporal succession of nows make possible or are the grounds of human experience. For Heidegger, human beings experience the world most primordially through a finite temporality shaped not by theory but by the fact that human beings are always already being-towards-death. Any and all theoretical interpretations of the world are less primordial than (if not derived from) this lived experience of human existence as finite.[9]

If these reasons why Heidegger focuses on human action are kept in mind, we may begin to compare his approach to Alfarabi's in a fruitful manner. At first, it might appear that Alfarabi, like the Scholastics, is forgetful of *metaphysica generalis* or the Being question. Indeed, the Being question is not writ large on every page of Alfarabi as it is on every page of Heidegger. But while, it might appear that Alfarabi focuses on *metaphysica specialis* or theology at the expense of *metaphysica generalis,* this appearance is deceptive. Although he is concerned with theology, he is not concerned to provide proofs of God's existence. Rather, he is concerned with the political role that theology plays. He pursues theology not with an eye to providing a demonstrative ground for politics. Far from serving as a ground, his theology is a rhetorical *defense* of his politics. Perhaps Alfarabi's particular kind of concern with *metaphysica specialis* distinguishes him from Heidegger's history of metaphysics.

Alfarabi's Plato begins, like Heidegger, not with the eternal (Ideas) but with the merely human. Furthermore, rather than begin with contemplation, Plato also begins with human action. Heidegger and Plato approach human action from a different perspective, however. Heidegger focuses first and foremost on our most everyday experiences, for example, the swinging of a hammer.[10] Surprisingly, through these humblest and most immediate forms of experience, we gain access to our being-towards-death or our finitude. Heidegger's purpose in beginning with these forms of action is to gain access to Being unmediated by metaphysical presuppositions. In contrast, Alfarabi's Plato focuses first and foremost on *political* action. In other words, he focuses on what, at least in his time, was perhaps the least humble form of action.[11]

Historical differences, no doubt, play an important role in Alfarabi's and Heidegger's differences of focus. Alfarabi's Plato lived in a world permeated by politics; Heidegger's world as well as ours distinguishes between state and society or public and private. The state is distant from us and our immediate, private experiences. Thus, it is understandable that Heidegger focuses on immediate and humble action rather than politics. The question remains, however, whether this focus precludes him from gaining a full understanding of less-humble political action. Can one understand less-humble forms of action in terms of more-humble forms?

The separation between state and society, which led to Heidegger's neglect of politics, was the product of the Enlightenment attempt to separate politics and religion–the state being the public realm of politics and society the realm of religion and other private matters. Today, society has come to be viewed as the real locus of human experience. This realm is filled with personal, religious, cultural, and social commitments. In contrast, the state is viewed more and more as a neutral realm of administration. The Western positivistic view that the only scientifically relevant matters are facts rather than values and that the highest manifestation of political rationality is bureaucratic order has contributed to the conviction that politics is cold, neutral, and free of commitments or beliefs.[12] Heidegger, despite his profound critique of positivism, is struck with the positivist's blindness to the role of belief in politics (as opposed to social life).[13]

Because Alfarabi lived in a medieval community that made no claims to separate religion and politics, he was more attuned than we are to the role that beliefs or commitments play in politics. No doubt, postmodernists will balk at my including commitments together with beliefs. Postmodernists (precisely as post-*modernists* or the antithesis of *modern* rationalists) inadvertently share some Enlightenment prejudices, for instance, its hatred of religion and its view that the Middle Ages were the "Dark Ages." Unfortunately, these prejudices prevent them from recognizing the kinship between the commitments they themselves champion and the medieval beliefs they despise. I believe that postmodernists would do well to leave aside these prejudices, because they, like Heidegger and the rest of us, could learn a great deal from Alfarabi and Plato about matters to which we have all grown oblivious–above all, the role that beliefs play in politics.

To repeat, Alfarabi's Plato, like Heidegger, is in a crucial sense phenomenological. To understand political things, Plato inquires into the things themselves without metaphysical presuppositions. In the *Summary* these things are the commonly accepted opinions about divine law and its origins. The *Laws* opens with the question: Who causes the laws? Insofar as the laws are divine, the most obvious and just answer is that the laws are caused by the god. But matters prove more complicated. Not only a god but also a semidivine hero is a cause. Having begun at inconclusive theological heights, the conversation between the Athenian Stranger and his Cretan and Lacedaemonian interlocutors descends to the question, What is the purpose of the laws? Only through an inquiry into the purpose or final cause of the laws will they arrive at an answer about their maker or efficient cause. The bulk of the *Laws* is devoted to the former investigation. The ultimate conclusion will be that their purpose is to teach the citizens how properly to honor their souls. The highest purpose is not, as one might expect, theological but psychological. If human beings prove capable of determining how to honor their souls, then they will be the makers of their own laws. There is, however, something divine about this capability. Few people are capable of being true doctors of the soul. Laws alone are not capable of teaching what the soul's health is, because they are concerned first and foremost with the body. Obedience to the laws is indispensable to the well-being of the city and the body, and their well-being in turn is indispensable to that of the soul. Alfarabi's Plato supplements the laws proper with an art of rhetoric regarding the gods that persuades citizens to obey the laws. This supplement is placed before the law in the form of preludes. According to Alfarabi, the preludes also contain dialectical arguments that lead the virtuous to inquire into the health of their own souls.

Although the preludes provide the laws with theological support, this theology is intended as a rhetorical argument rather than as a demonstrative metaphysical foundation. If the Athenian Stranger's laws have any foundation, they are psychological. Although the soul is in a sense the foundation of the laws, it is not a metaphysical foundation because, for Plato, the human soul is not also the foundation of the whole as, for instance, the Ego is for Descartes. The soul cannot be such a foundation because the human things are different in kind from the natural whole. In contrast, the Christian natural law tradition, like revealed religion, assumes that the human things may be derived from a (metaphysical) account of the whole: Thomas derives his natural (political) law from his eternal (metaphysical) law.

What need is there for a theology such as the Athenian Stranger lays down? The soul's economy depends upon it. According to the Stranger, human beings desire "to have things happen in accordance with the commands of [their] own soul—preferably all things, but if not that, then at least the human things." Our desire for command derives from our frustration at our own inability to know the whole. This desire for command leads us to pray. We pray with a view to persuading the power who rules the whole to order the whole in accordance with the vision we have of it. Without such a theology, human beings would not engage in spirited action for fear that their actions would not be justly rewarded. In contrast, human health requires the recognition of our inadequate knowledge of the whole and of the need to continue the pursuit of such knowledge. The life in pursuit of such knowledge is philosophy. Political action, however, cannot await such health. It requires some basis for spirited action: a theology. Not any theology, however, will do. Theologies that promise that God will deliver all of one's enemies into one's hands either raise irrational hopes or weaken resolve. From this it is not difficult to infer what kind of theology is most fitting. In conclusion, according to Alfarabi, Plato's account of politics cannot be inferred from metaphysical foundations. On the contrary, matters are the reverse: his theology may be inferred from his politics.

If I am correct that Alfarabi's Plato inquires into the political phenomena themselves without the crutch of metaphysical assumptions, then Heidegger is wrong in tracing metaphysics back to Plato. Furthermore, if I am correct, rationalism as such does not need the Heideggerian corrective. Rather, the natural law tradition, because it is responsible for originating such dogmatism, may need such a corrective. My task will be to describe an alternative to Heidegger's analysis of human action—one that begins not with the more humble forms of action but with the less humble ones. Because we live in a time in which politics or the state is so remote from us, it is useful to turn to Alfarabi's Plato, for whom politics is immediate. We will turn to Alfarabi with confidence that as a member of a community ruled by divine law, he will not ignore the crucial influence that belief has on politics in Plato's thought. As members of a community in which belief has a way of concealing itself, we have much to gain from the study of Alfarabi's Plato.

ACKNOWLEDGMENTS

I dedicate this book to Ralph Lerner for cultivating in me a love of the forgotten art of *kalâm*, an art whose importance will become apparent in the following pages. More generally, I am grateful to him for doing so much as a teacher to enhance my strengths as a scholar and a writer. Finally, I appreciate his care and discernment in reading earlier versions of this book.

I am grateful to Nathan Tarcov for his attentive readings of earlier versions of this book. And I am indebted to him for offering a graduate course at the University of Chicago on Plato's *Laws* and Alfarabi's *Summary*, which he taught along with Hillel Fradkin and Ralph Lerner. One of Tarcov's leading themes for that course was that over the course of the *Laws* the Athenian Stranger bows more and more to the demands made on cities by war, and less and less to the demands made by philosophy. This argument has become part of the very fabric of this book.

I owe a great deal to Muhsin Mahdi for taking me under his wing during a year at Harvard while I finished up an earlier version of this book. The influence on me of his pathbreaking writings on Alfarabi is evident on nearly every page. I am also deeply grateful for his painstaking care in reading and suggesting revisions for earlier versions of this book.

I want to thank Hillel Fradkin for a course he offered at the University of Chicago on Maimonides' *Eight Chapters*. The theme of that course was the health of the soul, which is also the central theme of this book, and especially of part three. This book owes a great deal to Fradkin's treatment of that theme. I am grateful to Charles Butterworth for having fostered my interest in medieval

Islamic political philosophy since I took my first course with him on the subject in 1986. I am especially appreciative of the care with which he has read and the support he has given to my research over the years.

I want to thank the Mellon Foundation for the support it gave me while writing an earlier version of this book in 1991–92. I also want to thank the Carthage Foundation for enabling me to revise the preface and chapter one of this book in 1992–93. And I appreciate the extreme care Jerry Weinberger took in suggesting revisions of a much earlier version of the preface. I am pleased to thank the Moshe Dayan Center for Middle Eastern and African Studies of Tel Aviv University, the Lynde and Harry Bradley Foundation, Joel Kraemer, and Asher Susser for giving me the opportunity to revise this book in 1993–94. And I thank the Department of Government of Georgetown University, (once again) the Bradley Foundation, and Walter Berns for enabling me to copyedit and proofread the final drafts of this book in 1994–95.

HarperCollins Publishers has granted me permission to reprint words and phrases from Thomas Pangle's translation *The Laws of Plato*, originally published in 1980 by Basic Books (now a division of HarperCollins), and now reprinted by the University of Chicago Press, 1988. It is an honor to thank Muhsin Mahdi for allowing me to reprint words and phrases from his unpublished translation of Alfarabi's *Summary*, which should be forthcoming in the revised edition of *Medieval Political Philosophy* by Ralph Lerner and Muhsin Mahdi. And I am grateful to Thérèse-Anne Druart for allowing me to reprint words and phrases from her critical Arabic edition of the *Summary*, forthcoming in *Bulletin d'Études Orientales* (Damascus), 47 (1995). Finally, I thank the *American Political Science Review* for allowing me to reprint passages from my March 1994 article, "Multiculturalism and the Problem of Particularism."

INTRODUCTION

1. The uniqueness of the Summary of Plato's "Laws"

Until the nineteenth century, with the exception of Galen's lost compendium no commentary was written on the *Laws* except for Alfarabi's *Summary*. Works by Aristotle and Cicero addressed the *Laws* but were by no means commentaries. The Platonic corpus was lost to the Christian West until the Neoplatonic revival of the study of Plato in Renaissance Italy. For reasons that will become apparent in later chapters, the *Laws* appears to have held no interest for these Neoplatonists, just as it seems to have held none for Plotinus and his followers.

The *Summary*, then, is unique. As Muhsin Mahdi has noted, it is "the only commentary by a Muslim author on a Platonic writing of which we possess the original Arabic text."[1] Moreover, the *Summary* is the only commentary on the *Laws* prior to the nineteenth century of which we have a full text. At present we possess only one very brief fragment of Galen's "Synopsis of the *Laws*," the fourth and last treatise of his *Synopses of Plato's Works*.[2]

Aristotle briefly comments directly on the *Laws* in his *Politics* in bk. 2, chap. 6 (1265a1–1266a3) (as well as, on occasion in other passages, such as 1274b8–15). I say that Aristotle commented "directly" in these passages because I believe that much of the *Politics* is, at least to some extent, his indirect response to the *Laws*; however, as his choice to write the *Politics* rather than a commentary on the *Laws* indicates, Aristotle disagrees at least with the emphasis of the *Laws*. He criticizes the *Laws* for dealing mainly with the laws rather than the regime (*politeia*). The *Politics*, as one might expect from its title, deals mainly with the regime. Aristotle is far less interested in law, not to mention divine law, than are Plato and Alfarabi.

Cicero does not present his own *Laws* as a commentary on Plato's *Laws*. Nevertheless, Cicero's *Laws* comes closer to being a commentary on Plato's *Laws* than does his *Republic* to being a commentary on Plato's *Republic*. As Cicero explains in his *Republic* (2.52), the city described therein is "actually possible" in contrast to the city in Plato's *Republic*, which is merely "to be desired rather than hoped for." Cicero's *Republic* describes the "regime" of the best politically possible city, and his *Laws* describes the laws of this same city. Thus, Cicero is able to present his *Laws* as a sequel to his *Republic*. In contrast, because Plato's *Laws* is his account of the best politically possible city and his *Republic* is his account of the best city simply, his *Laws* cannot be construed as a mere sequel to his *Republic*.

Cicero proceeds in his *Republic* and *Laws* as if he took Aristotle's criticism of Plato's *Laws*—that it fails to deal sufficiently with the regime of the city—seriously enough that he decided to write two books about the two fundamental aspects of the same (best politically possible) city, namely, its regime and laws. Because Plato's *Laws*, as opposed to his *Republic*, presents his best politically possible city, one could say that both Cicero's *Republic* and *Laws* are commentaries of a sort on Plato's *Laws*. No doubt one could benefit greatly from a comparison of Cicero's *Laws* and *Republic* with Plato's *Laws*.

Cicero in his *Laws* and Alfarabi in his *Summary* share one important thing in common: Each of them adapts the Platonic political teaching of the *Laws* to his own time and place. Although the *Summary* is a commentary on the *Laws*, Cicero's *Laws* is more of an imitation of Plato's. One reason why the *Summary* is less of an imitation than a commentary is that one of Alfarabi's leading methods of commenting on the *Laws* is to omit reference to subjects discussed by Plato. In contrast, the subjects omitted by Alfarabi appear prominently in Cicero's *Laws*.[3] Alfarabi says his purpose is, to reveal Plato's intention; Cicero's purpose is to reproduce the effects of Plato's intention. Of course, such a reproduction in a different time and place is possible only if one understands the intention behind them. Although Cicero and Alfarabi need the same understanding of the *Laws*, the latter has chosen to communicate this knowledge more directly.

Other than the indirect treatments of the *Laws* in Aristotle's *Politics* and Cicero's *Laws* and the lost compendium by Galen, we have only fragmentary quotations of the *Laws*. In the Muslim tradition, we have al-Bîrûnî's highly fragmentary yet accurate quotations in Arabic.[4] É. des Places has collected the quotations in the Christian (and pagan) tradition for the first six books of the *Laws* in his "La tradition indirecte des *Lois* de Platon (livres 1-6)." Des Places detects the emergence of an interesting pattern: Leaving aside the great diversity of brief passages quoted, there is one passage that is without compare in the frequency with which both pagan and Christian authors quote it: the passage on "God and justice" at 715e7-716a3.[5] As I indicated in note 3, this passage is conspicuously absent from Alfarabi's *Summary*. Alfarabi's understanding of the divine character of the *Laws* differs from the traditional understanding.

With these reasons for believing that Alfarabi is uniquely positioned to be our guide to the *Laws*, the question arises as to why so little attention has been given to his *Summary*. The first modern edition of the Arabic text of the *Summary* appeared in 1952. It should have been of much interest to both Plato scholars and Arabists. Plato scholars in general should have given it their attention because, to my knowledge, it is the sole extant premodern commentary on the *Laws*. Their inattention, however, is understandable, because Plato scholars very rarely read Arabic and therefore rely upon Arabists to give them access to such a text. The inattention of Arabists is more difficult to understand, because the *Summary* is the sole commentary on Plato's *Laws* by a Muslim philosopher. Although it is widely acknowledged that Plato exerted a profound influence on Alfarabi's political philosophy, those Arabists who acknowledge Plato's influence usually limit this influence to the peculiarly Platonic conception of the philosopher-king. In other words, Plato's influence is usually equated with the influence of his *Republic* or rather with the influence of a central "doctrine" of his *Republic*. But Islam is a revealed religion in which the divine law is central, and it is Plato's *Laws* rather than his *Republic* that contains his discussion of divine law. One would therefore expect the *Laws* to have had an even greater bearing than the *Republic* on medieval Islam. Avicenna gives evidence in his *On the Divisions of the Rational Sciences* that the *Laws* was viewed this way by the Muslim philosophers.[6] In view of these facts, the neglect of the *Summary* by Arabists is initially perplexing.

A perusal of two of the half-dozen reviews of the 1952 edition of the *Summary* will give us a better idea as to why it has suffered such neglect both by Plato scholars and Arabists.[7] According to W. Montgomery Watt's 1953 review, "While al-Fârâbî neglects many Platonic doctrines and misinterprets some, there are a suprisingly large number which he correctly reproduces. This book will not contribute to our knowledge of Plato's views, but it is an important source for any one assessing the extent of Greek influence on the Arabic philosophers and particularly on al-Fârâbî."[8] According to this leading Arabist, the *Summary* deserves little attention because Alfarabi's grasp of Plato is tenuous at best. Yet objections to this can be raised. On the one hand, Watt assures us that Alfarabi combines faithful reproduction of certain "Platonic doctrines" with misinterpretation of others. On the other hand, he assures us that we have nothing to learn from Alfarabi. Only if we know what Plato's doctrines are, could we determine that Alfarabi misinterprets certain "Platonic doctrines." If we know what Plato's doctrines are, then why should we expect to learn anything from Alfarabi about Plato's teaching? There is reason to doubt Watt's assumption that we have a sufficient knowledge of what Plato's doctrines are to judge whether Alfarabi misinterprets the *Laws*. What I mean can best be understood by looking at another review.

In his 1955 review, S. M. Stern says the following: "The present little 'Compendium of the Laws,' of some forty pages, gives an extremely imperfect rendering of the contents of [the *Laws*]. Here and there some ideas seem to have been rightly understood, sometimes the cause of the erroneous translation can be traced, but there are passages that are quite baffling and do not seem to refer to anything in the Greek original."[9] I assume that what Stern means by "passages that are quite baffling"–though it appears in the context of a far less charitable overall assessment of the *Summary* than Watt's–is what Watt means by "misinterpretations of Platonic doctrine." Passages are baffling, according to Stern, when they do not reproduce the "Greek original." Presumably, Watt would also maintain that Alfarabi misinterprets Platonic doctrine, when he fails to reproduce the Greek original. Both Stern and Watt assume that the Platonic teaching is easily found in the mouth of one or the other of the participants of his dialogue. A good interpretation of the *Laws* would therefore merely reproduce the arguments of the participants in the dialogue–as if Plato could have written treatises and chose perhaps as a stylistic whim to write in the dialogue form. The view that Plato's characters are his spokesmen might be an acceptable assumption, if Alfarabi himself did not indicate otherwise in his introduction to the *Summary*. Neither Watt nor Stern has taken seriously Alfarabi's guidance about how to read Plato's dialogues.

Watt has noticed Alfarabi's rather striking introduction and says, "After an introduction in which he explains how Plato, though usually speaking symbolically, sometimes speaks plainly, and therefore is difficult to interpret, al-Fârâbî gives a summary, book by book, of the first nine books of the *Laws*." But to say that Plato usually speaks symbolically does not merely mean that Plato's dialogues are "difficult to interpret." It means that reproducing the arguments of interlocutors is not reproducing Plato's meaning but reproducing Plato's "symbols." Because Plato usually does not "speak plainly," only rarely would reproducing the argument of a Platonic character reproduce Plato's meaning. It is apparent that we must understand more about how Alfarabi reads Plato before we may conclude, as Watt does, that we have nothing to learn from the *Summary* about Plato's teaching. If we conclude that we may learn something about the *Laws* by reading the *Summary* in conjunction with it, then we will have more incentive for reading the *Summary* than the mere antiquarian reason Watt left us with, namely, "assessing the extent of Greek influence on the Arabic philosophers and particularly on al-Fârâbî."

2. *Alfarabi's unmethodical method of reading Plato*

Let us turn now to Alfarabi's introduction in which he discusses how to read Plato. Alfarabi notes that human beings discern between the useful and the useless on the basis of experience. Human beings reflect upon particular events and infer from the various particular events certain universal characteristics. Of course, the more experiences one has, the more one is able to infer universal characteristics correctly. But individuals may misjudge experiences and therefore infer universals from them incorrectly. In this case, quantity of experience, of course, does not make up for poor "judgment" (*ḥukm*). The wise (*ḥukamâ'*) are those who have had "experiences that are true and valid." The wise possess a more accurate judgment of the experiences they have. Not only are the ignorant poorer at judging the experiences they have, but they also infer universals from particulars prematurely. They infer that something always happens in the way it has happened to them on a few occasions. Alfarabi provides two examples of incorrect universalization on the basis of limited experience. First, people infer from the fact that someone has told the truth or told a lie on one, two, or more occasions that that person always tells the truth or always lies. Second, people infer from the fact that they have seen someone act in a courageous or cowardly manner on a number of occasions that that person is a courageous or cowardly person. People hasten to make universal judgments on the basis of limited experience of both the words and the deeds of other people.

Not only do the wise recognize that most people are disposed to make such premature judgments, but they also take advantage of this disposition by repeatedly acting in certain ways so that they will acquire the reputation for always acting in such ways. In the course of his analysis of the difference between the judgment of the wise and of most people, Alfarabi does not say why the wise might feel the need to make use of most people's disposition to make premature judgments. Consequently, when Alfarabi turns abruptly from this rather scientific analysis to an enchanting analogy about an ascetic who is compelled to lie in deed because of fear for his life, we cannot help but search the analogy for clues as to why the wise might feel the need to mislead most people.

Alfarabi's abstemious ascetic (*ba'ḍ al-zuhhâd al-mutaqashshifîn*) was widely known in his city for his probity (*ṣalâḥ*), propriety (*sadâd),* asceticism (*zuhd),* and worship (*'ibâdah*). As Alfarabi's redundancy about the asceticism of the ascetic indicates, he was an exemplary ascetic. No explicit reason is given for his flight from the city, but it appears that his extreme asceticism made him popular among the people, and thus a threat to the tyrant who ruled his city. Realizing that he could not escape through the gates of the city undisguised, the ascetic donned the garb of a vagabond. He approached the gate in the early evening, acting like a drunk and singing to the accompaniment of his own cymbal. When the gatekeeper asked him who he was, he replied jokingly that he was so-and-so the ascetic. Comparing his words with his deeds, the gatekeeper concluded that he was just making fun of him, and he allowed him to pass out of the city unharmed. Although the ascetic avoided lying in speech, he lied in deed.

With Alfarabi's guidance let us begin analyzing this analogy between the ascetic and the wise human being. The wise Plato employed symbols (*ramz*), riddles (*alghâz*), obscurity (*ta'miyyah*), and difficulty (*taṣ'īb*) frequently enough that he came to be widely known for employing these devices. Just as the ascetic became known for his probity, propriety, asceticism, and worship, so Plato became known for his symbols, riddles, obscurity, and difficulty. Most people inferred from their limited experience of these qualities of the ascetic that he always acted in this manner. Similarly, most people inferred from their limited experience of Plato's writings that he always employed symbols. Thus, Plato made it possible for himself to state things openly and literally on occasion because most people would assume that he was speaking symbolically.

I still have not established why Plato, like other wise human beings, might feel the need to mislead most people. According to Alfarabi, Plato uses symbols and other devices to prevent "knowledge" or science (*'ilm*) from falling "into the hands of those who do not deserve it [*ilâ ghayr ahlihi*] and [from] be[ing] deformed [*yatabaddal*], or [from] fall[ing] into the hands of someone who does not know its worth [*man lâ ya'rifu qadrahu*] or who uses it improperly [*aw yasta'milu fī ghayr mawḍi'ihi*]." As a master of logic, Alfarabi recognizes the limits of analogies. As a nondemonstrative form of argument, the analogy necessarily contains certain inconsistencies between the analogy and that to which the analogy is drawn. The thinker who is able to reason logically is capable of making use of both the consistencies and inconsistencies between the analogy and that to which the analogy is being drawn. The ascetic established a reputation for probity, and so forth. It was as a result of this reputation that he came to fear that the tyrant might take away his life. In contrast, Plato established a reputation for the use of symbols. There is no evidence that he came to fear persecution as a result of his reputation for using symbols. On the contrary, his use of symbols, unlike the probity of the ascetic, was cultivated from the start as a way of protecting science. The ascetic lacks the foresight in the cultivation of his reputation that Plato possesses. Furthermore, the ascetic cultivates a reputation for probity, a moral quality from which he must deviate, even if only in deed, to save his life. But Plato cultivates a reputation for the quality of secretiveness, and any deviation from it toward openness is not a moral deviation, or at least not a deviation in the direction of immorality. Both the ascetic and Plato employ deception, but whereas the ascetic contradicts his own principle of action, Plato does not.[10]

Plato protects science in two ways: first, by presenting science indirectly through symbols and riddles; second, by cultivating the reputation for the use of these devices so that he can present science openly and literally on occasion but be misinterpreted as presenting it symbolically. Perhaps Plato needs to express science directly on occasion, so that the attentive reader might have a ready means of access to science not provided by symbols. Plato is said to prevent science from, first, falling into the hands of those who do not deserve it because they might deform it; second, falling into the hands of someone who does not know its worth; and third, falling into the hands of someone who uses it improperly. Some people possess an insufficient grasp of knowledge and therefore are incapable of conveying it to others in anything other than a deformed state. Other people may possess knowledge of something but do not recognize the worth of that knowledge. They in turn give others, who are not worthy of it, free and easy access to this knowledge. Yet other people may possess knowledge of something without knowing how to use that knowledge. These people run the risk both of using their knowledge improperly themselves and of teaching others how to misuse this knowledge.

Because Alfarabi provides persuasive arguments in favor of Plato's concealment of the sciences and he never denies the need to conceal them, I assume that he also engages in such concealment.

Having now nearly completed my analysis of Alfarabi's instructions about how to read Plato's dialogues, I recall the criticisms of Watt and Stern, the reviewers of the 1952 edition of the *Summary.* These two reviewers seemed to agree that when Alfarabi fails to reproduce the speech of one or the other speaker in the *Laws* he is misinterpreting the text. If Plato presents his own views most frequently by means of symbols and riddles, however, would it not be more proper to say, on the contrary, that merely to reproduce the speech of a participant in the dialogue is usually to misinterpret Plato's meaning? Alfarabi often does not reproduce the Greek original, because it does not reveal Plato's meaning on its surface. Because these reviewers failed to attend to Alfarabi's instructions about how to read Plato, they were driven to despair about the *Summary*'s usefulness.

According to Alfarabi, the *Summary* was written for two reasons: first, as an aid to those who want to know Plato's book, and second, as sufficient in itself for "whoever cannot bear the hardship of study and reflection." The *Summary* is intended both as a guide into the secrets of the *Laws* for those who are capable of undergoing the hardship involved in uncovering these secrets and as a substitute for or reproduction of the *Laws* for the lazy. All those who have dismissed the *Summary* for its inadequacy as a reproduction of the Greek original have overlooked its primary purpose: as a guide to the secrets of the *Laws.* Those who have condemned the *Summary* as an inadequate reproduction of the *Laws* include not only Stern, Watt, and the editor of the 1952 edition, Francesco Gabrieli, but also two contemporary Arabists: Thérèse-Anne Druart and Dimitri Gutas.

Druart follows Gabrieli in asserting that the *Summary* must be based on some intermediary compendium. Gutas follows Stern in asserting that the *Summary* must not have been written by Alfarabi, although he does not appear to do so for the same reason as Stern, namely, out of recognition of Alfarabi's excellence as a thinker. I will return to both Druart's and especially Gutas's arguments shortly. First, let me try to give a brief sketch of how one might read the *Summary* as a guide to the secrets of the *Laws.*

Alfarabi's text appears baffling if one assumes that his task is to reproduce the "original Greek," but it is less baffling if Alfarabi's task is to reveal the secrets of the *Laws*. Perhaps Alfarabi should be viewed as directly presenting the unadulterated truth that Plato strives to conceal. But that would run contrary to Alfarabi's own recognition that one must conceal science from most people. Alfarabi himself must employ symbols and riddles, in his own manner; but insofar as the *Summary* is intended as an aid to the diligent and able reader, Alfarabi must not merely reproduce Plato's obscurity. (Ironically, if he had merely reproduced this obscurity, perhaps some readers would have been satisfied with the *Summary* as a mere paraphrase of the *Laws*.) Alfarabi's secondary purpose—reproducing the *Laws*—is intentionally achieved in such a defective manner that the diligent and able are directed away from substituting the *Summary* for the *Laws*, as they might be first inclined to do.

In the *Summary*'s conclusion, Alfarabi indicates that his purpose in summarizing the *Laws* was to reveal what Plato "had intended [*qaṣada ilâ*] to explain." Alfarabi reveals Plato's intentions, although not straightforwardly. Purveyors of crossword puzzles sometimes offer hints to the solution of their puzzles, Alfarabi's style of writing provides hints for the solution of Plato's riddles and hints as to when Plato is expressing his own views explicitly. Alfarabi's style of writing in the *Summary* is obscure not only if one expects a paraphrase, but if one expects an explicit statement by Alfarabi of secrets that both he and Plato recognize need to be kept secret from many readers.

Although Alfarabi gives reasons why it is necessary to conceal science, he does not give rules or a methodology for using his hints to uncover the science contained in the *Laws*. On the one hand, it is possible to bemoan this fact as a great misfortune. On the other hand, it is evident that Alfarabi is merely exercising precautions necessary for the sake of science. If he were to offer such a methodology, science would not for long remain secure against misuse and misappropriation. Therefore, it is incumbent to look on this obstacle to our understanding as a challenge to be overcome.[11]

Although Alfarabi provides no mechanical rules for using his hints, there are some general guidelines that we can infer from what he does say: First, the only way to properly make use of his hints is to compare the *Summary* with the *Laws*. Thus, in the introduction he describes the *Summary* as "an aid to whoever wants to know that book [the *Laws*]." Similarly, he emphasizes the need to compare it with the *Laws* when he says that a subject he has been summarizing is "not hard for anyone to know who studies the original book on which this book is based [*fî aṣl hadhâ al-kitâb*] and reflects a little . . ." (disc. 4.2).

Second, whenever Alfarabi's text deviates from Plato's text, we must begin by assuming that the deviation is meaningful. We should not assume automatically, as did the reviewers of the Gabrieli edition and others, that any deviation is merely a failure on Alfarabi's part to reproduce Plato's original. Of course, in taking deviations so seriously we may run the risk of giving Alfarabi too much credit. Nevertheless, my above discussion of the original reception of the 1952 edition provides ample evidence that there is a far greater danger of not giving Alfarabi enough credit. Because the only way to give Alfarabi the benefit of the doubt is to compare his text closely with the *Laws* and because we do not possess a copy of the Arabic translation he may have used, we run the risk of assuming without justification that the *Summary* is based on our copy of the *Laws*. Although we cannot be certain about what text of the *Laws* Alfarabi had in front of him, later in the introduction I will adduce what evidence there is about the kind of text he might have had access to. The reader with a merely philological interest in the *Summary* is not likely to be persuaded by such evidence to undertake the arduous process of comparing the *Summary* with the *Laws*. Those of us who are also interested in the *Summary* for what it can teach us about the *Laws* must make do with what we have. I begin therefore by assuming that Alfarabi's deviations from Plato's text, as we have it, are meaningful rather than meaningless. If after giving Alfarabi's text the benefit of the doubt I find that I am unable to detect any meaning in a particular Alfarabian deviation, then I may treat such a deviation as meaningless–but not before. Furthermore, even when I fail to detect any meaning myself, I do not rule out the possibility that a future, perhaps more capable, interpreter will detect some meaning.

Third, in interpreting any passage of the *Laws* Alfarabi may reproduce the passage, represent it with deviations, or omit it. (In a variation on representing it with deviations, Alfarabi may also add material that has no obvious correlate in Plato's text.) The third hermeneutic rule is that reproduction, deviation, or omission does not always have the same meaning in every context. This rule implies that there are no scientific rules for understanding Alfarabi's interpretation. If such rules existed, then Alfarabi would fail to live up to the Platonic and Alfarabian requirement that those who are familiar with science should avoid making it easily accessible to most people.[12] For instance, one *cannot* assume that when Alfarabi reproduces a passage from the *Laws* that he is always showing his approval of it; that when Alfarabi represents a passage from the *Laws* with deviations, the said deviations always constitute Alfarabi's revision of Plato's teaching; and that when Alfarabi omits any reference to a passage from the *Laws*, he is always expressing his disapproval of it.

For example, when Alfarabi summarizes the Athenian Stranger's discussion of the ancient Persian monarchy and the ancient Athenian democracy, he scrupulously avoids making any mention of the Athenian democracy–even though the discussion of the two regimes is of a piece. One can interpret this omission in one of two ways: Either Alfarabi believes that his community is capable of improving on the Athenian's attempt to combine monarchy and democracy by moving further in the direction of monarchy than does the Athenian, or he believes that his community is incapable of making use of democracy because of certain deficiencies present in its political conditions but absent in the Athenian's community. We cannot decide how to interpret this omission on the basis of it alone. We must see what other passages of the *Summary* teach about the monarchy Alfarabi envisions to know how to interpret it. The same can be said about any particular case of reproduction, deviation, or addition.

Fourth, when I compare the *Summary* with the *Laws*, I am not merely superimposing the former on the latter. To apprise the reader of the contents of the *Summary* and of the *Laws*, I describe the contents of the passages from the respective works. Then I compare these two descriptions and attempt to arrive at a plausible interpretation of Alfarabi's view of Plato's intention. Admittedly, this process of interpreting a commentary on a text is highly convoluted. The interpretation of texts is by definition not an exact science. When one enters into the equation the added convolution of interpreting a commentary on another text, it is necessary to admit that any such interpretation is bound to be even less exact. Nonetheless, the possible benefits of gaining a greater understanding of Plato's *Laws* outweigh the costs of such inexactness.

Finally, I must emphasize that when I speak of Alfarabi's omissions, I do not have in mind Alfarabian "silences" of the sort that might interest a deconstructionist. Alfarabi and I agree that Plato had an intention when he wrote his dialogues. Furthermore, we both agree that when we read the *Laws*, what we are interested in is understanding this intention. I am interested in Alfarabi's omissions for what they teach me about his understanding of Plato's intentions and what they teach me about his own. I am not interested, like the deconstructionist, in such omissions for what they reveal about the purportedly unthought premises of Plato's (or Alfarabi's) thought. Indeed, one of the leading intentions of this book is to show that Plato is not subject to the unthought metaphysical premises that deconstructionists frequently ascribe to him.

3. *Alfarabi's access to the* Laws

In addition to the reasons given above, the *Summary* has received so little scholarly attention because we lack the kind of antecedents to it that modern philologically oriented scholarship demands. It is generally assumed that Alfarabi did not read Greek. Because we no longer possess copies of the Arabic translation of the *Laws* that Alfarabi is likely to have used, scholars are tempted to give up on inquiring into the *Summary* before having gotten started. They assume that its peculiarities and oddities can be readily explained as the product of the translation he used, and without the translation no sense can be made of the *Summary*. This scholarly decision to neglect the *Summary* reflects an old and deep-seated prejudgment among many orientalists that the peculiarities and oddities of a text by a medieval Muslim thinker must be the product of external historical forces or of as yet undiscovered (preferably non-Muslim) predecessors rather than of the mind of the thinker. This prejudgment is an odd combination of the modern, democratic tendency to overstate history's power over the individual, described by Tocqueville,[13] and of the view that Muslim thinkers in particular are constrained by their tradition from thinking independently.[14]

Because we know that Galen wrote a "Synopsis" of the *Laws*, scholars suppose that if Alfarabi did not use a defective translation of the *Laws*, he must surely have taken over wholesale the oddities and peculiarities of this "Synopsis." That Galen's compendium is lost but for an insignificant fragment gives them unlimited license for such speculation.

Is there reason to assume that the translation Alfarabi used—if in fact he could not read Greek and was therefore compelled to use a translation—was defective? Is there reason to assume from what little we know of Galen's compendium that Alfarabi relied on it? These assumptions here must not be left unchallenged. To evaluate them, we must inquire into the textual tradition of the *Laws* (both in the West up to the present and in the medieval Muslim world) and of the *Summary* (up to the present). I will show that the evidence does not favor the assumption that the peculiarities of Alfarabi's text are the product of his use of a defective translation or of Galen's compendium.

Because no copy of an Arabic translation of the *Laws* has come down to us (and because copies of Arabic translations of almost all Aristotelian works have come down to us), some readers of the *Summary* are ready to assume that no such translation existed in Alfarabi's time. The absence of such a translation, combined with many readers' expectation that the *Summary* be a mere paraphrase of the *Laws*, has led them to dismiss the *Summary* as a paraphrase of a poor summary or of a defective copy.[15] It is impossible to determine whether Alfarabi had access to the *Laws* merely by a casual comparison of the *Summary* with our text of the *Laws*, because the *Summary* is not meant to be a mere paraphrase that reproduces in abbreviated form the literal text of the *Laws*. Only by a minute comparison of the *Summary* with the *Laws* can the reader arrive at an informed decision about Alfarabi's access to it. First, however, it is useful to review the ways in which Alfarabi is likely to have had access. Perhaps there is reason to believe that Alfarabi had access to the *Laws* and to an uncorrupted copy of it.

There are two ways in which Alfarabi was likely to have had access to the *Laws*: Either in the form of one of the two translations about whose existence we have reliable testimony or in the form of a translation or a copy of the Greek original to which Alfarabi may have had access when he traveled to Byzantium. I begin with the former possibility.

Ibn al-Nadîm explains in his *Fihrist*, which was written shortly after Alfarabi's death, that two translations of the *Laws* had been made: one by Ḥunayn b. Isḥâq and one by Alfarabi's own student Yaḥyâ b. 'Adî.[16] We cannot be certain whether Ḥunayn's translation was into Arabic or merely into Syriac; Yaḥyâ, however, was known as a translator into Arabic of Syriac texts that had originally been in Greek.[17] In light of the proximity of the two translations (Ḥunayn died in 260/873 and Yaḥyâ died in 364/974), it is likely that Yaḥyâ translated into Arabic Ḥunayn's Syriac translation rather than that Yaḥyâ simply repeated the work already done by Ḥunayn—assuming for the sake of argument that the former read Greek.[18] The material that Ḥunayn used was most likely to have been one or more of those Greek texts collected by emissaries sent out during the ninth century by the caliph al-Ma'mûn, who ruled during part of his lifetime.[19]

As luck would have it, the two primary manuscripts on which the modern critical edition of the *Laws* by des Places is based are ninth-century Byzantine manuscripts: *Parisinus graecus* 1807 and *Vaticanus graecus* 1.[20] Of course, we cannot be certain as to the difference in quality between the manuscripts to which des Places had access and those to which Ḥunayn had access; however, the text to which we have access and the text to which Alfarabi would have had access, according to this scenario, are surprisingly close in both date and place of origin.

The second scenario is that Alfarabi had access to a presumably good translation or a copy of the Greek original when he studied in Byzantium. According to al-Khaṭṭâbî's report of Alfarabi's own account of his studies, Alfarabi spent eight years in the "land of the Greeks" (*bilâd al-rûm*).[21] He may mean by this one of two things: either that Alfarabi studied in Byzantium proper or in one of the areas near the border of Byzantium. Some of these border areas, technically under Islamic rule, were populated primarily not by Muslims but by Syrian Christians (and Sabians) such as Antioch and Ḥarrân. Al-Khaṭṭâbî also indicates that Alfarabi traveled to Ḥarrân with Yûḥannâ b. Ḥaylân, the teacher with whom he had studied in Central Asia where he was born.

In light of Alfarabi's evident desire to master the philosophy of Plato and Aristotle, one would expect that if he had traveled to Byzantium he would have made every effort to consult the best possible manuscripts. To do so, it is likely that he would have had to learn Greek. If, on the other hand, he merely traveled to Ḥarrân, recent evidence indicates that he may have come into contact either with Greek or Syriac versions of the Platonic corpus. According to reports both in works by al-Mas'ûdî and Ibn abî Uṣaybi'a (based on Alfarabi's lost *On the Appearance of Philosophy*), Alfarabi viewed himself as one in a line of philosophers that could be traced to the Alexandrian school.[22] Until recently, it was believed that the Alexandrian school was transferred to Antioch when the Muslims invaded Alexandria. Now it appears more likely that the Alexandrian school as well as the Athenian Academy were exiled from Byzantium in the sixth century, prior to the Muslim invasion. Damascius, the last Athenian head of the Academy, led the exiles to Ḥarrân. It is possible that members of the Academy were able to bring Platonic texts with them.[23] It is even possible that Alfarabi learned something of use for his political philosophy from whatever vestiges of the Academy existed in Ḥarrân.[24]

Either through direct knowledge of the original Greek or through a Syriac intermediary, then, it is likely that Alfarabi would have had access to a text of the *Laws* similar, if not identical, to our own.

4. The Summary*'s textual tradition: The contemporary debate*

Let us turn now to the contemporary debate over the textual tradition of the *Summary*. The first modern printed edition of the *Summary*, edited by Francesco Gabrieli, appeared in 1952.[25] Gabrieli's edition was based on a single manuscript: Leiden MS *Golius* 133 (A.D. 1292–93). In 1961 Muhsin Mahdi wrote an article that supplied not only corrections to Gabrieli's reading of the manuscript but also an extensive discussion of what substantive approach should be taken in interpreting the *Summary*.[26] At some time after 1961, Mahdi discovered that Gabrieli had not availed himself of all of the manuscripts available to him: In 1941, prior to the publication of Gabrieli's edition, Hartwig Derenbourg had established the existence of another manuscript in his Escurial catalog. I say merely "another manuscript" because a debate exists as to the proper identity of this manuscript. On the one hand, Professors Druart and Mahdi hold that the Escurial MS *Casiri* 883 (at least ca. A.D. 1277–78), an abridged version of Alfarabi's *Summary*, predates the Leiden MS[27] and offers in some cases better readings than those found in the Leiden MS, and therefore can be helpful in producing a critical Arabic edition. On the other hand, Dimitri Gutas has proposed the thesis that both the Escurial MS and the Leiden MS are based on a third text, which he hypothesizes is Galen's lost "Synopsis of Plato's *Laws*."[28]

Gutas's thesis rests upon what appears to be a misreading of the 1977 article by Druart in which she first proposed the thesis that the Escurial MS (*E*) is an abridged version of Alfarabi's *Summary*.[29] In that article Druart suggests that *E* is an abridged version of the *Summary* and, that it predates the Leiden MS (*L*). In other words, she proposes that *E* is an abridgment of a copy of the *Summary* that was made prior to the copying of *L*. Since *E* is based on an earlier copy of the *Summary*, which was bound to have undergone less textual corruption, it should come as no surprise that, despite the fact that *E* is an abridgment, it contains some readings of the *Summary* that are better than those in *L*. Despite Druart's assertion that *E* predates *L*, Gutas speaks, for whatever reason, as if Druart views *E* as an abridgment of *L* rather than as an abridgment of an earlier and less corrupt copy of the *Summary*. Indeed, Gutas speaks of *L* as if it were the original manuscript by Alfarabi rather than a scribe's copy made over three centuries after Alfarabi wrote the *Summary*.[30] Because Gutas argues as if *L* were Alfarabi's original, and because he, like Druart, recognizes that *E* contains better readings than *L*, he concludes that *E* cannot be an abridgment of Alfarabi's *Summary* (in reality of *L*) but must be an abridgment of some other work (namely, Galen's lost "Synopsis of the *Laws*") and that Alfarabi's *Summary* (or rather *L*) is also a version of this other work. Both Gutas and Druart posit a third text. Druart's third text is the original of the *Summary*. According to her, *L* and *E* are both copies of it, and *L* was copied later and probably from a more corrupt text than *E*. In contrast, Gutas's third text is Galen's "Synopsis." He says nothing about whether *L* appeared later than *E*, or vice versa. Overlooking the difference between *L* and Alfarabi's original manuscript of the *Summary*, he hypothesizes a third non-Alfarabian text. Without Gutas's hypothesis, the scholar would with good reason assume that the 'third text' is Alfarabi's original of the *Summary*.[31]

Gutas claims that Galen's "Synopsis" must be the third text because he finds one passage (at least he supplies only one passage) in the *Summary* that has no literal parallel in the passage in the *Laws* on which Alfarabi seems to be commenting. This passage happens to show some similarities (although no literal parallels) to passages in a work by Galen entitled *Peri Ethon*. Gutas tries to lend credence to his claim by noting that Galen was a student of Posidonius's writings. In *On the Emotions*, Posidonius criticized Plato for being longwinded in the *Laws*. Gutas takes this criticism to be the inspiration for Galen's "Synopsis" or at least for the brevity of the "Synopsis," of which we have proof (he supposes) in the brevity of Alfarabi's *Summary*.[32] Now, we know from the testimony of Ḥunayn b. Isḥâq that Galen's "Synopsis" was brief,[33] and Gutas thinks that the brevity of the *Summary* derives from the brevity of its purported source, Galen's "Synopsis." Gutas's thesis concerning the "third text," then, rests upon the shared brevity of Galen's "Synopsis" and Alfarabi's *Summary* and the fact that there is one passage in the *Summary* that seems to be similar to a passage from a work by Galen, a work other than the no longer extant "Synopsis."

Little need be said about the first argument. Shared brevity is so formal that it could be used to justify the argument that a brief Marxist compendium on a text which preceded in print a brief liberal democratic compendium must have served as the inspiration for the latter text.

The second argument requires a more involved response. First, it is not difficult to find parallels between some passages from the *Summary* and any of a large number of ancient works on ethics and politics. One cannot, however, infer from this that it is an imitation of these various works and the same holds for the "Synopsis."

More importantly, one can question the claim that Alfarabi relied so heavily on Galen that he did little more than reproduce his "Synopsis." In his recourse to Galen, Gutas assumes that when Alfarabi summarized the *Laws* his aim was merely to extract passages and reproduce them. In other words, Alfarabi was little more than an abridger of arguments, a glorified scribe, i.e., someone like the abridger of the *Summary* who produced *E*.[34] He slavishly reproduces either the *Laws* or Galen's "Synopsis." In resorting to Galen's "Synopsis," Gutas is pursuing a line of inquiry already suggested by Gabrieli and in turn Stern[35] for essentially the same reason: namely, that the *Summary* does not suffice as a paraphrase. Although Alfarabi says in the conclusion that "we extracted [*istakhrajnâ*] those of [the *Laws*'] notions [*ma'ânî*] that dawned on us," he does not speak of extracting passages literally. On the contrary, he indicates that he is communicating not the statements of Platonic characters, whether they be from the mouth of the Athenian Stranger or from the mouths of his interlocutors, but rather those things that "the wise [Plato] had intended to explain [*qaṣada ilâ bayânihi*]." It is not by chance that the majority of passages in the *Summary* begin with the phrase "[Plato] explained" (*bayyana*) rather than "[Plato] said" (*qâla*).[36]

Finally, there is some evidence that Alfarabi's *Summary* not only is not a slavish reproduction of Galen's "Synopsis" but was composed in opposition to Galen's "Synopsis." According to Ḥunayn b. Isḥâq, whose remarks Gutas cites in the course of his construction of the third text, Galen's "Synopsis" contains (according to Gutas's translation) the "essential concepts [*jumal ma'ânî*] of the twelve books on the *Laws* by Plato." Apparently, Galen had access to all twelve books of the *Laws* and commented on all of them. Alfarabi, however, claims to be ignorant of the number of books in the *Laws* (conclusion), and he comments only on the first nine books. Alfarabi's innovative omission is incompatible with Gutas's portrayal of him as a scribe reproducing Galen's "Synopsis." Furthermore and more importantly, the parts of the *Laws* Alfarabi chooses to summarize are precisely those parts that Posidonius (Galen's teacher and inspiration) viewed as a waste of time (see above, n. 32). Perhaps Gutas would argue that Alfarabi only had access to Galen's synopsis of the first nine books of the *Laws*. The likelihood that he did not have access to the whole "Synopsis," however, is not great, because it was translated by a disciple of Ḥunayn b. Isḥâq, named 'Isâ b. Yaḥyâ, who lived shortly before Alfarabi (Ḥunayn b. Isḥâq died in 260/873 and Alfarabi died in 339/950). Even if Alfarabi did not have access to the whole of the "Synopsis," there is every reason to believe that he would at least have known Ḥunayn b. Isḥâq's account of the "Synopsis," to which even we still have access, which indicates that the number of books summarized by Galen was twelve. Alfarabi supplies a hint that indeed he knows the number of books in the *Laws* but has chosen to depart from Galen by summarizing only the first nine books: He says that, according to some, the *Laws* contains ten books and according to others it contains fourteen books. On the one hand, Alfarabi leads the reader to believe that he did not have access to Galen's "Synopsis" by not citing Galen's view that there are twelve books in the *Laws*; on the other hand, he hints that he knows that there are twelve books in the *Laws* by choosing the two numbers whose mean is twelve.[37]

Thus, we see that not only is there every reason to view the *Summary* itself as the purportedly mysterious "third text" from which *E* and *L* have been derived, but there is positive evidence against the supposition that Alfarabi slavishly copied bits and pieces of a lost "Synopsis of the *Laws*" by Galen.

Having come to see how doubtful it is that Alfarabi based his *Summary* on Galen's "Synopsis," let us return to the more vexing question of the relation between the *Summary* and the *Laws*. Not only Gutas but Druart doubts that the *Summary* was based on the *Laws*. Indeed, Druart, despite her belief that the "third text" is the *Summary*, is also lured into the trap of suggesting that Alfarabi must have based his *Summary* on some other summary, and in lieu of any other summary to point to, she also suggests Galen's "Synopsis." She adduces the following evidence that Alfarabi's *Summary* could not have been based on the *Laws* but was a summary of a summary: On the third MS of the *Summary* (the Kabul MS–of which I have made no mention so far because it plays no active part in the debate between Druart and Gutas outlined above, since it is for the most part identical to *L*) is inscribed the following title: "Summary of the Compendium of the Laws of Plato" (*Talkhîṣ jawâmi' nawâmîs al-Aflâṭûn* [*sic*]). As Druart herself suggests, however, this title was inscribed by a different scribe than the one who copied the Kabul MS.[38] Even on purely philological grounds such evidence is of questionable worth. Presumably, Druart was motivated by more than this to conclude that Alfarabi's *Summary* cannot be a summary of the *Laws*. The relation between the *Summary* and the *Laws* is obscure. It begs to be solved by the simple statement that Alfarabi could not have had direct access to the *Laws*.

Despite the availability to Alfarabi of a translation by a translator of the stature of either Ḥunayn b. Isḥâq or Yaḥyâ b. 'Adî, Gutas attempts by sleight of hand to discredit the kind of translation to which Alfarabi would most likely have had access.[39] There remains open to us, however, only one way to determine with greater certainty whether Alfarabi had direct access to the *Laws*: to compare the *Summary* with the utmost care and in the utmost detail with the *Laws*, guided by Alfarabi's own instructions in his introduction. This book will be the occasion for just such a comparison.[40]

5. This book's structure

This book is divided into three parts. The first part concerns the identity of the foundations of law. It is commonly believed that Plato grounds his laws on a demonstrative *metaphysica specialis* or theology. In fact, the theology in bk.

10 contains Plato's rhetorical defense of law. This book shows that the true foundations of law are psychological. In other words, law does not have a metaphysical ground. The second part concerns the divergence between the city ruled by reason (the city in the *Republic*) and the city ruled by written law (the city in the *Laws*). The divergence between the former and the latter necessitates that law be defended not by strictly rational arguments but by subrational ones, which Alfarabi calls *kalâm*. The third part concerns the ascent from the rule of written law to the rule of reason. The purpose of the written law is to form human beings possessed of good breeding. Those possessed of good breeding may be capable of gaining access to the life ruled by reason. Plato gives the reader a means of access to this life–viz., the philosophic life–by attaching preludes to his laws.

A more detailed account in terms of chapters is as follows. In chapter 1, I explain that the foundations of the law are psychological rather than metaphysical. What appears to be Plato's metaphysics is, in fact, his rhetorical defense of law or his art of *kalâm*. Following the lead set by modern scholarship on medieval Christian philosophy, most students of Alfarabi have concluded that he is a Neoplatonist. Furthermore, they believe that he, like his Christian counterparts, understands Plato through a Neoplatonic lens. In chapter 2, I explain that they have treated Alfarabi's subrational defense of divine law, i.e., his *kalâm*, as if it were a metaphysical doctrine. In chapter 3, I show that despite the nineteenth-century decision to cease relying upon Neoplatonic commentaries to understand Plato, much of the secondary literature on the *Laws* views Plato through a Neoplatonic lens. In particular, Plato scholars also mistake his *kalâm* for a metaphysical doctrine.

If the foundations of law are metaphysical, then the intelligible order of the natural whole extends to the order of political things or the city–as natural law theorists such as Thomas Aquinas argue. Thus, many scholars conclude that for Plato the rule of law is the same thing as the rule of intellect. In chapter 4, I begin the process, ongoing throughout part 2, of clarifying the disjunction between the order of the natural whole and the order of the city. In particular, I explain that although intellect may order the natural whole, it does not rule in the city, especially the city ruled by law. Even the most "natural" city or the city ruled by intellect described in the *Republic* is not thoroughly "natural" or rational. The city ruled by law is even further from being permeated by intellect or a natural order. In chapter 5, because I cannot help but describe the general outlines of the city in the *Laws* when I describe the differences between a city ruled by law and a city ruled by intellect, I also take the occasion to describe the differences between Alfarabi's regime in the *Summary* and Plato's city in the *Laws*. These differences are the result of Alfarabi's adaptation of the teaching of the *Laws* to his own time and place. I return to the theme of the divergence between the rule of law and the rule of intellect in chapter 6. War reveals itself as a mark of the city's inevitable deviation from the rule of intellect. The end of producing a citizen body that is fit both in body and soul for waging war works at odds with the end of producing a citizen body that is fit for inquiry and intellect. Law cannot help but favor one of these ends at the expense of the other. As the military purpose of the education described in bk. 7 implies, the city necessarily squints toward the martial end. In chapter 7, the last chapter of part 2, I explore some of the means by which Alfarabi's Plato makes the rule of law more like the rule of intellect. One means is to try to find ways to modify law over the course of *time* without compromising law's authority. Another is to limit the size of the political body (*space*) over which the law rules. The success of these efforts to rationalize law, however, are limited. Law is irrational to the extent that it cannot accommodate crucial differences between individual human beings.

Although law proper cannot accommodate differences between individuals, I show in the third part that by adding preludes to the laws Plato and Alfarabi give some individuals access through the laws to a rational way of life. In chapter 8, it becomes apparent that the purpose of law must be to produce citizens who are capable not only of obeying law but of ruling. Law must be supplemented by human rulers if it is to draw more closely to the rule of intellect. Indeed, law cannot directly foster intellect. At best it can foster conditions that might give rise to intellect among its citizens. Good breeding is the condition among the citizens that approximates most closely to intellect without being intellect. Insofar as it is the overarching purpose of law to produce rulers possessed of good breeding, to understand a soul with good breeding is to grasp the purpose of law. But the life in accordance with good breeding, like the law that fosters this life, is not a strictly rational life. Can one truly understand good breeding and thus the leading purpose of law without having transcended good breeding? This question is answered in chapter 9. Finally, in chapter 10, poetry reveals itself as the entry point into that inquiry into law that makes rational innovation possible. Poetry rather than law gives one access to the psychological purposes of law. Plato mixes poetry with law proper by adding preludes to the laws. Finally, the inquirer into law must go beyond poetry to *kalâm* and ultimately dialectic in order to grasp fully the limits of law. Only by grasping precisely how the rule of law falls short of the rule of intellect can the inquirer fully grasp the necessity for *kalâm*, that is, for the defense of the law's roots.

6. This book's audience

It almost goes without saying that this book should be of interest to students of Alfarabi's political philosophy and of Arabic or Islamic political philosophy in general. Not only does it constitute the first full-length book on an individual Alfarabian work of political philosophy, it is on perhaps the least accessible of these writings, and as such it should be especially useful for Alfarabi scholars. Furthermore, as a study of Alfarabi's sole commentary on a work of Plato it will help to illuminate the relationship between the Arabic philosophic tradition and Plato.

Precisely because the obstacles to the profitable study of the *Summary* are even greater for the Plato scholar and classicists in general, this book should be especially welcome to such scholars. The benefits of studying the *Summary* are in many respects unique. As this introduction has tried to show, Alfarabi provides the reader not only with an account of how to read Plato but also with an example of such a reading. Any thoughtful reader of the Platonic dialogues is struck by the dialogical form that Plato's writings take. This form implies that Plato chose not to set forth his philosophy as an easily accessible doctrine. Beginning with simple observations of this kind, Alfarabi goes on not only to describe how we might read Plato but also to account for what could have motivated such a style of writing. Alfarabi's speculations about these motivations are not idle: they derive from an evident familiarity with the challenges confronting any philosopher who attempts to communicate knowledge to others.

It has become traditional for students of Plato's political philosophy to favor his *Republic* over his *Laws*. The reasons for this are readily apparent: First, the *Republic* is a more exciting dialogue. In this dialogue, Socrates engages some politically ambitious young men in a discussion. Consequently, the pace of the discussion is faster, and its political ambitions are greater. Second, in the West the *Republic* retained a currency while the *Laws* underwent neglect among the Neoplatonists (and in turn during the Renaissance) because the *Republic* appealed to the decidedly metaphysical and suprapolitical interests of the Neoplatonists. In striking contrast to the *Republic*, the *Laws* is a discussion among old men about a city that is to exist in deed rather than merely in speech (as is the city in the *Republic*). In spite of the pragmatic political character of the *Laws*, many modern interpreters of the *Laws* extend their Neoplatonic approach to Plato even to the *Laws*. I know of no other interpreter of the *Laws* who offers as convincing a correction of this Neoplatonic approach as does Alfarabi in his *Summary*.

For Islamicists, Islamists, theologians, and theorists in comparative religion, Alfarabi's analysis of the rhetorical and political role of theology should be thought provoking. Perhaps it will even serve as the basis for innovative new thinking about religion and politics. Alfarabi's heterodox view cannot help but stand in striking contrast to the more traditional view that theology provides a positive ground for all aspects of human existence. If theology, by definition, is essentially rhetorical, then what are the tasks and the limits of such rhetoric? If theology is rhetorical, then what other grounds for human existence might there be? As we will see, Alfarabi answers these questions.

Last but by no means least, this book should be of interest to students of Heidegger and of postmodernism. I argue that Heidegger has misrepresented Plato as the father of the history of metaphysics and that, contrary to Heidegger's Plato, Alfarabi's Plato possesses a phenomenology that can compete with Heidegger's own. Plato is not the father of metaphysics, because his intent in speculating about *metaphysica specialis* is not to provide a demonstrative metaphysical foundation for law but rather to provide a rhetorical defense of law. The phenomenology of Alfarabi's Plato can compete with Heidegger's, because its focus is the role of beliefs in politics. Because Heidegger lived—as we do today—in a time in which politics was remote, his phenomenological analysis was limited to an analysis of the role of belief or commitment in nonpolitical settings. In contrast, because Alfarabi lived in a community in which the role of belief was so prominent, he was better able than Heidegger to illuminate the role of beliefs in politics. Consequently, at least for the political scientist and legal theorist, I believe, Alfarabi's Plato provides a superior phenomenology. I hope that postmodernist political scientists and adherents of Critical Legal Studies will take this claim not as an idle boast but as a call for further debate and inquiry.

I.
Metaphysics as Rhetorical Foundation of Law

1
The Roots of the Laws

Perhaps the most ready assumption of any reader of the *Laws*–if only because of its title–is that its primary purpose is to provide a philosophically criticized code of law.[1] Although the mere quantity of words is not a sufficient indicator of the leading subject of a great written work, it is worth noting that, as E. B. England, the author of the most authoritative commentary on the Greek text of the *Laws* has observed, at least two-thirds of the *Laws* is taken up with "'talk about the laws'" as opposed to "actual legislation."[2] If jurisprudence is the art of "actual legislation," what is the bulk of the *Laws* concerned with when it is taken up with "talk about the laws"? In section 1, I distinguish the jurisprudential art of inferring laws from the rhetorical art of defending the opinions and actions that law inculcates (the art of *kalâm*). I also distinguish the popular art of defending these fundamental opinions and actions, or roots, from the philosophic art of defending them. The latter art presupposes an inquiry into the purposes of the laws, i.e., political science; the former art does not. Thus, the "talk about the laws" that takes place in this Platonic dialogue proves to be twofold: First, it is an inquiry into the roots (political science); second, it is an art of defending them (*kalâm*).

In section 2, I clarify *why* the leading subject of the *Laws* is not jurisprudence but rather political science and *kalâm*. Jurisprudence presupposes that the lawgiver has already laid down the law. According to Alfarabi, Plato's objective is more profound than merely inferring laws on the basis of the preexisting purposes of the lawgiver. By inquiring into the purposes of law, political science enables human beings to revise the law and to defend it properly.

In section 3, I explain that the philosophic defense of the revised law or the philosophic art of *kalâm* takes the form of a *metaphysica specialis* or theology. This theology is frequently misconstrued as if it were intended to be a demonstrative *metaphysica specialis* rather than a rhetorical defense of law. Alfarabi shows in his *Book of Letters* that even the theology in bk. *Lambda* of Aristotle's *Metaphysics* (which is still viewed generally as his attempt to provide a demonstrative *metaphysica specialis*) is a piece of *kalâm*. Even the apparently apolitical *Metaphysics* cannot escape the political task of defending the law. Aristotle in bk. *Lambda*, like Plato in bk. 10 of the *Laws*, presents a theology in which the gods show little concern for human things. Indeed, the gods seem to have only one task: the guidance of perhaps the most regular feature of nature, the motion of the heavenly bodies. Although the political content of Aristotle's theology is negative–astral gods are not concerned with the affairs of human beings–his theology is highly political. It promotes human self-reliance, especially in the realm of politics. Thus, the belief in astral gods promotes the formation of certain kind of souls. In sum, the purpose of this theology is essentially psychological or political.

In section 4, I offer crucial textual evidence from the *Summary* that the intention of Plato's theology is essentially political rather than metaphysical.

1. Jurisprudence and kalâm

In the *Enumeration of the Sciences*, Alfarabi defines the art of jurisprudence (*fiqh*) as inferring decisions from the laws already laid down by the Lawgiver (*wâḍi' al-sharî'ah*) as well as from his purpose in legislating. The Lawgiver's purpose is to inculcate belief in certain opinions and to command certain actions. Because religion and law are so inextricably bound up with one another in Islam, the opinions and actions that are inculcated and commanded are opinions "about God . . . and His attributes, about the world, and so forth, . . . actions by which God . . . is magnified, and . . . actions by means of which transactions are conducted in cities."[3] In the *Enumeration*, Alfarabi describes the political phenomena as he finds them in his community. The highest opinions–in this case the opinions about God–are the highest purpose of the Lawgiver. His highest purpose is not political. As has been suggested by others, this emphasis on the divine purpose is especially pronounced in the monotheistic religions. In such religions, the divine Law shapes political life for the sake of religion.[4]

After describing jurisprudence in the *Enumeration*, Alfarabi goes on to describe an art of "defending" (*nuṣrah*) these fundamental opinions and actions (or "roots") called *kalâm*. Of course, there are different ways of defending things. One may defend something with blind devotion and a willingness to use any weapons one might lay one's hands on. Or one might defend something only after having inquired into whether it is sound. The *Enumeration* describes an art of *kalâm* of the former kind. The practitioners of *kalâm* (*mutakallimûn*) described therein willingly adopt arguments that "our intellects reject" and themselves eagerly deny "the testimony . . . of the objects of sense."[5] These *mutakallimûn* by denying the evidence of the senses and the intellect prove that they are not friends of the philosophic sciences. Consequently, Alfarabi describes the sciences he presents in the *Enumeration*, including *kalâm*, as the "generally known" (*mashhûrah*) sciences.[6] Although the art of *kalâm* described in the *Enumeration* is hostile to the philosophic sciences, is it not possible that there exists an art of *kalâm* that is not hostile to the evidence provided by the senses and intellect?

In the opening of the ninth discourse of his *Summary*, Alfarabi says that the earlier books of the *Laws* (bks. 1-8) presented a "discussion" (*kalâm*) of the roots of the laws. In other words, bks. 1-8 contain Plato's art of *kalâm*. Because Plato is a philosopher, his art of *kalâm*, unlike that described by Alfarabi in the *Enumeration*, does not contradict the guidance of the intellect or sensation.[7] Not only does Plato avoid using whatever weapon comes to hand, he also begins by inquiring into the soundness of the roots before he takes the field in their defense. The Platonic art may be called the philosophic, as opposed to the "generally known," art of *kalâm*.

Alfarabi's announcement that bks. 1-8 present Plato's art of *kalâm*, however, is somewhat disconcerting. The Athenian Stranger offers his leading theological arguments in bk. 10. Is not *kalâm* usually understood to be "theology"? There seems to be a ready solution to this whole problem. In the conclusion of the *Summary*, Alfarabi says himself that there were discourses or books of the *Laws* that he was not in a position to copy. The *Summary* breaks off its interpretation of the *Laws* early in bk. 9 (864c10). Alfarabi, it appears, was simply ignorant of bk. 10. He must go to great lengths, then, to describe Plato's art of *kalâm* in his summary of bks. 1-8. As Leo Strauss has shown in his "How Farabi Read Plato's *Laws*," however, Alfarabi is highly reticent about God or the gods in discourses 1-8. Above all, although the Athenian presents his brief version of the theological prelude to the laws as a whole in bk. 4, Alfarabi in contrast is nearly silent about God or the gods (in disc. 4). He describes the books he summarizes, bks. 1-8, as Plato's "discussion" (*kalâm*) of the roots of the laws. Why then is he not more taken up with "theology"? To understand this riddle of riddles in the *Summary*, recall that Alfarabi's foremost purpose is not to reproduce the content of the *Laws* but rather to describe what Plato "intended" (*qaṣada ilâ*) to explain. Although Plato presents certain fundamental theological opinions and actions (or roots) in bk. 10 as well as bk. 4, his intention in doing so is political. His account of the gods in bk. 10 should not be construed, as his scientific doctrine about gods or demonstrative *metaphysica specialis*.

In the popular religion described in the *Enumeration*, the fundamental opinions and actions are synonymous with the ultimate purpose of the Lawgiver. His highest purpose is to inculcate certain beliefs about God. In contrast, in the philosophic religion described and defended in the *Laws*, the fundamental opinions and actions are not synonymous with the ultimate purpose of the philosophic legislator. The highest communal purpose of the philosophic legislator is instead the political well-being of the community. Alfarabi's object is to reveal the political purpose of Plato's *kalâm*. This inquiry into the political purpose of the law's roots is the element of the *Laws* that deserves to be called political science. The whole of the *Summary* deserves to be called political science.

Plato formulates a theology only in conjunction with an inquiry into the law's purpose. The popular *mutakallimûn* receive the religion they are given and defend it with unquestioning faith. In contrast, the philosophic *mutakallimûn* (like Plato) scrutinize their community's religious law with an eye to its political well-being. Because Plato's *kalâm* involves scrutiny or inquiry, the Athenian Stranger (the leader of the dialogue) describes bks. 1–8 as a process of "educating the citizens" (857e6). He contrasts this process of education with the juristic activity of inferring legislation. The inquirer into the purpose of the roots is compared to a doctor (who is a free man) treating free human beings. The latter engages the patient in a dialogue "using arguments that come close to philosophizing, grasping the disease from its source, and going back up to the whole nature of bodies" (857d2). As the doctor treats bodies, so does the legislator treat souls. Inquiring into the purposes of the roots is inquiring into the nature and the disease of the soul. This inquiry not only is a kind of prelude to the act of legislating, but it takes place within the preludes to the laws. Plato's free doctor was originally (in bk. 4) analogous to the prelude; the slave doctor was analogous to legislation proper. Thus, when in bk. 9 the Athenian describes his educational activity as a philosophic *mutakallim* on analogy to the activity of a free doctor, he is also alluding to the educational role of the prelude.

But in bk. 4 the prelude was said to be analogous to the free doctor not so much in his capacity as educator but as persuader. There the Athenian suggests that the prelude persuades where the law coerces. Alfarabi's interpretation of this passage in bk. 4 explains that preludes serve both an educational and a persuasive purpose. He describes a few kinds of preludes, only one of which is the Athenian's persuasive prelude. Alfarabi calls it the "imposed" (*taklîfiyyah*) prelude. Preludes of this kind "are like proclamations effected through discussion [*kalâm*] and clarifications by means of arguments [*mujâdalât*]" (disc. 4.16). The reader who attends to the bracketed Arabic terms will recognize this form of "discussion" as our art of *kalâm*. The other element, the arguments, are specifically dialectical arguments (dialectic is called *jadal* in Arabic). The inquiry into the purpose of the laws takes on a dialectical form in the *Laws* and *Summary.* Alfarabi's dialectic, like Plato's, takes as the premises of its arguments commonly accepted opinions about divine law and its purposes. This dialectical inquiry into the purposes of divine law is political science. The intimacy of the relation between *kalâm* and political science is exemplified by the fact that "discussion" (*kalâm*) and "[dialectical] arguments" (*mujâdalât*) are merely two different aspects of the prelude to the law.

In the *Laws* even the inquiry into the purposes of the law (political science) is therefore not strictly rational or demonstrative; rather, it is dialectical. The purposes themselves are not strictly rational, because the way of life advocated by the law is not strictly rational. Of course, if even the inquiry into the purposes is not strictly rational, we should hardly expect that the defense (*kalâm*) of this way of life would be strictly rational.[8] Although the purposes of the laws are essentially psychological rather than metaphysical, this does not make them rational. The closest the *Laws* comes to giving a rational description of a rational way of life is to point beyond the way of life advocated by the law to the philosophic way of life. (In contrast is the *Republic,* where the philosophic way of life is a prominent theme.)

In a discussion of *kalâm* that owes a great deal to Alfarabi's, Maimonides traces the historical origins of (generally known) *kalâm* in the Muslim community to the *kalâm* of the Christian community, especially in Greece and Syria where philosophic ideas had a wide currency. He suggests that *kalâm* arose in an effort to oppose philosophic opinions that "ruined the foundations (*qawâ'id*) of their Law."[9]

In Alfarabi's community (as well as Maimonides'), popular *kalâm* views philosophy as an enemy of the law. This is inevitable in view of the subphilosophic character of law. This animosity, however, is especially marked in monotheistic communities in general. Indeed, it may account for the fact that these communities have an independent art of *kalâm*–in contrast, for instance, to Plato's community. The animosity stems from each monotheistic community's claim to be the one true religion or divine law. This claim in turn stems from the belief that there is one and only one God rather than a loosely structured, often shifting pantheon of gods. The divine laws of the monotheistic communities lay claim to an incomparable degree of authority.[10] Any threat to the authority of such a law–and philosophy was perceived to be such a threat by the early Greek and Syrian Christians–was bound to evoke a greater response than it did in ancient Greece. Although a generally known *kalâm* did not have as distinct an existence in ancient Greece as it did in Alfarabi's community, I intend to show that Plato's *Laws* contains his philosophic art of *kalâm*.[11]

Perhaps one may wonder why we (members of modern secular regimes) cannot merely dispense with *kalâm* so that we might pursue independently the dialectical inquiry into the purposes of the law's roots or political science. The reason is that this inquiry runs the risk of undermining the law's authority.[12] All written laws rest upon certain fundamental moral opinions, whether they are explicitly religious in character or not. Although Alfarabi defines *kalâm* as an art that defends a divine law or religion, one need not argue that the U.S. Constitution rests upon a tacit civil religion in order to show that as a regime ruled by written laws our regime requires something like Alfarabi's *kalâm*. In the *Enumeration* Alfarabi includes among the roots that *kalâm* must defend not only opinions about God and actions directed toward God but also "actions by means of which transactions (*mu'âmalât*) are conducted in the cities."[13] Even a regime, such as ours, that does not concern itself with its citizens' opinions and actions concerning God must provide a subphilosophic defense of its roots concerning human transactions. Written law as such requires a subphilosophic defense. Only if written law could become strictly rational could one make do without such a defense.

2. *Why are the roots the theme of the* Laws *and the* Summary?

Although legislation is the subject matter of the *Laws* as well as the *Summary*, both of these books focus on the highest aspect of legislation: namely, the defense of and the inquiry into the purposes of the roots.[14] As we saw above, this defense and inquiry are the activities of the philosophic *mutakallim*. Why, the reader may ask, is philosophic *kalâm*, rather than the act of legislation, the subject matter of the *Laws*? Every legislator should take up the subject matter of philosophic *kalâm* prior to legislating. To know what to legislate, the legislator must know what the purposes of legislation are. The act of legislation itself merely engages the limited kind of prudence that should be possessed by the jurisprudent.[15] Once the purposes of legislation have been determined, then one needs merely a certain amount of experience with human beings to know what laws should be laid down to achieve these ends.

Let us turn to the opening of the *Laws* to understand better why the subject matter of philosophic *kalâm* is the subject matter of the *Laws* and *Summary*. The Athenian Stranger asks his interlocutors (Kleinias and Megillus, a Cretan and Spartan, respectively) the following opening question: Who is the "cause" (*aitia*) of your laws, a god or some human being? As Alfarabi explains, this inquiry into the "cause" (*sabab*) is an inquiry into a specific kind of cause, namely, that of the "maker" (or agent, *fâ'il*). The interchange between the Athenian Stranger and Kleinias offers a heterogeneous answer: First, Kleinias responds that it is most just to say that a god legislated the laws. Kleinias's answer seems to represent the most commonly accepted opinion among Cretans about the divine foundation of their laws. Thus, as stated in the introduction, Plato begins (in a phenomenological manner) with commonly accepted opinion (rather than with metaphysical presuppositions). Second, the Athenian suggests that a hero, Minos, joined with Zeus in legislating for Crete. In contrast, as if to denigrate the human role in legislation, the Athenian mentions only in passing Lycurgus's role in legislating the Spartan laws, so well known to the modern reader from Plutarch (632d4). The Athenian's mention of the semihuman hero, however, leaves us from the start with a heterogeneous and indecisive answer to the Athenian's own opening question.[16]

Why is it more just to say that the god, rather than some human being, legislated? The preliminary answer to this question is obvious. All people are more willing to obey a law that they believe is sanctioned, indeed legislated, by a god. The gods are more able to guarantee that the unjust–who, as anyone can see, frequently slip through the hands of the human authorities–will be punished. The gods should guarantee vengeance.

Leaving justice aside, who really legislates? This question also has an obvious preliminary answer for the modern reader. Let us restrain our desire for immediate answers, however. Although Plato and Alfarabi may have a similar answer to this question, the way in which they answer it is instructive. As I have said, Kleinias is led to answer in a heterogeneous manner the question of who is the cause of the laws. The very heterogeneity, and consequent insufficiency, of the answer leaves it as an unresolved matter. At first it might appear that this matter has been shunted into the background: The Athenian gains his companions' assent to undertake a discussion of the political regimes and laws. But, as the dramatic setting–an ascent to the cave where Minos received from Zeus the laws of Crete–suggests, the questions of how, in what sense, and why human beings are said to receive their laws from gods will continue to be addressed, if only in the background, throughout the dialogue. It is for this reason that the *Laws* was described by Alfarabi's student Avicenna as the treatment of prophecy and the divine Law.[17]

Not long after the opening section on the "maker" of the laws, Alfarabi takes up the question anew in the form of an inquiry into the identity of the true legislator (disc. 1.14). In the passage Alfarabi summarizes (639a2 ff.), the Athenian attempts to draw analogies between the sober ruler's art of rule over the drinking party and the art of rule of a goatherd over a herd, a captain over a ship, and a general over an army. Alfarabi treats the sober art of rule over the drinking party as analogous to the legislator's art. Alfarabi piously asserts that the true legislator is distinguished from the false one by virtue of his having been created (*khalq*) and equipped for his purpose by God (*Allâh*). Alfarabi does not say that God reveals the law to the true legislator, but merely that the true legislator (the sober ruler) is endowed differently from the false legislator (drunk ruler) from birth, as the term *khalq* suggests.[18] Although the endowment of a human individual could be the result of a miraculous intervention by an omnipotent God, it could just as easily be the result of a God with knowledge of universals or nature or chance. Some human beings are capable of legislating "true laws" and some are not. This much is certain: Alfarabi does not say that God gives laws to legislators as a mysterious act of will. It remains unclear, however, who Alfarabi considers to be the maker of the laws.

At the opening of the *Laws* the Athenian appears to drop the question as to who makes the law. After having answered the question about the "maker" of the laws inconclusively (and after vaguely describing the subject matter of their future discussion), the Athenian turns from the question about the "cause" as "maker" or "agent" to the question about the "cause" as "purpose." Answering the latter question is an indirect way of answering the former. If a human being is capable of determining what the proper purpose of law is, then that person would not find it difficult to legislate—let alone to revise received legislation. In other words, if a human being is capable of determining what the cause of law is, in the sense of its purpose, then that human being should be capable of being the cause of law, in the sense of its agent. This inquiry into the purpose and, above all, into the agent of the law, which plays such a central role in medieval Muslim (as well as Jewish) political philosophy, is sometimes referred to as prophetology.[19] Once again, Avicenna's description of the *Laws* shows itself to be apt.

The Athenian does not begin the inquiry into the purpose of the laws by asking his interlocutors, What is the proper purpose of law in general? but rather by asking them, What is the purpose of your laws—in particular, of your most distinctive laws concerning common meals, gymnastic, and the bearing of arms? Yet citizens stand in such a relation to their laws that they, like Kleinias, transform a question about their own laws into a question about laws as such (625e7 ff.). For citizens are taught to cherish their own laws as the best. Why should one obey the laws of one's city if one believes that there are other laws that are better? In the following pages the Athenian shows Kleinias that either Kleinias does not understand the purpose of his own laws (630e–32d8) or his own laws do not have the proper purpose (634c–35b6). In either case, Kleinias is in need of an education as to what the proper purpose of law is. This education in the purpose, rather than in the art, of legislation is the primary subject matter of the *Laws* and the *Summary*. As I suggested earlier in this chapter, the inquiry into the purposes of the laws is the part of political science that is indispensable to the philosophic *mutakallim*.

As we saw in section 1, the purpose of the philosophic law (including the laws proper and the preludes) is to cure the disease of the soul. Thus, proper legislation depends upon a proper understanding of the "whole nature of souls." The roots of the philosophic version of the divine law are specific opinions about God and the world, and so forth—namely, opinions that are compatible with the formation of certain kinds of souls. According to Thomas Pangle, "The science regarding soul is the same as the science regarding gods."[20] At least one possible meaning of this statement is that the kind of gods in which people believe determines to a great extent what kind of souls they will have. If people believe in an omnipotent God who is readily made jealous but who is merciful, they are likely to have humble souls. On the other hand, if they believe in a God who has a knowledge of universals and who suffers from no human passions, they are less likely to have humble souls. Of course, the humility or lack of humility of a city's population has a direct effect on its political life. Thus, the philosophic *mutakallim*'s concern with the soul translates into a concern with its gods. Once again, the difference between the way in which the philosophic *mutakallim* is concerned with the gods and the way in which the popular *mutakallim* is concerned with the gods is that the former focuses on that which promotes the right kind of souls and thus the political community's well-being, whereas the latter focuses on that which promotes the community's popularly accepted religious traditions.

What kinds of opinions about the gods, and thus about the human soul, are conducive to the political well-being of a community? This question will remain at the center of my inquiry throughout the rest of this study, especially in part 3. For the present let it suffice to say that a common but incorrect answer to this question is, that the community should depend upon the gods to give them victory in battle. Although such a vision of the gods might give rise to hopefulness among citizens about achieving victory in battle, it may fail to foster martial virtue by reducing human self-reliance. In general, one of the crucial ways, perhaps the crucial way, in which the philosophic *mutakallim* modifies the popularly accepted opinions about the gods is to reduce the amount of influence on political events popularly attributed to them. Certain philosophic *mutakallimûn* have been so successful in reducing the political role of the gods that *kalâm* has come to be misconstrued as their demonstrative *metaphysica specialis*.

3. *How philosophic* kalâm *becomes misconstrued as metaphysical doctrine*

Aristotle is the leading example of a philosophic *mutakallim* who has been so successful in reducing the political role of the gods that his *kalâm* has come to be construed as his metaphysical doctrine. Indeed, the accepted modern interpretation of bk. *Lambda* of his *Metaphysics* is that it presents what he intends to be his demonstrative *metaphysica specialis*. In contrast, Alfarabi explains in his *On the Purposes of Aristotle's Metaphysics* that bk. *Lambda* presents Aristotle's *kalâm*.[21] Alfarabi's own account of the intention of this *kalâm* is presented in the *Book of Letters*, his commentary on or interpretation of the *Metaphysics*. As Muhsin Mahdi has suggested, the second and middle section of the

Book of Letters is a commentary on one brief but striking passage in *Metaphysics*, bk. *Lambda* (1074a38-b14).[22] In this passage, Aristotle argues that in the most ancient religion among the Greeks there was a belief that the heavenly bodies are gods and that the natural whole is divine—a belief strikingly similar to the beliefs he defends in bk. *Lambda*. Modern human beings corrupted these purer beliefs by describing the gods as like human beings and animals to persuade the many "and as something useful for the laws and for matters of expediency." The usefulness and expediency for law of anthropomorphic gods is readily apparent: such gods give great immediacy to threats of punishment for disobedience to the city's laws.

Aristotle justifies his revised version of popular Greek religion by suggesting that his account of the astral gods is identical to the Greek religion that predated the anthropomorphic religion (*Metaphysics* 1074b1-14). In other words, he tries to persuade his reader that his account of the gods is more traditional than the tradition. He appeals to the prejudice in favor of tradition while revising the tradition. Alfarabi recapitulates this approach to *kalâm* in the *Book of Letters* in the following form: Philosophy precedes religion in time; philosophy is more traditional than the tradition.[23] Aristotle's claim that his theology is more traditional than the tradition has at least two politically salutary effects: he shields himself from persecution and, of greater interest at present, he revises the traditional understanding of the gods by substituting his more philosophic theology for the popular theology. He would be thoroughly irresponsible in making this substitution if the resulting theology could not at least accommodate a political teaching that would fill the political role traditionally played by the popular theology, namely, persuading the many "and as something useful for the laws and for matters of expediency." In other words, contrary to appearances, the *Metaphysics* must accommodate itself to politics even if it does not supply a political teaching. When one thinks of how that consummately political Socratic, Xenophon, portrays Socrates as arguing in favor of a teleological account of the whole (*Memorabilia* 4.3), one begins to wonder whether it is so implausible to suggest that even Aristotle's apparently apolitical teleological theology has a political purpose.

Alfarabi uses the myth[24] that philosophy precedes religion to defend philosophy in his community in the following manner: First, if philosophy is older than religion, then it deserves the respect accorded the old. Second, religion not only emerges after philosophy but is an imitation of philosophy. And because often one religion follows another and the one that follows imitates its predecessor, the further a religion is from its origins in philosophy the more distant an imitation it becomes. Alternatively, sometimes a religion will emerge that is an imitation of a false philosophy. In either case, such an account of the emergence of religion makes it highly likely that one's present religion is only a distant imitation of the truth or of true philosophy. Consequently, one should not be surprised if adherents of one's religion attack contemporary adherents of philosophy because of the great divergence between philosophy and a distant imitation of philosophy.[25] One should assume that philosophers are unjustly accused when they are accused of heresy.

I am less interested here in the defense of philosophy that Alfarabi achieves with Aristotle's myth, however, than I am in how this argument is, as Aristotle says, "useful for the laws." By treating religion as an imitation of philosophy, Alfarabi makes it possible for religion to be made in the image of philosophy. "Metaphysics" is the means by which Alfarabi achieves this rationalization of religion. By replacing anthropomorphic gods with astral gods (or separate intellects or angels), Aristotle (and Alfarabi) considerably weaken the immediacy of punishment threatened by law. Indeed, Aristotle's political intention–although it is a negative political intention–is to transform the traditional gods, who like human beings have a personal stake in the affairs of human beings, into politically disinterested astral gods (very much like Plato's astral gods in bk. 10 of the *Laws).* On the other hand, by describing astral gods as the ruling part of a teleologically arranged whole, they offer some support to the law.

4. The roots of the laws revisited

Bk. 10 contains Plato's *kalâm* in much the same way that Alfarabi says bk. *Lambda* of Aristotle's *Metaphysics,* contains Aristotle's *kalâm.* Alfarabi asserts, however, that Plato presents his "discussion" (*kalâm*) of the laws' roots in bks. 1-8 (disc. 9.1). To understand this apparent contradiction, we need only recall that although the roots and their purpose are both theological for the traditional *mutakallim,* the roots and their purpose are different for the philosophic *mutakallim.* For the latter, the roots are theological, but their purpose is political or psychological. Bk. 10 does not contain the roots of Plato's law if one means by roots the ultimate purpose of law. Accordingly, Alfarabi says that what follows the opening of bk. 9–in other words, most of bk. 9 and bks. 10-12–"explains things that adorn and embellish the law and things that are consequences of the roots" (disc. 9.2). Insofar as the roots are the purposes of the laws, the laws are themselves the consequences of the roots. Most of bk. 9 and bks. 11 and 12 are taken up with legislation proper. Presumably, that which adorns and embellishes the law is what is left over once we take away most of bk. 9 and bks. 11 and 12, namely, bk. 10. Kleinias (a spirited soul) asserts that the theological prelude presented in bk. 10 is "just about [the] noblest and best prelude on behalf of all the laws" (887c). In spite of Kleinias's possible objections, however, the theological prelude to the law contained in bk. 10 is an adornment. (This is not to say, however, that adornments may not have substantial purposes. An account of the gods of the sort described in bk. 10 may be indispensable for the cultivation of the indignant or spirited kind of soul that will rule in the second-best city described in the *Laws* [see especially disc. 5.9].) By omitting a summary of bk. 10, Alfarabi merely omits the adornments. This is unproblematic because Alfarabi's *Summary* strives, above all, to reveal Plato's intention rather than to recapitulate his text. Plato's highest intention is to understand the psychological or political purpose of the best laws. In summarizing the first nine books of the *Laws*, Alfarabi reveals the psychological purpose (or roots) of the laws. The heart of the *Summary* is bk. 5, whose leading theme is how to honor the soul. Plato presents the purpose of bk. 10 in bk. 5.

In bks. 4 and 5, the Athenian presents his, as opposed to Kleinias's, version of the prelude to the law as a whole. This version of the prelude falls into two parts or preludes along the line separating bk. 4 from bk. 5: First, in bk. 4 he presents a "prelude as regards the gods, those who come after the gods, and the living and dead ancestors" (724a). Second, in bk. 5 he presents a prelude as regards "how [human beings] should be serious and how they should relax as regards their own souls, their bodies, and their property" (724b). Alfarabi's interpretation of these two parts of the Athenian's prelude strips away the adornments of the law to reveal the purposes of the laws.

In his summary of the first part of the prelude, Alfarabi quickly undermines any inclination to view the account of the gods in this first part as belonging to the prelude to the law as a whole: He omits any mention of the striking opening of this part in which the Athenian announces that the god is the beginning, middle, and end of all things.[26] Alfarabi only notes that the gods are displeased with the arrogant human being (cf. disc. 4.9 with 716a4). Furthermore, he makes no mention, as Plato does, of people's need to sacrifice to, pray to, or serve the gods (cf. disc. 4.10 with 716c–18a). Their "support" is acquired, at least by the ruler, merely by his avoiding arrogance (which, as it so happens, is a way of serving other human beings rather than gods). The only things that Alfarabi suggests human beings need to care for are their own bodies, souls, and property; they should do so both for their own sake and for their family's sake (cf. 717c3). In other words, Alfarabi gives an account of the first part of the prelude (in bk. 4) that leaves it indistinguishable from the second part (in bk. 5). Finally, when Alfarabi turns to summarizing bk. 5, he does not mention the gods as those beings who must be honored before the human soul (disc. 5. 1).[27] He merely notes that the human soul ranks third in divinity, and he chooses to add that the human soul is the noblest of things. What remains of the Athenian's prelude is an account of human being, and above all of the human soul. By reflection on this prelude one can begin to acquire the knowledge of the disease of the soul and the whole nature of the souls, i.e., of the true foundation of the revised divine law.

In modern political philosophy, Machiavelli initiated a concerted attack against religion. His loud declamations against Christianity led not to the revision of popular religion but to its near obliteration. If I am correct that politics can never be strictly rational, however, the ambition to obliterate religion was misplaced. Belief, which disappeared in one form, reappeared in another, in some ways less salutary, form.[28] At the same time, Machiavelli's loud declamations led eventually to an obliviousness of the need for philosophic *kalâm*. The ultimate result was not that *kalâm* was annihilated but that it became so intermingled with political science as to become indistinguishable from it: political science became ideology. Although positivism maintains an illusion of objectivity and neutrality, it has developed a decided preference for modern egalitarian political regimes. Such regimes are said to manifest the orderliness, symmetry, and equality characteristic of positivistic social science itself.

Under the illusion that modern Western culture is different in kind from all previous traditional cultures,[29] positivistic political science has become oblivious of the need for an art such as *kalâm*. In reaction, postmodernism would have us believe that political science is nothing other than *kalâm*. Thus, the postmodernists generally advocate the study of rhetoric rather than metaphysics and science. In contrast to both of these extreme positions, Alfarabi, through his interpretation of the *Laws*, describes both a dialectical inquiry into the purpose of law (political science)–which necessarily points beyond the rule of law to the rule of reason–and a rhetorical defense of law (*kalâm*). As I will show, the rhetorical defense cannot be properly undertaken without a knowledge of the political science to which it is a supplement. On the other hand, political science is ill-equipped to make policy recommendations without a full recognition of the limitations political life places on rationality, limitations that circumscribe the subrational defense of law.

2
Alfarabi's Platonism

This chapter treats the secondary literature on Alfarabi's corpus as a whole rather than just on the *Summary*, because there is only one substantive treatment of the *Summary*, namely, a brief article by Leo Strauss.[1] The purpose of this chapter, however, is to correct certain common and persistent misunderstandings of Alfarabi. In spite of the readily apparent anachronism involved, I will discuss the secondary literature on Alfarabi before that on the *Laws*, because the former provides easier access to insights that are of use in reading the latter. In particular, most of the literature on Alfarabi openly describes him as a Neoplatonist and thus as a metaphysical dogmatist. In contrast, the secondary literature on Plato is less explicit in identifying him as such a dogmatist.

To some extent the attribution of Neoplatonism to Alfarabi was to be expected because the example followed in scholarship on medieval Islamic philosophy was scholarship on medieval Christian philosophy. And Neoplatonism had served as the model for much of medieval Christian philosophy. Consequently, scholars of medieval Islamic philosophy were predisposed to view their subject also as essentially Neoplatonic. More specifically, medieval Christian philosophy since Augustine had come to view Plato through the eyes of the Neoplatonists, and consequently, scholars assumed that medieval Islamic philosophy viewed Plato through the same Neoplatonic lens.

The Neoplatonic character of most of the nineteenth- and twentieth-century scholarship on Plato's political philosophy is far more difficult to detect, especially since the German scholarship that was initiated by Schleiermacher prided itself on forgoing the Renaissance reliance on Neoplatonic commentaries for understanding Plato. I will show that, in spite of its claims, a large portion of the modern scholarship on the *Laws* has failed to free itself from the Neoplatonic tradition. Finally, I have chosen to focus primarily on the tendency to view Plato and Alfarabi through a Neoplatonic lens because a major concern of this study is to demonstrate that neither Plato nor Alfarabi (nor Alfarabi's Plato) is a metaphysical dogmatist, as are the Neoplatonists. What appear to be their respective metaphysical dogmas are in fact their arts of *kalâm*.

1. *Alfarabi as metaphysical Neoplatonist*

Those students of Alfarabi who treat him as a Neoplatonist are inspired, at least in part, by their familiarity with the importance of Neoplatonism for the medieval Christian tradition. The influence of Neoplatonism reached the Aristotelian Thomas Aquinas by way of Augustine, who frequently notes the kinship between the teaching of Christianity and the teaching of Neoplatonism.[2] Indeed, Augustine goes so far in his admiration of Neoplatonism as to admit that the only worthy opponent of Christian doctrine (or theology) is Neoplatonism.[3] According to Augustine, Neoplatonism and Christianity shared a central doctrine in common: the belief that this world of appearances (including politics) mirrors or should mirror a superior metaphysical or divine order. More importantly for us, Augustine attributed this view not only to the Neoplatonists but also to Plato.[4] As I will show, Alfarabi's Plato in no way subscribes to this view. At the same time, I will explain why Alfarabi waxes Neoplatonic in his emanationist theology in the opening sections of the *Virtuous City* and the *Political Regime*.[5]

In general, the secondary literature on Alfarabi regards his metaphysics as Neoplatonic.[6] For my purposes, the single most important fact about Neoplatonists is their studied lack of concern for political or worldly affairs. This lack of concern is complemented by the undivided attention they pay to metaphysical matters, above all to *metaphysica specialis* or theology. The difficulty with characterizing Alfarabi as a Neoplatonist is that his attention to metaphysical matters is never undivided. He presents his own *metaphysica specialis* only in works whose leading subject matter is politics.[7] Consequently, even if Alfarabi were a Neoplatonist as regards his metaphysics, he would not be an orthodox Neoplatonist. Certain aspects of his Neoplatonic heterodoxy are widely recognized in some of the secondary literature. The secondary literature, however, because of its roots in nineteenth-century German historical scholarship, understands its enterprise in such a way that heterodoxy is necessarily reduced to eclecticism. Alfarabi is thought to combine a Neoplatonic *metaphysica specialis* with a Platonic political philosophy, no matter how incompatible these elements might be.

The heterodoxy of Alfarabi's purported Neoplatonism should be taken seriously. It appears in works such as the *Political Regime* and the *Virtuous City,* in which Alfarabi presents a Neoplatonic theology and then a strikingly parallel description of the political order he envisions. In effect, the hierarchy that characterizes the virtuous regimes finds divine support in an equally hierarchical and orderly account of the divine beings. At first glance, his account of political things shares much with the view that would gain ascendancy four centuries later with Thomas Aquinas: The order that rules the heavens extends not only to the earth but to the human things. Or in the words of Majid Fakhry, for Alfarabi politics is "an extension or development of metaphysics or its highest manifestation, theology. . . ."[8]

Alfarabi's *Summary,* as a commentary on Plato, provides a useful counterpoint to the first impression left by the *Political Regime* and the *Virtuous City.* It confronts us with one massive fact: In Alfarabi's sole commentary on Plato, that is, in the context in which one would most expect him to view Plato through a Neoplatonic lens, there is not a trace of Neoplatonism.[9] Alfarabi does not summarize the one passage of the *Laws* that could be an extraordinary vehicle for a Neoplatonist commentator, namely, the account of the astral gods given in bk. 10. Indeed, the gods are ever-present in the *Laws* in a manner unparalleled in the rest of the Platonic corpus, yet Alfarabi chooses to omit the most striking accounts of their role.

In his commentary on the *Laws* (and in his commentary on the *Metaphysics)* Alfarabi never recapitulates Plato's (or Aristotle's respective) proofs of god's existence–the very heart of *metaphysica specialis* and what came to be the very centerpiece of medieval Scholasticism. Alfarabi is profoundly silent about the theology of Plato in the *Summary* for the same reason he is silent about Aristotle's theology in the *Book of Letters*: Both of these commentaries are meant to convey the intention of their respective authors. Because their intentions were political rather than metaphysical, Alfarabi is silent about their theologies but describes their political import. In contrast, Alfarabi presents his own art of *kalâm* in the opening of the *Political Regime* and of the *Virtuous City.*[10] In these works which he wrote under his own name–viz., in a highly exposed setting–Alfarabi presents his own criticisms and revisions of the regimes and laws adhered to in his own time. In such a context, these regimes and laws require the kind of theological defense Plato provided for his own revised regime in the *Laws.* Although in the *Summary* Alfarabi adapts Plato's regime in the *Laws* to his own time, he does so in a setting in which all divergences from the regimes of his own time and place can be dismissed as deviations deriving from the pagan Plato. Furthermore, he makes such adaptations primarily to make the teaching of the *Laws* accessible to his contemporaries rather than to serve as a political blueprint.

Even when Alfarabi does present his equivalent to the *metaphysica specialis* of Plato and Aristotle, his theology is intentionally presented in an even less demonstrative fashion than in their theologies. His various versions of this theology are, at best, descriptions of the divine order rather than attempts to provide rational proofs of God's existence. Far from making any effort to appear to present proofs, Alfarabi's method of argumentation can only be described as rhetorical. Perhaps Alfarabi, in reviewing the effect of Aristotle's and Plato's proofs of god's existence, arrived at the conclusion that it would be better to avoid even the appearance of presenting demonstrative proofs of God's existence.

There is no doubt that in the theological passages of the *Political Regime* and the *Virtuous City,* Alfarabi uses Neoplatonist imagery. What is at issue, however, is whether he uses this as imagery for political purposes (i.e., as rhetorical *kalâm*) or views it (as the Neoplatonists viewed similar but not identical teachings) as the truth (i.e., demonstrative *metaphysica specialis*). To see that Alfarabi uses such accounts merely as imagery, one need only recall the political context in which they appear. The parallels that exist between the metaphysical account and the account of political life in each case are obvious: The metaphysical world is said to be ruled by a self-sufficient unique being who rules absolutely over a hierarchal order; and the political world, in the best case, is said to be ruled by the philosopher-king who rules absolutely over a hierarchical order. The primary difference between these parallel accounts is that what is supposed to be necessarily the case in the first account is only so in the best case in the latter account. There is perhaps no more persuasive rhetorical argument for striving in the direction of the best case (philosophic rule) than a description of a necessary and therefore inevitable (theological or metaphysical) hierarchy. Thus, the metaphysical account is intended as a model or an analogy for the account of political life.

Alfarabi never attempts to use demonstrative arguments to prove that the city is ordered in the same way as is the metaphysical order. He only draws an analogy (a form of rhetorical argument) between the metaphysical order and the political order. There are obvious problems with this analogy, however. The city is the home of—and itself a product of—the arts that produce artificial rather than natural things. Any philosopher deserving of the name would not be willing to rest satisfied with the mere assumption that the city has the same order as that underlying the natural whole. Alfarabi's use of the imagery of metaphysics for political purposes is far removed from the medieval Christian "natural law" teaching articulated most clearly by Thomas Aquinas. This teaching assumes that the order underlying the natural whole as dictated by the "eternal law" extends itself to the political realm in the form of the "natural law" (*Summa Theologiae,* 1a2ae.91, 1 and 2).

Despite rhetorical appearances to the contrary, Alfarabi makes an inquiry into political things that makes no assumptions about the naturalness of political things. Indeed, he acknowledges that the human or political things are voluntary rather than necessary.[11] Like Plato and Aristotle, however, in his political works he frequently describes the natural whole as teleological and hierarchically ordered to persuade his readers that the city should possess a similar teleological and hierarchical order. In modernity, Spinoza engaged in a concerted effort to undermine the ancient claim that the natural whole has a teleological order, even though he affirmed the existence of a hierarchy of human ends. Ironically, the attack on teleology in the natural sciences led by degrees to a denial of the possibility that there is a hierarchy of human ends.[12] Perhaps, after all is said and done, Alfarabi's teleological metaphysical imagery is not such a bad way to persuade human beings of the reasonableness of his account of the best political order. Furthermore, perhaps his account of the metaphysical order, although not truly philosophical or rational, may constitute a substantially more rational account of the whole than that which is popularly accepted. Finally, by setting the metaphysical order above the political order, Alfarabi elevates the rank of inquiry into the order of nature in the eyes of those ambitious persons who might otherwise aspire to tyranny.

2. *Alfarabi as political Middle Platonist: Richard Walzer*

Richard Walzer proposes a related but more refined interpretation of Alfarabi's corpus than the one I have just criticized. He recognizes the Neoplatonic character of Alfarabi's "metaphysics," but he also detects an incompatibility between Plotinian Neoplatonic metaphysics and the amount of attention that Alfarabi lavishes on politics.[13] He does not consider Alfarabi to be indebted in metaphysical questions (especially the possibility of emanation from the Active Intellect to the human intellect) to the "mystically minded" Neoplatonists of the Athenian Academy but rather to a "moderate Neoplatonist" of the sixth-century school of Alexandria.[14] As far as politics is concerned, Walzer assigns Alfarabi's presumed debt in this area to a purported "Middle Platonist" predecessor. The best example he is able to supply of a Middle Platonist with Alfarabi's interest in politics is Cicero. There is no evidence, however, that Cicero's works reached the Arabic-speaking world by Alfarabi's time. Walzer attributes Alfarabi's interest in the question of the possibility of a nation encompassing the entire inhabited world, to his supposed Middle Platonic predecessor's having lived at the end of the Roman Empire.[15] But as Ralph Lerner has suggested, Alfarabi's "'great' perfect political association . . . did not require the model of Rome or Persia but could have referred to the monotheistic universal religions whose claims seemed to supersede the statesmen's and philosophers' *nomos*."[16]

Walzer's view is an improvement over those of his predecessors who viewed Alfarabi as a Plotinian Neoplatonist. He acknowledges that Plotinian Neoplatonism is incompatible with a substantive interest in political things. Nevertheless, he is compelled to have recourse to eclecticism to explain the uniqueness of Alfarabi's concern with political things in the medieval world of his time. Especially because Alfarabi lived in the Islamic world, Walzer believes he must have slavishly adopted one contemporary tradition or another in metaphysics and one tradition or another in political philosophy, even though we possess no traces of said traditions. Above all, Walzer is unwilling to entertain the possibility that Alfarabi chooses elements of, for example, Neoplatonic doctrines and manipulates them to achieve an effect. He views Alfarabi as enthralled to a confluence of traditions rather than as a master manipulator of them. On the one hand, Alfarabi must be indebted to some unidentified Middle Platonist who took a peculiarly political approach to Plato's *Republic* and *Laws*. On the other hand, he must be indebted to a moderate Neoplatonism in metaphysics that can somehow be reconciled with this political Platonism. Is it not possible that Alfarabi rediscovered the original meaning of Plato's political thought, after its having lain dormant for centuries? Could he not have understood things about Plato's thought that were lost on many of Plato's own disciples in the Academy after his death? Could he not have grasped something that the Christian world had neglected–something that lay dormant, so to speak, within its own breast? Perhaps Alfarabi was a thoroughgoing Platonist who merely made use of Neoplatonic imagery because changed religious conditions demanded it of him.

Let us take the example of an Alfarabian work, *Harmonization of the Opinions of the Two Sages: Plato, the Divine, and Aristotle*, which no doubt contributed to Walzer's view that Alfarabi was a moderate Neoplatonist-Middle Platonist hybrid. According to Walzer, Alfarabi "[like] many Greek thinkers, . . . believed in the ultimate identity of Plato's and Aristotle's views. He based himself on Aristotle, as understood by the Greek commentators of late antiquity, in logic, natural science, psychology, metaphysics (these metaphysics however understood and developed on moderate Neoplatonic lines)."[17] In the *Harmonization*, Alfarabi attempts to harmonize the opinions of Plato, the divine, and Aristotle by means of Neoplatonic mediation. He attempts to harmonize them, however, for a reason that should make it clear that his primary interest is not in the truth of what he says: The apparent disagreement between the philosophers has become a source of "doubt and suspicion."[18] Evidently, the dialectical theologians attempted to use the apparent divergence between the philosophers to raise doubts about the compatibility of such a teaching with the one true teaching, namely, Islam. To harmonize Plato, the divine, and Aristotle, Alfarabi makes recourse to a writing that we now know to be Neoplatonic, the *Theology of Aristotle*. Many scholars have assumed that Alfarabi failed to realize that this work is Neoplatonic rather than genuinely Aristotelian.[19] In her article "A Re-examination of al-Fârâbî's Neoplatonism," Miriam Galston adduces reasons for believing that, contrary to appearances, Alfarabi did not consider the *Theology of Aristotle* to be genuinely Aristotelian but realized that it was a Neoplatonic work. To begin with, Alfarabi makes no mention of the *Theology* or of its doctrines in his comprehensive treatment of the works of Aristotle in his *Philosophy of Aristotle*.[20] Galston also argues that the interest that the Aristotle of the *Theology* displays in 'metaphysical questions' is to be contrasted with the interests of the Aristotle of the *Philosophy of Aristotle*. In the latter text, Aristotle–like the Aristotle in the *Book of Letters*, Alfarabi's Plato in the *Philosophy of Plato*, and, I would argue, Alfarabi's Plato in the *Summary*–has almost nothing to say about "divine science." Above all, he has nothing to say about the third part of "divine science," i.e., the account of god and the separate intellects or the bodiless beings.[21]

One could argue that Alfarabi is practically silent about Aristotle's "true" Neoplatonic opinions concerning the bodiless beings in his *Philosophy of Aristotle* because he has already expressed his Neoplatonic understanding of Aristotle's metaphysics in the *Harmonization* and in his political writings. There are, at least, two considerations that argue against this interpretation. First, even a cursory logical analysis of the *Harmonization* and the *Philosophy of Aristotle* shows that the *Harmonization* is the far more rhetorical work; it aims to provide an apology for philosophy rather than an accurate presentation of the thought of a philosopher.[22] Second, and this is a factor that Galston seems to have neglected, in the *Harmonization* Alfarabi harmonizes not the purported opinions of Aristotle and those of Plato but of Aristotle and Plato *the divine*.[23] As Galston mentions, "In the *Harmonization* [Alfarabi] notes that in several places in the *Theology* Aristotle supports the view that forms have an independent existence in a separate, divine world–a Platonic doctrine against which Aristotle presents repeated and strong objections in his other works."[24] When we recall Alfarabi's silence in the *Philosophy of Plato* about the so-called theory of Ideas, it becomes obvious that Alfarabi is harmonizing a false Neoplatonic Aristotle not with an authentic Plato but with Plato *the divine*, whose authenticity is equally in doubt. As Galston suggests, precisely because the *Harmonization* does not treat the true philosophy of Aristotle (and, I would add, of Plato), we cannot determine on the basis of the *Harmonization* whether Alfarabi regards Plato's and Aristotle's views on metaphysics to be substantially different. To determine this, one would have to turn to Alfarabi's *Philosophy of Plato and Aristotle*. Above all, this writing shows that Alfarabi does not regard Plato's and Aristotle's views on metaphysics as Neoplatonic or dogmatic in character.[25] As for the *Harmonization*, one is merely able to determine that Alfarabi intends to make it appear that Plato and Aristotle agree with one another and, perhaps more crucially, as Galston points out, with the opinions of revealed religion on metaphysical matters.[26] The most glaring evidence that one of the primary purposes of the *Harmonization* is to create a mere appearance of harmony between philosophy and revealed religion is his attempt to persuade the reader that Aristotle did not think that the world is eternal.[27]

I have happened upon the reason why Alfarabi's "metaphysics" takes on a Neoplatonic character rather than, for example, the character of Aristotle's "theology" in bk. *Lambda* of the *Metaphysics*. Druart has argued that Alfarabi's emanationism is his innovation on Aristotle. She suggests that the primary mark of the innovation is that whereas Aristotle's Prime Mover is merely a principle of change, Alfarabi's First Cause is a principle of existence. Or put more elaborately, "Most of the attributes of al-Farabi's first cause are missing in Aristotle, since the prime mover is a final cause of motion but does not bestow being, oneness, and truth on any other being."[28] I admit that this is an innovation; however, Alfarabi is compelled to afford God at a minimum the powers of an efficient cause in order to accommodate philosophy to *revealed* religion.[29]

I have shown that, contrary to Walzer's view that Alfarabi is a passive recipient of a dogmatic (yet moderate!) Neoplatonism, he is a master manipulator of Neoplatonism. Furthermore, if he is in any sense a Middle Platonist, he is not a political Middle Platonist. Rather he may be a metaphysical Middle Platonist. And by this I do not mean that he reconciles Plato's metaphysical dogmatism with Aristotle's metaphysical dogmatism. On the contrary, Alfarabi seems to detect a nondogmatic approach to metaphysics not only in the thought of Plato but even in the thought of Aristotle. He harmonizes a Neoplatonic Aristotle with a Neoplatonic Plato only in the *Harmonization*, whose leading purpose is to harmonize philosophy with revealed religion.

3. *Alfarabi as political Aristotelian: Galston's* Politics and Excellence

Although Galston's large and closely argued work obviously deserves more attention than I can give it in this context,[30] no assessment of the secondary literature on Alfarabi, and in particular no assessment of Alfarabi's Platonism, can be made without addressing this ambitious piece of scholarship. One of the inexplicit but leading arguments of this book is that Alfarabi's political philosophy owes more to Aristotle than it does to Plato. At the same time, Galston graciously acknowledges her neglect of the *Summary* (p. 221).[31] Furthermore, in light of this neglect, she acknowledges that a final understanding of Alfarabi's political philosophy is not yet at hand. Because the *Summary* is the sole commentary we have by Alfarabi on a Platonic or Aristotelian political work, I am justified in a study on the *Summary* in raising doubts about the purported Aristotelianism of Alfarabi's political philosophy.[32] Galston's arguments for his Aristotelianism depend, above all, upon the importance she attributes to his *Apho-*

risms. In the *Aphorisms,* he clearly draws material from Aristotle's *Nicomachean Ethics,* but–this is crucial–it is not a commentary on the *Ethics.*[33] The *Aphorisms* does not present Alfarabi's interpretation of Aristotle's political philosophy so much as an imitation of his popular ethical teaching.

The first, and perhaps the boldest, step in Galston's attempt to disprove Alfarabi's Platonism is a methodological or interpretive one. Galston claims to have uncovered an as yet neglected and more correct method of reading Alfarabi. For the sake of convenience, I will call this method the "dialectical method." According to this method, the reader is obligated to view all of Alfarabi's texts as a working out of various, often contradictory, "doctrines." These "doctrines" and their "consequences" in each of Alfarabi's texts should be treated with "equal care" (pp. 51, 54). Indeed, the highest task of the reader is to compare the contradictory "doctrines" and their contradictory "consequences" with one another. Galston's hope is that by playing them off one another in dialectical fashion the reader might arrive at some insight as to which "doctrines" and "consequences" are demonstrative. Galston's method enables her to compare contradictory formulations in different Alfarabian texts. It also enables her to view the Alfarabian corpus as one whole in which the difference between parts (i.e., texts) is little more than the difference between opposing arguments that one might play off one another in one text. Consequently, she does not see it as her task to analyze each of his texts as if it were an integrated whole that must be understood as a whole before it is compared with his other texts. How can the reader, however, know beforehand that all of Alfarabi's "doctrines" and "consequences" are of equal rank? Are not different Alfarabian texts argued at different levels of logical rigor? (For instance, to take again perhaps the most revealing contrast within the corpus, it is useful to compare the *Harmonization* with the *Philosophy of Plato and Aristotle.*)

Galston contrasts her method with Leo Strauss's esoteric "method," in which, according to her, a polarization between the surface and the depth is assumed as a matter of "conviction" (p. 51).[34] She fails to distinguish clearly between two distinct senses of the opposition between surface and depth. She focuses on the opposition Strauss draws between more and less exoteric works, since her dialectical method applies particularly to the comparison of different statements by Alfarabi in different texts, and she tends to neglect the opposition he draws between more and less esoteric statements within a given text (p. 51). She tends to neglect this latter sense because her method leads her to neglect the integrity of each Alfarabian text. In the name of understanding the whole Alfarabian corpus, she passes over what must surely be a preliminary task, namely, the understanding of each text as a whole. It is not surprising that Galston rejects Strauss's distinction between more and less exoteric works,[35] because her method appears to assume that the Alfarabian corpus is essentially homogeneous.

I will mention only one example of what results from neglecting to see each of Alfarabi's texts as an independent whole. In the third chapter in section C, entitled "The Ruling Types and Their Activities," Galston compares the "divergent portraits of the supreme ruler" (p. 127) or the supreme ruler as seen from different "point[s] of view." Do Alfarabi's different texts present different portraits of the same supreme ruler or of different supreme rulers? Can one compare Alfarabi's "supreme ruler without qualification" (identified with the philosopher-king) described in the *Political Regime* with the "supreme ruler" in the *Aphorisms,* or even with the "supreme ruler" in the *Virtuous City,* as if they were equivalent? But for the fact that Alfarabi adds the specification "without qualification" (a specification that Galston neglects in this section) to his identification of the "supreme ruler" in the *Political Regime,* we would be thrown back on a resource that Alfarabi constantly reminds us we must use, namely, the awareness that words have a multiplicity of connotations. We can determine what kind of "supreme ruler" Alfarabi is talking about only by first determining what kind of city (or cities) is under discussion in each writing. And the difference in kind between "supreme rulers" in Alfarabi's different writings is often not just a difference in "point of view" but of rank.

The most obvious indicator of Galston's tendency to homogenize Alfarabi's writings is the undue weight she gives to the *Aphorisms* and to its description of the supreme ruler. She uses the *Aphorisms* to bolster a quietly argued but crucial thesis of her book: Although the theoretical virtues are higher in rank than the practical, they are both equally indispensable for human happiness. Following Alfarabi, she does not mean by practical virtues the theoretical understanding of political things or political philosophy but rather the virtues of a human being experienced in political affairs (p. 94). I cannot agree that the practical virtues are, according to Alfarabi, equally indispensable for human happiness.

The audience of the *Aphorisms,* like that of Aristotle's *Nicomachean Ethics,* which it often seems to paraphrase, is potential statesmen. The aphoristic style of the *Aphorisms* is especially well suited to the potential statesman who is impatient with the long and at times laborious study demanded by philosophic inquiry. One of the main purposes of the *Ethics* is to teach the statesman to prefer both the moral political life and the philosophic life to the immoral political life, i.e., the life of the tyrant. Such a teaching achieves two things at once: a respect for the philosophic life and a willingness to avoid pursuing the pleasures of a tyrant's life. The undue weight that Galston gives to the *Aphorisms* is consonant with her relative neglect of the Platonic element in Alfarabi's political philosophy. What Galston finds troublesome in the thought of Plato and in the highest expressions of Alfarabi's political philosophy is that Plato never devoted as much effort as did Aristotle to proving the superiority of the moral political life to the immoral political life with respect to happiness (which is not to say that Socrates did not frequently offer myths in favor of this argument); Plato merely proved the superiority of the philosophic life to the immoral (and by implication the moral) political life with respect to happiness (cf. pp. 13–14). Ironically, Galston readily admits that even in the *Aphorisms*, where Alfarabi assigns the highest rank he ever assigns to moral virtue, Alfarabi stops short of Aristotle in the crucial respect: He omits the requirement that "actions . . . be chosen for their own sake to qualify as moral" (p. 172). In other words, moral actions are not ends but means. Why Galston goes on to assert that such a view of the morality of actions is incompatible with the thought of Plato (pp. 172–73) is unclear to me.

Briefly, let us consider what effect Galston's dialectical method has on her interpretation of what I have called Alfarabi's metaphysical imagery in the opening of the *Political Regime* (and the *Virtuous City*). Rather than attempt to determine what the unified purpose of the *Political Regime* is, she suggests that it be viewed as "a work that presents theoretical philosophy *alongside* political philosophy" (Galston's italics) (p. 181, n. 5). It is difficult to understand why Alfarabi would have presented the two "parts" of this writing as forming a seamless whole unless he intended them to be viewed as an integrated whole with a unified purpose. What is the difference between setting these parts of one writing alongside one another and setting two completely different Alfarabian texts alongside one another? If Galston's "dialectical method" of reading is to be followed, then we are left without any means of answering that question. Alfarabi is far too fine a writer to leave such questions open.

In conclusion, on the basis of the popular Aristotelianism of Alfarabi's *Aphorisms* we are left with doubts about the wisdom of dispensing with what has become the more generally accepted view that Alfarabi's political philosophy is Platonic. I have myself indulged in this chapter in a sampling of a wide variety of Alfarabian texts, thus coming close to falling into the trap I have accused Galston of falling into. After the secondary literature on the *Laws* is discussed in the next chapter, however, we will turn to a single Alfarabian text, the *Summary*, with the hope that through it we might gain at least a glimpse of the whole Alfarabian world.

3
Natural Right versus Natural Law

If this book were solely dedicated to interpreting Plato's *Laws*, a chapter on the secondary literature on the *Laws* would be expected to provide a comprehensive review of that literature. Because this study, however, is dedicated to explaining Alfarabi's interpretation of the *Laws*, my object in this chapter will be merely to highlight a part of the literature whose interpretations of the *Laws* are a useful counterpoint to Alfarabi's. The two interpretations I will discuss are variants of essentially the same understanding. Both hold that Plato presents a theory of natural law in the *Laws*. In the first, he is purported to have an ethical theory of natural law and, in the second, a legalistic theory. Both share the view that Plato believes the order of political things rests upon or is derived from the order underlying the natural things. If this were so, then metaphysical knowledge would be a prerequisite for applying reason to the ordering of political life. This interpretation of the *Laws* is graced with a simple and easy harmony between the metaphysical and the political, but it also demands of human beings that they possess godlike metaphysical knowledge. By raising doubts about these two interpretations of the *Laws*, I will open up the possibility that one can acquire knowledge of how to order political life without possessing metaphysical knowledge.

Another consequence of the view that the order of political things and the order underlying natural things are in harmony is that the reason pervading the natural whole pervades the political things. Consequently, natural law is said by these interpreters to be synonymous with reason. Thus, the city ruled by natural law is the best city. One of the leading purposes of this book is to show that, according to Plato and Alfarabi, written law (even laws such as the second table of the Decalogue, which Thomas Aquinas considers to be natural) does not rule the best city but merely the second-best city. The best city is ruled by unconstrained reason. The gulf between the best city and the second-best city contributes to the need for the art of *kalâm*.[1] If reason were synonymous with written law, there would be no need for this art. Even in modernity, when natural law theory became possible without God, thinkers continued to believe in this harmony between written law and reason. Thus, the present-day forgetfulness of *kalâm* may to some extent be the result of the ultimate success of natural law theory.

In the preface, I mentioned that the most influential contemporary proponent of the view that Plato derives his politics from his metaphysics is Martin Heidegger. The reader might wonder why I do not discuss Heidegger's interpretation of Plato in this chapter. The reason is that Heidegger, like his Neoplatonic predecessors, pays little or no attention to the *Laws*. He is far more interested in Plato's more "metaphysical" dialogues such as the *Sophist* and in those passages from other dialogues such as the *Republic* and *Phaedrus* that seem to evince a quasi-Augustinian or Neoplatonic belief in a dichotomy between this world and a higher metaphysical world.[2] The natural law theorists whom I will discuss here hold a similar metaphysical view of Plato; however, they are more interested in developing the implications of this view than in deconstructing it, as is Heidegger.

It is not difficult to surmise how the metaphysical view of Plato has gained ascendancy in everyone from the natural law theorists to Heidegger. A brief historical review of the study of Plato through the ages in the Christian or Western world reveals how this view has taken hold. Although Plato had substantial influence on Christianity during the era of the church fathers and Augustine by way of Neoplatonism, his influence was meager during the Middle Ages. Christians then knew little more of his writings than the *Timaeus*. Christianity's emphasis on religious dogma rather than divine law no doubt contributed to its appropriation of this relatively metaphysical writings of Plato's. In a complementary fashion, medieval Christianity looked almost solely to Aristotle for the formulation of its political science: Aristotle's emphasis on ethics was well suited to Christianity's emphasis on ethical counsels rather than divine laws. Not until the Renaissance was interest in Plato revived, and even then the interest remained largely in the Neoplatonic commentators on Plato. The next major revival of interest in Plato occurred in Germany in the nineteenth century. The renewed interest was largely limited to students of philology rather than of philosophy. Although they eschewed the use of Neoplatonic commentators, their leading substantive interest was still in Plato's metaphysics. To this day, even thinkers as profound as Heidegger and his postmodern followers have remained largely under the influence of this approach. Many postmodernists have come to assume that for all philosophers in the Western tradition, and above all Plato, metaphysics provides the ground for politics.[3] Although theology provides this ground in the revealed religions, Alfarabi shows that Plato diverges from the revealed religions in this respect. (Heidegger makes evident his belief that revealed religion and the whole history of Western thought share the view that theology or metaphysics provides the groundwork for politics by his use of the term "ontotheological" to describe the Western tradition.) Ironically, Heidegger's project is precisely to deconstruct the metaphysical presuppositions underlying the Western analysis of human action. Heidegger traces these presuppositions to Plato's doorstep, but perhaps he was led by his predecessors' desire for a metaphysical foundation of politics to find such a foundation where there was none. And perhaps Heidegger is not the only thinker to have undertaken an analysis of human action freed from the chains of metaphysical dogmatism.

1. Plato as ethical theorist of natural law

Beginning in 1942 a series of books and articles appeared on the *Laws* heralding a renewed interest in the dialogue. The basis of the renewed interest was the claim that Plato offers therein a natural law theory. In the past, it had been suggested that natural law theory first made its appearance among the Stoic philosophers. In this series of articles, a new version of the traditional metaphysical view of Plato became manifest. Just as the Ideas serve as the metaphysical ground of Platonic politics in his early writings, so the gods serve as a metaphysical ground in his late writings, especially the *Laws*. In his *Plato's Theology*, Friedrich Solmsen made the first major contribution to this new reading of the *Laws*. The focus of his analysis was bk. 10 (introduction). He attempted to prove that Plato possessed a natural law theory by arguing that the account of the gods in bk. 10 provides the metaphysical foundation for his law or ethics.[4] Of course, the medieval Christian theory of natural law exemplified in the thought of Thomas Aquinas rests its account of law or ethics on just such a metaphysical foundation.[5]

The reader will have noticed with some unease that when discussing the Christian natural law teaching I have spoken as if the legal and the ethical are interchangeable. I have spoken in this way because, at least for some of the modern interpreters of Plato whose understanding of the natural law teaching is synonymous with the Christian natural law teaching, natural law is not a strictly legal or political theory but rather a moral or ethical theory. Indeed, according to Solmsen, there are two antithetical threads in the thought of Plato presented in the *Laws*: one is political, particularistic, and archaic and the other is ethical, universalistic, and "progressive."[6] The theory of natural law that begins to emerge in the *Laws* is said to be a part of the universal, progressive ethical element in the thought of Plato that obviously foreshadows the Christian conception of a universal natural law. The purportedly archaic element is that "alliance between the terrestrial and spiritual power" which characterizes the political teaching of the *Laws* as well as the classic Greek polis.[7] Of course, progress being inherently preferable to conservation, Solmsen can dispense with the archaic element and devote his full attention to the progressive element. Before I raise any doubts about such an approach to the thought of Plato, I must elaborate more fully Solmsen's view that bk. 10 provides a foundation for a universal natural law teaching.

Solmsen recognizes that bk. 10's account of astral gods is at odds with the traditional Greek teaching about gods who have an interest in the well-being of a particular political community and of particular human beings.[8] Solmsen refers correctly to the astral gods as "cosmic" rather than political gods. Unlike the Muslim and Jewish philosophers who consequently raise the problem as to whether such gods would have any interest in the actions of individual communities or human beings, Solmsen infers that although such a "cosmic" conception of god is incompatible with the existence of "political deities," it is not incompatible with the existence of a god who endows all human beings with certain ethical principles or principles of practical reason.[9] Solmsen presents the traditional natural law teaching in a somewhat crude form, but he makes it clear that bk. 10 as a theological or metaphysical teaching is a more comfortable foundation for a universal ethical teaching than for a particular political law.[10] We can respond to this incompatibility between the particularistic political teaching and the universalistic theology of the *Laws* in two ways: (1) by using the universalistic theology as the basis of a universal ethical teaching and dispensing with the political teaching, as Solmsen does, or (2) by attempting to reconcile these two incompatible threads in the argument of the *Laws*. Insofar as the latter approach gives Plato the benefit of the doubt when it comes to judging whether the *Laws* is a unified writing or not, it has much to recommend it. Alfarabi hints at this latter approach by refusing to treat bk. 10 as the account of the foundations (or purposes) of the law.

If Alfarabi not only omitted a summary of bk. 10 but also omitted any mention of the gods, I might have been able to say that Alfarabi has gone to the opposite extreme of Solmsen and dispensed with Plato's universal theological teaching and taken up his particularistic political teaching. But he does not go this far. He merely makes it clear that he does not consider the theological account in bk. 10 to be the foundation or ultimate purpose of the laws.

2. *Plato as legalistic theorist of natural law*

There is another leading argument, made by students of legal philosophy, that Plato has a natural law theory. These students, as is to be expected, take a more legalistic approach to natural law than the one taken by Solmsen. This approach is taken by three authors: Jerome Hall in his "Plato's Legal Philosophy" (1956), Huntington Cairns in his *Legal Philosophy from Plato to Hegel* (1949), and Werner Jaeger (who is not, strictly speaking, a student of legal philosophy) in his "Praise of Law" (1947). Although Hall diverges from Cairns and Jaeger in the texts he cites and thus in some of the arguments he uses to prove his point, all three authors understand Plato's purported conception of "natural law" to be that of an ideal law that can serve as a model for positive law.

Because Hall denies the authenticity of the *Minos*, a passage of which serves as the basis of Cairns's and Jaeger's arguments that Plato has a theory of natural law, I will begin by describing Hall's argument separately. The driving animus of Hall's article is to disprove Ernest Barker's argument in *Greek Political Theory* that there is an opposition between Plato's supposed affirmation of the sovereignty of law in the *Laws* and the *Crito* and his apparent disdain of law in the *Republic* and *Statesman*. Hall tries to disprove Barker's argument by showing that the *Republic* and the *Statesman* in fact acknowledge the sovereignty of law. As a legalist, Hall is bent on vindicating law. His argument is that the negative remarks made about law, especially in the *Republic*, are negative remarks about positive law and not about the ideal or natural law. Indeed, Hall goes so far as to say that "In Plato's scheme, the perfect ruler, the philosopher-king and the Athenian Stranger represent God, perfect knowledge, justice, the ideal, the Good, and, as will appear, Natural Law."[11] I agree with Hall's suggestion that Barker is wrong in taking the dichotomy between the *Laws* and the *Republic* so far as to deny that the *Laws* as the second-best city still looks to the *Republic* as the best city. More importantly, however, I cannot agree that "true law" is synonymous with "perfect wisdom."[12]

Generally, Hall makes his case by citing passages from the *Republic* and the *Laws* in which a theory of natural law seems to be suggested by the close proximity of references to nature and to law.[13] The closest he comes to giving a reasoned argument proving that Plato adheres to natural law theory is logically questionable. Hall says that students of rhetoric such as Callicles and Sophists such as Antiphon set up a dichotomy between nature and law, and since Socrates disagrees with Callicles's dichotomy between nature and law, therefore (Socrates) Plato must have a theory of natural law.[14] Arguments that fall short of asserting the existence of natural law can still be responses to Callicles' understanding of "natural right." According to Callicles, natural right is the right of the "superior" (*kreittôn*) (by which he seems to mean "the few") to rule over the inferior (by which he seems to mean "the many"), but the inferior contrive laws or conventions in order to cheat the superior of their natural rights (*Gorgias* 489c, 488b5). Socrates' response to Callicles does not entail the rejection of natural right (and its replacement by natural law) but the clarification and in turn the modification of Callicles' version of natural right. Although

Socrates' version of natural right is not equivalent to natural law, it does entail a greater reconciliation of nature and law or convention than does Callicles'. Socrates attempts to show Callicles that the highest natural right is the right of those superior in intellect rather than in physical strength and upbringing–both of which Callicles seems eager to prove he possesses (489d–90b). Furthermore, Socrates attempts to show him that the inferior, i.e., the many, are in fact the superior from the point of view of strength (cf. *Laws* 627b). Such a definition of natural right is, of course, completely compatible with the rule of the philosopher-king in the best city described in the *Republic,* but it is also compatible with the rule of law described in the second-best city in the *Laws.*

In bk. 6 of the *Laws* the Athenian describes two kinds of equality: on the one hand, "natural equality" (757d6) or "strict justice" (757e3) that affords unequal honors (including offices) to those of unequal merits, and, on the other, the equality of the lot that affords equal honors to those who are not equal. The laws that rule the second-best regime find their original source in the natural right of intellect to rule the city but quickly admit the foremost counterclaim to intellect: the demand of the majority for the equality of the lot. In the hands of the majority the counterclaim of the lot represents the title to rule of the stronger. If it were not for the reconciliation with the majority's claim of strength, the city would be consumed by civil war (757d8–10). Towards the beginning of the *Laws,* Plato gives evidence that he identifies the rule of law with the reconciliation of such conflicting claims and the rule of the philosopher-king with the absolute subordination of the claim of strength to the claim of intellect. At 627e the Athenian identifies three different kinds of judges: the one who destroys the wicked and sets the better to rule themselves, the one who makes the worthy rule the worse with voluntary submission, and the one who reconciles the conflicting claims by laying down laws. According to Alfarabi, the middle choice is the best and is synonymous with the rule of the philosopher-king in the *Republic.* The third choice, which is synonymous with the rule of law described in the *Laws,* is the worst. Law cannot be synonymous with reason, because it reconciles other claims to rule with the claim of reason.

Let us now turn to the more legalistic argument made by both Cairns and Jaeger, which relies heavily on a striking argument made in Plato's *Minos.* (Jaeger, like Hall, rejects the authenticity of the *Minos* but unlike Hall feels obliged to use it because he is writing an article dedicated to the memory of a legal scholar who viewed it as authentic.) Both Cairns and Jaeger hold that Socrates argues in the *Minos* that only a good law deserves to be called a law. And because the laws in the cities are constantly being changed, they must be bad laws (315b) and thus nonlaws. From this Jaeger, for instance, infers the existence of a dichotomy between positive law and natural law.[15] In their haste to confirm this interpretation, both latch on to Socrates' assertion that law "wishes to be the discovery of what is" (315a4). But to suit their purposes they both, each in his own way, come to ignore the difference between the assertion that law *wishes to be* the discovery of what is and the assertion that law *is* the discovery of what is.[16] Insofar as the assertion that law wishes to be the discovery of truth follows upon Socrates' immediately previous assertions that if law is opinion it must be worthy and thus true opinion, and insofar as opinion even if true is not the same thing as knowledge, it should be evident that Socrates does not mean that law is the discovery of what is but rather it wishes to be that discovery. Once again, the legalistic argument that Plato has a theory of natural law relies upon the dubious assumption that law is synonymous with reason or intellect.[17] As I will show later, Alfarabi repeatedly makes it apparent that for Plato a substantial distance exists between intellect and law.

Whatever their disagreements, the adherents of the legalist and the ethical view of natural law agree that natural law in the Platonic corpus rests upon a metaphysical foundation.[18] The legalists' claim that the metaphysical order that underlies the cosmos underlies the law might seem to undermine their concern with the laws of a particular political community. In contrast, for the adherents of the ethical view, the supposition that the natural law receives cosmic support compels them to deny the direct bearing of the natural law on 'particularistic' political life and to affirm its bearing on universal ethical life. But the legalists are able to assert that the order underlying the law is the same as the order underlying the cosmos by maintaining the distinction between the positive laws of a particular political community and the natural law that is a model for all communities.

No one would deny that it is at least one of the primary rhetorical purposes of Plato's corpus to establish confidence in the view that there is a natural order that underlies the cosmos that also underlies the order of the human things. There is reason to believe that the Western Christian tradition has raised this rhetorical purpose to the level of a philosophical doctrine, exemplified above all by Christian Neoplatonism. That Alfarabi views this aspect of the Platonic corpus more as a politically salutary argument than a philosophical doctrine is evident, because he does not summarize bk. 10 of the *Laws* in the *Summary.* Alfarabi views Plato through a Neoplatonic lens the least just where one would expect him to view him that way the most. On the other hand, Alfarabi does use Neoplatonic imagery in works such as the *Political Regime* and the *Virtuous City,* that are not commentaries on a work by Plato: He seems to affirm that there is a hierarchy among the natural things that can and should serve as the model for the ordering of the human things.

Is it possible that Alfarabi shared Anaxagoras's view that the heavenly bodies were nothing more than stone, while he affirmed for political purposes that they possess souls that are hierarchically organized? The previous chapter showed that Alfarabi's supposed Neoplatonism in these other works, unlike

Neoplatonism itself, does not serve a theoretical purpose but rather serves a salutary political purpose. Alfarabi does not rest his account of the human or political things on a metaphysical foundation; rather he engages in an inquiry into them without making metaphysical assumptions.

II.

The Divergence Between Law and Intellect

4
Is the Best City Ruled by Law?

As I explained in chapter 1, the divergence between written law and intellect is at least in part what necessitates the existence of the art of *kalâm*. If political life could be made strictly rational, then we could dispense with the art of *kalâm*. But even the virtuous city, the city ruled by intellect, must have recourse to opinions that are generally accepted rather than rationally demonstrated. Generally accepted opinions cannot be defended by the art of demonstration and must be defended by a subdemonstrative art of *kalâm*. The rule of written law makes recourse to *kalâm* even more necessary than it would be in the virtuous city.

Maimonides adumbrates the gap between the rational way of life and the way of life ruled by written law. The Law (i.e., written divine law) is concerned with the welfare of the generality of human beings, not with the rare exceptions. Indeed, it attempts to eliminate differences among its adherents so that they might live together in harmony. Furthermore, it ignores the changes in temperament of its adherents that arise over time. The art of legislation can be contrasted with the art of medicine, which modifies its treatment in accordance with the disposition of each patient and with changes in their temperaments (*Guide*, 3. 34). With an eye to the well-being of the city as a whole, the Law must overlook the well-being of individuals, especially of extraordinary individuals. In looking to the well-being of the whole, the Law is not strictly rational in its treatment of individuals. The rational treatment of individuals' souls must be an art of treatment analogous to the medical treatment of the body. In his *Eight Chapters*, Maimonides describes this medical treatment of the soul.

In the *Laws* and *Summary*, the medical treatment of the soul is a distant goal. The art of persuading citizens to obey the law, viz., the art of *kalâm*, is a far more pressing matter. Nonetheless, the philosopher's art of *kalâm* should be distinguished from the popular art of *kalâm,* because it not only persuades the citizens to obey the laws but also leads those who are able to learn to care rationally for their own souls. Furthermore, the philosopher's *kalâm* persuades citizens to obey not merely the traditional law but a revised version of it. Without such revision, it would be far more difficult for individuals to learn to care rationally for their own souls. In the third part, I will explain how the philosophic art of *kalâm* can begin to lead to the medical treatment of one's own soul. First, however, let us examine the divergence between written law and intellect so that we might better understand why the art of *kalâm* is necessary.

In the Alfarabian corpus there are two different accounts of the city in the *Laws* . One appears in the *Summary;* the other is a terse one-sentence reference to this city in the *Philosophy of Plato.* The *Plato* appears to suggest that the city in the *Laws* is the same as the city in the *Republic.* In this chapter, I will demonstrate, that although it is useful for the inhabitants of the city ruled by written law to believe that their city (the city in the *Laws*) is the best city (the city in the *Republic*), closer analysis of the passage in the *Plato* will show that Alfarabi does not teach the identity of these two cities.

In the *Summary,* Alfarabi is also reticent about distinguishing the city in the *Laws* from the city in the *Republic* or about identifying the city in the *Laws* as the second-best city. Because to assert that the city ruled by written law is as such second-best is to imply that the divine Law revealed by the Prophet is second-best. It has been suggested that the monotheistic religions view the rule of the living Prophet as preferable to the rule of his written law in the same way that the philosophic tradition views the rule of the philosopher-king as preferable to the rule of even the best written law.[1] Yet let us reflect on some examples. Moses requires that not a letter of the Law he receives from God should be changed (Deuteronomy 13:1). Muhammad claims that the Law is the sole miracle of the faith he brings. The revealed religions are so strict about the unalterability of the Law not merely because of their desire to avoid future internal dissension but also because they view the Law as the revelation of the Divine Mind. If the Divine Mind intended that different things be demanded of people at different times, then it would have provided an unending series of legislator-prophets. In effect, the revealed religions agree with Thomas Aquinas that the laws in the second part of the Decalogue are "natural" or universal and permanent laws.

1. *According to the* Philosophy of Plato

In the *Philosophy of Plato,* Alfarabi speaks quite briefly and cryptically about the *Laws* and the city described therein. He limits his description to the following: "Then he [Plato] presented in the *Laws* the virtuous ways of life that the inhabitants of this city should be made to follow."[2] By placing his description of the *Laws* after that of the *Timaeus* (which itself follows that of the *Republic*), Alfarabi seems to imply that the city, which he vaguely refers to as "this city," is identical with the city in the *Timaeus*–which is, of course, identical with the city in the *Republic*.[3] Thus, in his first assessment of the *Philosophy of Plato*, Leo Strauss reads Alfarabi perhaps too literally:

> [Farabi] conceives of the *Laws*, not, as Plato himself had done, as a correction of the *Republic*, but as a supplement of the *Republic*: whereas according to Plato the *Republic* and the *Laws* deal with essentially different political orders . . . , Farabi's view is closely akin to that of Cicero . . . , according to whom the *Republic* deals with the best political order and the *Laws* deals with the best laws belonging to the very same best political order.[4]

Strauss asserts that Alfarabi understood the relation between the *Republic* and the *Laws* differently from Plato. In other words, he asserts that Alfarabi misinterprets Plato. As we will see shortly, Strauss was to go on to alter the view expressed in this passage. But the view expressed here is instructive. Here Alfarabi is said to identify the city in the *Republic* with the city in the *Laws*. In doing so, he interprets the *Laws* as a rational law theorist would: He identifies the best rule with the rule of the ideal law, i.e., the natural law. Thus, he appears to equate the rule of living intellect with the rule of written law.[5]

Before turning to Strauss's later interpretation, I must say something about what might have led him to the above misinterpretation. Leaving aside for the moment what appears to be the literal meaning of the passage from the *Plato*, throughout his writings Alfarabi hints that the author of the divine Law, i.e., the prophet, should be the philosopher-legislator. Thus, the author of the written divine Law should be the same as the philosopher-king who rules the best city. Similarly, Aristotle identifies the Athenian Stranger, viz., the legislator in the *Laws*, as Socrates.[6] Furthermore, Aristotle suggests that Socrates strives to bring "the regime of the *Laws* by degrees around to the regime of the *Republic*."[7] Nonetheless, there are limits to the extent to which the regime of the *Laws* can be brought around. As Thomas Pangle points out, those limits are set by the rule that Plato has imposed upon himself in the *Laws* (as opposed to the *Republic*), i.e, "that the *Laws* remain within the bounds of the politically possible."[8] Despite the fact that the philosopher is the legislator in the *Laws*, he is legislating for a different city from the city of the philosopher-king. Above all, although he may be the legislator, he is not the ruler.[9]

In the *Political Regime*, Alfarabi distinguishes the city ruled by living wisdom from that ruled by written law. Referring to the philosopher-king as the "supreme ruler without qualification," he explains that this ruler can change any law as he sees fit and so can his successors. Such an approach to law can be sustained as long as all of his successors are of his caliber.[10]

> But if it does not happen that a man exists with these qualifications, then one will have to adopt the Laws prescribed by the earlier ones, write them down, preserve them, and govern the city by them. The ruler who governs the city according to the written Laws received from the past imams will be the prince of the law ([or tradition] *sunnah*).[11]

Just as laws in the city ruled by the "ruler without qualification" are unwritten, so the laws in Plato's *Republic* are unwritten.[12] And just as the city ruled by the "prince of the tradition" is characterized by the petrification of law in written form, so the laws under discussion throughout the *Laws* (with the exception of bk. 7) are written laws.[13] The "prince of the tradition" cannot change the laws as he sees fit, because they are written down to be preserved unchanged or almost unchanged.[14] Although the most desirable form of rule is that of living wisdom that can modify the unwritten law as it sees fit, in lieu of a philosopher able or willing to rule, human beings should settle for the rule of written law and less-than-philosophic rulers.[15]

Now we may turn to Strauss's later interpretation of the cryptic description of the *Laws* in Alfarabi's *Philosophy of Plato*. In *What is Political Philosophy?* he offers a far more subtle and complicated interpretation than he had in "Farabi's Plato."[16] He still acknowledges that Alfarabi intends for us to think of the city in the *Laws* as the "virtuous city described in the *Republic*"; however, reading the passage (in a sense) more literally than he had in his earlier interpretation, he notes a striking incongruity: Alfarabi when referring to the *Laws* makes no mention of the "obvious and guiding theme of the *Laws*, namely, the laws." Instead, he mentions the virtuous ways of life. Alfarabi distinguishes between obedience to law and the virtuous ways of life (disc. 9.7). If such a dichotomy exists, then why does Alfarabi attribute to the *Laws* a discussion of the virtuous ways of life rather than of the law? There is one other reference to the *Laws* in the *Plato*. As Strauss notes, in this reference Alfarabi distinguishes (once again cryptically) between the science and art embodied in the *Laws*, which he attributes to Socrates, and the science and art embodied in the *Timaeus*, which he attributes to Timaeus. "If we combine [this information with the former information about the virtuous ways of life] we reach the conclusion that Socrates was silent about the laws. . . ." Thus, the former cryptic reference to the "virtuous ways of life" is not so much a report of what the contents of the *Laws* is as an account of what the contents of the *Laws* would have to be if it were Socratic (or philosophic). As Strauss mentions, the *Laws* is the only Platonic dialogue in which Socrates does not appear.[17] In summary, Strauss's later interpretation of the *Plato* is that Alfarabi does not believe that the two cities in the *Laws* and the *Republic* are the same. If they were, the *Laws* would have to make its obvious theme the virtuous ways of life rather than the laws.

2. *According to the* Summary

In the *Laws*, the relation between these two cities is first alluded to in the Athenian's discussion of the three judges in bk. 1 (627e ff.). The Athenian asks Kleinias which (of the two) he would deem a "better" (*ameinôn*) judge: the one who would destroy the "bad" (*kakoi*) and leave the "better" (*beltious*) to rule themselves or the one who would make the better rule and the "worse" (*cheirous*) willing to be ruled? As the direct interrogative "which (of the two)" (*poteros*) that leads off this passage implies, his question was initially intended to be limited to these two alternatives. Whether the Athenian goes on to offer a third alternative because Kleinias does not answer the question as asked or because the Athenian prefers a third alternative, as is suggested by at least one interpreter,[18] is not immediately clear. It is clear, however, that the third alternative he adds is the judge who would reconcile the better and the worse by laying down laws for them "for the rest of time" and securing their friendship for one another. This friendship would enable them to disavow the destruction of any member of the group much as a family would not think of destroying its "black sheep."

Perhaps Kleinias did not answer the question as first put because he did not find either alternative acceptable. Later in the dialogue, Kleinias voices a healthy Cretan rejection of all tyranny (710c). He is not interested in choosing between a tyrannical judge who destroys all of the bad and one who makes the worse willing to be ruled by the better. Indeed, he is not even willing to answer the question until he is given the alternative to tyranny of rule by law.[19] Finally, when the Athenian restates his question about which judge is better, he no longer mentions the second judge as an option (628b6). By omitting the more desirable of the two options, he draws our attention to Kleinias's prejudice against tyranny.

Although E. B. England believes (as Kleinias seems to believe) that the Athenian means by "third with respect to virtue" that the highest rank of virtue goes to the third judge, Alfarabi understands the Athenian (or Plato) to mean that the lowest rank of virtue goes to this judge. At least according to Alfarabi, Plato does not believe the best city is ruled by the third judge: The "virtuous city [*al-madînah al-fâḍilah*] . . . conquers [or tyrannizes,[20] *ghâlibah*] by virtue of truth and rightness" (*ṣawâb*)[21] (disc. 1.6). Alfarabi distinguishes this judge from the one he calls the "agreeable" (*murḍī*) judge. The Athenian's first two judges, whether by destroying the worse or "making" (*poieô*) the worse willing to be ruled, apply force tyrannically or without being constrained by laws.[22] Alfarabi captures the contrary procedure of the third judge when he says that the agreeable judge "conducts himself . . . [in the way of] gentleness and good administration." Because the agreeable judge rules in accordance with law, he does not "conquer by virtue of truth and rightness," i.e., what is highest; rather he begins by looking to "what is most needed, namely, the lowest." The more agreeable judge (who rules by law) is more agreeable not because he is better but because he is gentler.

The contrast between the gentle but worse rule that is subordinate to law (of the city in the *Laws*) and the harsh but better rule of the good tyrant (of the city in the *Republic*) is taken up again in bk. 4 (709e ff.). The Athenian does not make this contrast explicitly; however, Plato represents it dramatically by the Athenian's call for a good, young tyrant to assist the legislator and, as was mentioned earlier, by Kleinias's negative reaction to this call and implied preference for the rule of law (710c). The Athenian sets the stage for his call with the admission that legislation is only to the slightest extent in the hands of the human beings who call themselves legislators. Human art is capable at best of grasping a fortunate occasion if it is to achieve anything politically good. Tyrants whose actions are not constrained by law are more capable of "cooperating with the opportune moment in the midst of a gale" (709c4) than are gentler rulers who submit their rule to this constraint. The tyrant the Athenian calls for is already to some extent constrained by law, however, because he is subordinate to a presumably older legislator. It is fortunate that this tyrant (unlike the philosopher-king in the *Republic* [485b–87a5]) is so subordinated, because he lacks some of the qualities the truly good tyrant would need, viz., gracefulness, love of truth and justice, and perhaps even the needed kind of moderation.[23] As long as the older legislator is the Athenian Stranger, a philosopher, we can be certain that the young tyrant will be supplemented as he should be. Although Kleinias may possess the needed gracefulness and love of justice, it is not as clear that he, or a legislator like him, would possess the requisite love of truth or its complementary form of moderation.

Bk. 4 marks the beginning of the explicit search for laws to be laid down at the founding of Magnesia. The founding of the city is the opportune moment that occasions the call for the young tyrant. More specifically, the opportune moment is the moment when the composition of the citizen body is determined (707e ff). According to Alfarabi, the proper citizen body, namely, the one that will be receptive to the laws being given to the city, is the leading "precondition" (*sharṭ*) of the city (disc. 4.1). Indeed, he acknowledges that happening upon such a citizen body (not just possessing a good legislator–709c9) is a matter of good fortune (disc. 4.3). As we will see shortly, the other discussion of tyranny arises in connection with this same problem (735d3).

The composition of the citizen body gives rise to the call for the young tyrant. The tyrant's harshness is needed to deal properly with the citizen body, which is, as it were, his raw material. According to Alfarabi, "tyranny" (or despotism, *taghallub*) is necessary to deal with human beings who lack fine "natural dispositions" (*ṭibâʿ*) (disc. 4.4). Of course, the harshness of tyranny is not inherently desirable but rather necessary because of what the Athenian referred to earlier as the "bad men" (*kakoi*). In contrast, as was implied in my discussion of the opposition between the prelude to the law and the law proper, gentleness is preferable in dealing with those with fine natural dispositions. Kleinias's city-to-be has potentially severe problems with the composition of its citizen body. When the Athenian practically implores Kleinias not to tell him that the people who are to colonize Magnesia are coming from sources over which the founder-legislators have little or no control, he cannot avoid doing so (707e–708d6).

The problem posed by the arbitrary manner in which colonists are acquired for Magnesia leads us to the other treatment of tyranny, in bk. 5 (735d ff.). After the Athenian has laid down the prelude to the laws as a whole, he is ready to turn to a discussion of what is usually referred to as the regime (*politeia*), namely, the ruling offices. The topic of the regime needs to be discussed before the laws can begin to be laid down in earnest. But, as happens so often in this dialogue, before he can even begin to discuss the regime proper, he must digress to solve the problem posed by the arbitrary manner in which the colonists are acquired. The problem of the composition of the citizen body is part of the regime problem more broadly understood.[24] Although this problem encompasses the laying down of the ruling offices, it also encompasses an account of the ruled. In a city whose population is drawn from heterogeneous sources in an uncontrolled manner, such an account cannot be neglected.[25]

In the second discussion of tyranny, the tyrannical rule (of the second judge), which sets the better to rule over the worse, is opposed to the rule limited by law (of the third judge). Despite the concession that the Athenian made to law in his previous discussion of tyranny (namely, the subordination of the young tyrant to a legislator), the Athenian acknowledges again the preferability of the harsher rule of tyranny (735b ff.). Kleinias's instinctive tendency to defend the rule of law in good Cretan fashion has been tempered. It may be that he can raise no objections to the claim that the harshest purge is the best purge because the Athenian does not give him the opportunity to do so.[26] It is more likely, however, that the Athenian has succeeded in persuading Kleinias that tyranny is not inherently bad. In between his last and the present discussion of tyranny, the Athenian has argued that benevolent tyranny is conceivable, if not politically practicable. First, he capitalized on Kleinias's ignorance of Homer

(680c3-6) by persuading him that Nestor was a conceivable though barely attainable exemplar of the moderate tyrant (711d7-12b, esp. 711e6-10).[27] Second, and to some extent in contradiction, he underlined the political impracticability of benevolent tyranny by treating Kronos, a god rather than a mere human being, as the exemplar of such tyranny (713a7-14b2).[28]

As was the case earlier in the discussion of the three judges (627e), the best purge is the purge that does not destroy all the bad, only the incurably bad (735e4). According to Alfarabi, those who must be purged are those "whose diligence, behavior, art and zeal act in opposition to the rulers" (disc. 5.12). Apparently, the merely bad are obedient. The only difference between the merely bad people and the (merely) good people, who need to be given the example set by the punishment of the incurably bad, is economic.[29] The (merely) good people whose goodness depends upon their wealth and obedience should be contrasted with the truly good or, as Alfarabi calls them, the "virtuous" (disc. 9.2, 9.7). The goodness of the "virtuous" does not depend upon their obedience to law. In this crucial respect, the "virtuous" resemble the "incurably bad" more than they do the "merely bad."

Despite the preferability of the harsh ruler, who, like the second judge, stops short of destroying all of the worse and setting the better to rule over themselves, an even milder rule and purge must be applied to the colonists. Why is it that the better and harsher purge cannot be applied, especially in light of Kleinias's apparent willingness to entertain at least the possibility of (benevolent) tyrannical rule? As the *Republic* amply demonstrates, although the harsher purge is conceivable, it is not politically practicable. (Where could one find rulers able and willing to institute or citizens willing to be subjected to Socrates' planned exile of everyone over the age of ten [541a])? The harsher purge is abandoned in accordance with Plato's self-imposed rule in the *Laws* not to stray beyond the politically practicable.

Yet there are other dramatic reasons why the harsher purge is abandoned; as Alfarabi suggests, "there is not a genuine and urgent need" for it (disc. 5.13). The Athenian would have us believe that no purge, not even the gentler purge, need be applied to colonize Magnesia. (This gentler purge, euphemistically called colonization, is gentler by virtue of the fact that the incurably bad, i.e, the bold poor, need not be destroyed: they can be expelled.) Because Magnesia is to be newly founded, it has no need to purge a preexisting citizen body; the founders need only exclude the undesirable colonists and include the desirable. Although it may not be necessary to apply either purge to the city once it is colonized,[30] according to Alfarabi,[31] the colonists prior to their arrival are likely to have left (or been driven from) their own cities because of the pressing need of the disenfranchised to migrate and the poor to acquire some livelihood (disc. 5.13). In other words, the bulk of the colonists are likely to be precisely the "incurably bad" who have been expelled in the "gentler purge" euphemistically called "colonization." In light of the kinship between the "incurably bad" and the "virtuous" noted above, this is not all bad. The "incurably bad" are not obedient, but, of course, obedience is not a particularly desirable quality among founders.[32]

The virtues of the "incurably bad" should not be overstated, however. It had appeared that the Magnesians were to be spared the grim choice between the harshest best purge and one of the gentler worse purges. Although the founders can exclude undesirable colonists, the pool of potential citizens on which they must draw is severely limited beforehand: The "incurably bad" are predisposed as a result of the harsh circumstances under which they lived in their "mother city" to be devoted money-lovers.[33] According to the Athenian just a few moments later, the love of money is the leading impediment to the formation of a just city (737a6).

If not for the limitation posed by the colonists' greed, one might think that the Magnesian founders' process of selection would produce a city approximating closely to that produced by the best purge. Alfarabi capitalizes on our tendency to view colonists as blank slates by leading us to think that the city founded on such colonization can be "a virtuous city"–an appellation the Athenian, in contrast, does not use in this context. It is of the utmost importance that Alfarabi does not identify this city as "the" but as "a" virtuous city. (Contrast the reference to "the virtuous city" in disc. 1.6.) Alfarabi has pressing reasons for concealing the difference between the colony ruled by law and the best (or virtuous) city.

A reader of Alfarabi's *Summary* with some familiarity with Islam is likely to think that Alfarabi has Islam in mind when discussing this virtuous city founded upon migration.[34] Yet Alfarabi does not speak of the Islamic "emigration" (*hijrah*); rather he merely speaks of a "migration" (or relocation, *intiqâl*). In the next paragraph Alfarabi merely lists topics the Athenian discusses at some length. Among the topics he mentions are "companions" (*aṣḥâb*) and "mosques" (*masâjid*) (cf. disc. 5.14 with 737c–38e9). "Companions" as well as "brothers" alludes to the correct distribution of population (737d), if for no other reason than because the prior item on the list, "land and territories," alludes to the distribution of land and houses (737c6) and the following item, "provisions and nourishments [or nourishment]," to the provision of food (737d2).[35] Both these terms also appear connected with Islam. The term "companions" (*aṣḥâb*) reminds us of the "companions" (*ṣaḥâbah*) of the Prophet, Muhammad.[36] While, the term "mosques" (*masâjid*) is even less ambiguously Islamic than is "companions" (*aṣḥâb*). Furthermore, it should be assumed that Alfarabi uses "mosques" (*masâjid*) rather self-consciously here, because he uses the more generic term "temples" (*hayâkil*) elsewhere in the *Summary* (for instance, disc. 8.7). By incremental steps Alfarabi alludes more and more boldly to Islam.

Alfarabi merely alludes to rather than mentions Islam explicitly here because this virtuous city founded on migration is at the most second-best to the city founded on the harshest purge. If one were to identify explicitly the former city as Islam, this would be tantamount to suggesting that Islam is not *the* virtuous city but merely *a* virtuous one. By simply alluding to Islam, Alfarabi hints at something that it would be inappropriate for him to state explicitly.[37]

Alfarabi's wish to deemphasize the distinction between the best and the second-best cities becomes readily apparent in the next paragraph (disc. 5.15). It summarizes the Athenian's explicit treatment of the divergence between the best city and the second-best city with regard to virtue (739a–e9). Although he appears to quote Plato's text (something he rarely does), Alfarabi mentions only one city. He conceals the difference between the best city and the second-best city. In addition, whereas the Athenian describes the recourse to the second-best city as akin to the draught player's deviation from the "sacred line" (739a),[38] Alfarabi has Plato say, "This is the city whose existence we wanted from the start." Alfarabi can be understood to be both inaccurately and accurately representing what "Plato says." He misrepresents Plato's (or the Athenian's) suggestion that the second-best city is a deviation from the "sacred line." But he accurately represents the inquiry into the regime and laws of regimes ruled by written law—the subject of the *Laws* from the very start. Choosing not to mention that Plato discusses two cities in the passage being summarized and that one of the two cities is a deviation from the other has the same effect: to gloss over the difference between the two cities.

The Athenian distinguishes between these two cities with regard to their immortality (739e7). By suggesting that the best city is inhabited by gods or children of gods (739e), he implies that it does not have an inherent tendency to decay. The citizens of the second-best city, however, are human beings rather than gods. This politically possible city has an inherent tendency to decay.

Earlier, too, Alfarabi affirmed the inherent tendency of the city ruled by law to decay (disc. 3.1). What the Athenian portrays as an account of the coming into being and passing away of political regimes, Alfarabi summarizes as an account of the coming into being and passing away of legislation. Although the Athenian explicitly identifies one cause of the destruction of regimes—natural disasters—Alfarabi elucidates two causes of the destruction of laws. The second cause is natural cataclysms, but the first cause is simply the passage of time. In other words, regimes ruled by written law have an inherent tendency to decay. The reason that the best city can endure is not so much that the rulers and ruled are divine, however, as that the uninterrupted rule of philosophy would be characterized by the uninterrupted ability of intellect to adjust its rule in accordance with changing times (and differing places). In contrast, the second-best city has an inherent tendency to decay because the written law as written does not accommodate such adjustments for change.

Written law can be made to imitate intellect by adding preludes to the laws. Preludes or rather certain preludes ("imposed preludes") make the law more like intellect by teaching rulers, who might otherwise be willing to accept all that tradition dictates, to inquire into the roots of law (disc. 4.16). Only by human intervention on the part of rulers and legislators can written law be protected from the vagaries of time. Indeed, the influence of time is great enough that Alfarabi, unlike the Athenian, portrays its passage as a form of "natural prelude" to or condition of law's existence (disc. 4.16).

When Alfarabi turns from discourse 5 to discourse 6, he initially appears to continue to maintain the fiction that his *Summary* and the *Laws* concern the virtuous city. He says that Plato "had resolved to explain" (*qad 'azama . . . an yubayyina*) that the virtuous city will not endure unless its "rulers and rule" (or regime, *ri'âsah*)[39] are ordered fairly and naturally. That Plato had resolved to explain something about the virtuous city does not mean that he ever does. In fact, he discusses the second-best regime. Furthermore, he, unlike Alfarabi, talks about the need to order the rulers and the *laws* fairly and naturally (715a–c). Alfarabi ignores the laws so that he can focus on the rulers and their regime. The rulers, by means of the preludes to the laws rather than the laws proper, will prove to be the law's salvation.

Alfarabi also confirms that the Athenian is no longer talking about the best city—in spite of Plato's purported intention to discuss the best city—when he extends the ordering of the legislator beyond the "rulers" to include the "judges" and "companions" (*aṣḥâb*). By this reference to the companions, we are reminded once again of Islam. Furthermore, the difficulties that confront it at its founding signal that this colony is not the virtuous city. It is resistant to accepting those "regimes" (*siyâsât*) and that order imposed on it by the legislator owing to the ignorance, "lack of sophistication" (*ghayr muḥtanikîn*), and childishness of its citizens (disc. 6.2). That it is, in fact, resistant to these things is evident in the legislator's recourse to a "contrivance" (or ruse, *ḥîlah*) to achieve their acceptance (disc. 6.3). In addition, Alfarabi does not suggest that *some* of the citizens are "ignorant, unsophisticated and childish" but simply that the citizens (as a whole) are. He also confirms what we had suspected when discussing the harshest and gentler purges: the colonists are themselves castoffs from other cities or the product of a gentler purge, euphemistically called "colonization." Although he referred to this colony earlier as "a virtuous city" (disc. 5.13), one thing is clear: This city cannot be the city ruled by the "supreme ruler without qualification." At best it is the city ruled by the "prince of the tradition," which Alfarabi also seems to classify as a virtuous city.[40]

Another indicator of how great the divide is between the best city ruled by the philosopher-king and the second-best city ruled by certain citizens under the constraint of law is the composition of the most powerful ruling body of the second-best city, the Guardians of the Laws. These Guardians, who are to be the means by which the acceptance of the laws is contrived by the legislator, are not only not philosophers but not even young tyrants with some philosophic qualities. At least at the beginning, they are to be old men from Knossos who share some of Kleinias's good qualities but who also possess his deficiencies. Like Kleinias, they lack experience with many of the laws being laid down by the Athenian. Above all, they are unfamiliar with laws whose ends include anything other than war. Not only are they inexperienced with such laws, but as old men, they lack the desire of the young to be educated about them. At best, they can hope to reacquire their youthful eagerness to learn to a modest degree by taking part in drinking parties (disc. 6.3 end and cf. 671b8 ff.). The task of prodding these old men to inquire into the roots of the law will no doubt be formidable. If they succumb to their preference for tradition rather than hearken to the call of the preludes to rethink their laws when necessary, their city, unlike the virtuous city, is doomed to decay.

According to Alfarabi's understanding of the *Laws*, the city under discussion in the *Laws* is the second-best city. For reasons that I have made amply clear in this chapter, he is reticent about the divergence between the best and the second-best city. Nevertheless, he is fully aware of this divergence. As we will see in part 3, the level of treatment the diseased soul is capable of acquiring in the second-best city diverges as far from the philosophic treatment of the soul in the best city as the second-best diverges from the best city. Although the knowledge of the nature and the disease of the human soul is the foundation of the law, the law itself does not give us access to this knowledge and thus to the medical treatment of the soul.

5
Plato's City and Alfarabi's Regime

In the previous chapter we saw that, on the one hand, Alfarabi understands the difference between the best city and the second-best city in essentially the same way as Plato does. But he has reasons for concealing that understanding and makes certain noteworthy modifications of Plato's teaching. In the *Virtuous City*, he suggests that two other, larger political associations are virtuous in a manner at least akin to the best city: the virtuous nation and the virtuous association of the inhabited world (*ma'mûrah*).[1] Muhsin Mahdi has shown that these are not essential modifications of the Platonic teaching. The virtuous nation is composed of virtuous cities, and the virtuous association of the inhabited world is composed of virtuous nations. A nation does not become virtuous merely by the subjugation of ignorant cities by one virtuous city; each city must itself be virtuous.[2] Does Alfarabi's account of a virtuous nation and association of the inhabited world indicate that he has been carried away with the hopes and aspirations of his Islamic community (which are shared ultimately by all the monotheistic religions) to extend the rule of its law over the entire earth? One would answer this question affirmatively only if one believed that he is far more sanguine than Plato about the political practicability of the virtuous city. Furthermore, the possibility of both of these larger regimes is dependent upon not only the possibility of the virtuous city but also the possibility of a multiplicity of virtuous cities at any one time. If we assume that Alfarabi (following Socrates in the *Republic* [592a5-b6]) believed that the virtuous city is politically impossible, then it follows a fortiori that his two larger regimes are even more probably politically impossible. Consequently, when inquiring into the politically practicable, Alfarabi, like Plato, is compelled to look to a second-best city (or nation) ruled by written law.

Although Alfarabi does not list three different sizes of second-best regime (a small, a medium, and a large one) in the *Summary,* as he listed three sizes of best regime in the *Virtuous City,* there is evidence that he does in the case of the second-best what he does in the case of the best: He modifies or extends the teaching of the *Laws* about the second-best city to make it apposite to the aspirations and hopes of his own political community. As we will see, he extends what Plato teaches about this city to either a far larger city or a second-best nation. I hope to show that although he may extend it to a nation, he does not go so far as to extend it to an association of the inhabited world.

There is nothing dangerous in extending what Plato teaches about the virtuous city to a virtuous association of the inhabited world, as Alfarabi does in the *Virtuous City*. As I have explained, this association of the inhabited world is even more strictly a regime in speech than the virtuous city. Besides, Alfarabi prevents this association from being used to justify efforts to extend one faith over the entire earth by implying that there are a multiplicity of virtuous cities and a multiplicity of virtuous religions. He never speaks of a homogeneous virtuous association of the inhabited world; he always speaks of such an association as heterogeneous.[3] In contrast, in the *Summary* Alfarabi talks about one "city." His city, however, appears at first to have no clear borders; for this very reason, I have chosen to refer to it with the size-neutral term "regime" rather than "city." Unlike the virtuous nation or association of nations, his second-best regime appears not to be an association of cities or nations. Indeed, he never speaks of the regime as being constituted of more than one city.[4]

Because the *Summary* concerns a politically practicable regime, it reads far more like Avicenna's down-to-earth treatment of his own religious community in the *Healing*: metaphysics 10, chapter 5 than the *Virtuous City*. Some have noted, however, that Alfarabi, unlike Avicenna, never refers specifically to Islam or to the Prophet, Muhammad, in his political writings. His reticence about Islam becomes especially thought-provoking in the *Summary*. In this work he is closer to the everyday realities of his own community than he is in any of his other political writings. Because it treats the second-best regime, it is an occasion for Alfarabi to deal with mundane matters such as commerce and access to water. Above all, the *Summary* is at least in part a work of *kalâm*: it provides a defense of a particular community. As such it is more particularistic than his other works of political philosophy. It, however, is supposed to be a summary of a work whose subject is a pagan city with deep roots in its own time and place. Assimilating Islam to the Athenian's second-best city will prove to be more complicated than assimilating it to the far less earthbound city of the *Republic*. Although there are no citations of Scripture or references to the Prophet in the *Summary*, there are a number of references (in addition to those cited in the previous chapter) that lead me to believe that he has Islam in mind in this work.

First, Alfarabi seems to be at pains to avoid mentioning more than one god as lawgiver–as if Zeus were merely the Greek equivalent of the monotheistic God (disc. 1.1). Although he later goes on to admit the existence of a multiplicity of laws, he is reticent to admit, as Kleinias does, that Apollo is said to be the maker of the Lacedaimonian law (cf. disc. 1.2 with 624a4). Not much later, Alfarabi even refers to God (*Allâh*) using the traditional Islamic honorifics of "the mighty and the majestic" (*'izz wa-jall*) (disc. 1.7). When he finally does mention Apollo, he does so in close conjunction with Zeus. Initially, he speaks of "their two laws" (*nâmûsîhimâ*), but then he switches to speak of the statutes of "their Law" (*sharî'atihimâ*)–as if their two *nomoi* (laws) had become one *sharî'ah* (divine Law) (disc. 1.9). Of course, it cannot be denied that Alfarabi allows himself to speak of a multiplicity of gods in the *Summary*. Indeed, on occasion he even goes so far as to speak of a multiplicity of gods when the Athenian only speaks of one god.[5] Had he not mentioned a multiplicity of gods in summarizing a work so steeped in pagan religion, one would have wondered whether he suffered from a fear of discussing any god but the one God. Leaving this aside, he seems to be intent upon creating the initial impression that the work he is summarizing can be assimilated to Islam.

Second, Alfarabi introduces the subject of taxation, which has no parallel in the *Laws* (disc. 6.17). His discussion of "taxes" (*furûḍ*) makes use of three categories that, although not all Islamic in origin, play an Islamic or rather particularistic role. He mentions "alms" (*zakawât*), "land taxes" (*kharâjât*), and the "poll tax" (*jizyah*). Of course, the giving of "alms" is one of the five pillars of Islam. One might think that Alfarabi means by a poll tax simply a personal tax, as opposed to a tax on land. He indicates, however, that these taxes have two purposes: for levying natural resources (evidently for distribution to the poor) and "for humiliation in order to keep the juveniles [*ṣibyân*] from inclining toward practices other than those of the followers of laws and toward different ways of life and laws of the citizens." The poll tax was levied in his time only on non-Muslim people of the Book, the "protected people" (*dhimmîs*). He seems to recognize the need to maintain a tax that will prevent members of the Islamic community from following other faiths. (This tax contrasts favorably with the practice of killing apostates common among medieval monotheistic communities.)

Other passages indicate that even if Alfarabi is not thinking exclusively of Islam, he is at least thinking in mundane terms that have special pertinence to the regions ruled by Islam. He seems to have the "climatic region" (*iqlîm*) of the Islamic community in mind, for instance, when he goes into such great detail about the problem of providing water to a community and in particular to those who travel (disc. 6.15–16).[6] One can hardly imagine the Athenian Stranger asserting, as Alfarabi does, that water is "one of the greatest factors causing cities to exist and to flourish and their renown to last" (contrast 761a8–c5 and 763d2–7). Similarly, Alfarabi's abandonment of most of the Athenian's harsh strictures on artisanry, trade, and commerce reflects his need to admit occupations other than farming into a regime that is located in a climatic region where citizens often cannot draw their livelihood from agriculture (cf. disc. 4.1 with 705a–c; disc. 5.18[a] with 742b; and disc. 8.10 with 846d).

Finally, we need only recall the reasons for Alfarabi's reticence about the divergence between the best and the second-best city, discussed in the previous chapter, to understand why he might not feel free to refer explicitly to Islam in the *Summary.*

However this may be, having seen that Alfarabi extends the Platonic teaching about the second-best city to a second-best regime or perhaps a nation, we are led to wonder how he envisions the rule of such a regime. There are certain differences between the rule of the second-best city and second-best nation that one does not find between the rule of the best city and the best nation or association of the inhabited world. The best or virtuous city is ruled by a philosopher-king, and analogously the virtuous nation or association of the inhabited world would be ruled by a philosopher-king. In contrast, although Plato's second-best city has a democratic (or republican) form of rule, Alfarabi's second-best regime is monarchical. The greater size of Alfarabi's regime makes democratic rule impracticable.[7]

In section 1, I will explore the textual evidence that seems at first to support the view that Alfarabi's regime is more like the best city in the *Republic* than the Athenian's city. Although Alfarabi shows a preference for monarchy, closer inspection reveals that this monarchy is not synonymous with the rule of the philosopher-king in the *Republic.* In section 2, I will inspect the titles to rule in Alfarabi's regime for further evidence of the kind of regime he envisions. Wisdom or the love of wisdom (philosophy) is not among these titles. Furthermore, wealth in particular ascends in importance here. In section 3, I will explain that the political offices in the *Summary* are more monarchic than are the offices in the *Laws.* Their monarchic character is determined less by any aspiration to the centralized rule of philosophy than by the recognition that a large regime requires more centralization than Plato envisions in the *Laws.* Furthermore, the character of the citizen body in Alfarabi's regime—above all, its concern with trade and moneymaking—is not compatible with the view that his regime in the *Summary* is his best regime. In section 4, I will show that, on the one hand, Alfarabi does not confine his regime to the narrow limits of the ancient polis, and, on the other, he offers a severe critique of the monotheistic law's aspiration to world rule. I conclude that he intends his second-best regime to be a nation rather than an association of the inhabited world.

A fuller description of the second-best regime will make more salient the differences between its leading ways of life and that of the best regime. Consequently, we should be better able to understand why the scientific analysis of the regime ruled by law must be supplemented by *kalâm*, the subrational defense of law.

1. Persian monarchy and Athenian democracy

Alfarabi appears to show a preference for Persian monarchy as opposed to Athenian democracy, since he remains almost completely silent about the latter. His preference, however, is for ancient rather than contemporary Persian monarchy. At times the former looks like the best city in the *Republic*. Closer inspection shows, however, that even this monarchical standard is merely second-best. Although the Athenian gives the initial impression that ancient Persian monarchy and ancient Athenian democracy are equally indispensable models, closer inspection shows that he shares Alfarabi's preference for the ancient Persian monarchy.

According to the Athenian, monarchy and democracy are "as it were, two mothers of regimes" (693d). Furthermore, the Persia of his day is the extreme embodiment of monarchy and the Athens of his day of democracy. Democracy and monarchy are two mothers of regimes because the presence of both guarantees the presence of three crucial things in the city: freedom, friendship, and prudence (693e). Because the Athenian asserts that the extreme of democracy represented by contemporary Athens is the home of extreme freedom, the reader is led to expect that the extreme of monarchy represented by contemporary Persia is the home of extreme friendship or prudence or both. This expectation is not fulfilled. The Athenian merely asserts redundantly that Persia is the nation that delights too exclusively in monarchy (693e5-8). Perhaps this expectation was misguided, for as Socrates shows in the *Republic*, friendship (not to mention prudence) cannot be an evil for a city as freedom can be. Later, the Athenian confirms that this expectation was misguided when he asserts that the contemporary Persians have "by going too far in depriving the populace of freedom, and by bringing in more despotism than is appropriate, . . . destroyed the friendship and community within the city " (697c8-9, and see 698a5). Extreme monarchy leads to slavery rather than to friendship and prudence. Thus, the two mothers of regimes, democracy and monarchy, when taken to their extremes embody excessive freedom and excessive slavery, respectively. What has become of friendship and prudence? According to the Athenian, the ancient Persian monarchy, which mixed freedom and slavery judiciously, possessed all three of the desirable characteristics: freedom, friendship, and prudence (694a5-b7).

It is less clear that the ancient Athenian democracy possessed these characteristics. If the ancient Athenians were free, the Athenian Stranger never says so. He consistently says that they were enslaved, in awe, and fearful of both their laws and the gods (698b4–d3). Not only is he silent about their freedom, but he also says that their friendship was based on fear (698c). To my knowledge, the Athenian never says that ancient Athens or its rulers were prudent. The closest he comes to this is to speak of the rulers or the judges at musical contests as the educated (700c5). The ancient Persian monarchy, then, is portrayed by the Athenian more favorably than is ancient Athenian democracy.

The ancient Persian monarchy made possible freedom, friendship, and prudence, at least among the king and his counsellors. Furthermore, their friendship was not merely derived from the fear of external enemies, as was the case among the Athenians, but also from their appreciation of one another's ability to give good counsel. It derived from the most elevated form of freedom, freedom of speech (*parrêsia*). Here it is not the merely educated who have the right to speak but the prudent. The monarch or rather king (*basileus*) is so judicious and so free of envy in the use that he makes of his counsellors that the Athenian speaks of a multiplicity of "rulers" (*archontes*) (694a7). And these rulers "drew toward [*agontes epi*] equality." Yet this equality was not what we today think of as equality, namely, giving the same thing to everyone. Rather it afforded to those who were "prudent and capable of giving counsel" the right to speak freely with the monarch.

The Athenian goes on to discuss this latter kind of equality as of monarchic origin (in bk. 6. 757c). (Consequently, I will refer to this as "monarchic equality.") It is distributed by Zeus (757b7), the highest ruling and most kingly god who educated Minos about legislation. Presumably, Zeus's monarchy based on wisdom is to be distinguished from the kind of monarchy ruling the contemporary Persian regime.[8] The latter monarchy prohibits subjects from addressing the monarch as an equal in counsel. (Thus, according to Averroës, whose discussion of Alfarabi's views on the ancient Persian monarchy will be discussed shortly, the kind of monarchy ruling the contemporary Persian regime requires that that honor be given to the monarch alone.)

Just as the Athenian appears initially to portray monarchy and democracy as equal "mothers of regimes" (here in bk. 3), so he initially portrays "monarchic equality" as if it were not clearly distinguishable from what we understand to be equality today—let us call it, somewhat redundantly, "democratic equality" (in bk. 6. 757c).[9] And just as Alfarabi displays a preference for monarchy (here in disc. 3.13–15), so he is far more explicit than is the Athenian about the preferability of monarchic to democratic equality (in disc. 6.7). Evidently, the Athenian feels a greater need than Alfarabi to be evenhanded in his treatment of monarchy and democracy. Perhaps he feels this need because of the antityrannical passions of his interlocutors discussed in the previous chapter.

The ancient Persian monarchy is preferable to ancient Athenian democracy because in it one is able to distribute honors on the basis of merit, in particular, prudence. As the Athenian says in the interlude between his description of ancient Persia and his description of ancient Athens, honors should be distributed on this basis rather than on the basis of wealth (696b). Eventually, however, the Athenian will be compelled to give distinctions of wealth such a role as well (see 744b ff.). Thus, just as ancient Athens came to be divided into four property classes, so will the city in the *Laws* come to be divided into such classes. This concession to wealth is, however indirectly, a concession to the claims of democracy.[10] In spite of this concession, the Athenian seems to share Alfarabi's preference for the ancient Persian monarchy.

Throughout his summary of the Athenian's discussion of the genesis of Persian monarchy and Athenian democracy, Alfarabi makes no mention of the latter. Consequently, he is silent about combining the two mothers of regimes, monarchy and democracy, as a necessary condition for the existence of freedom, friendship, and prudence in the city (disc. 3.13). Instead, he describes the presence of friendship and freedom as the necessary condition of quick and easy establishment of the laws.[11] Later, the Athenian indicates that their establishment is made possible by "tyranny" (*taghallub*) (710b6 and 9, 711a3 and c8, 712a9; disc. 4.5).[12] Expediency may be at the root of Alfarabi's preference for monarchy rather than a desire to establish the most exalted form of monarchy akin to Zeus's.

Alfarabi mentions one fault of the Athenian's contemporary Persian regime that I have already mentioned, i.e., an excess of slavery (cf. disc. 3.14 with 697c9). Unlike the Athenian, however, Alfarabi does not imply that it is best to have a mixture of freedom and slavery. In other words, he seems simply to favor freedom over slavery. At the same time, he advocates a more extreme form of monarchy than that of ancient Persia: He claims that "a multiplicity of rulers will corrupt the matter and that the aim of the lawgiver must be exclusive rule" (disc. 3.13). In advocating such rule, Alfarabi comes closer to the Persia of the Athenian's time than to ancient Persia. As we recall, the hallmark of the Persia of the Athenian's time was enslavement of all subjects to the king. Perhaps Alfarabi mixes slavery and freedom after all. One thing is certain: Alfarabi's regime tends more toward extreme monarchy than does the regime in the *Laws*.

Alfarabi's views on ancient Persian monarchy were discussed by at least two later medieval Muslim political philosophers, Ibn Bâjjah and Averroës. Neither author, however, specifies where Alfarabi expressed these views. It is uncertain, therefore, whether they are discussing the views he expresses in the *Summary*. Indeed, at times it appears that he must have presented another discussion of the ancient Persian regime in which he did not stray so far from this ideal as he does in the *Summary*.[13]

In the *Governance of the Solitary*, Ibn Bâjjah describes the city in the *Republic* as an even more insurmountable goal than Plato's city. According to Ibn Bâjjah's description, in this city all opinions are true—in other words, there seems to be no need for noble lies. The absolute insurmountability of this goal necessitates that the philosopher seek solitude in the imperfect cities in which human beings live. Most imperfect cities are a mix of the four imperfect regimes described by Plato in the *Republic* (timocracy, oligarchy, democracy, and tyranny), except for the ancient Persian regime, which was an unmixed mean between the imperfect regimes and the perfect (i.e., virtuous) regime. Thus, according to Ibn Bâjjah the ancient Persian regime proves to be a second-best regime.

In the *Commentary on the "Rhetoric,"* Averroës explicitly refers to the ancient Persian regime described by Abû Naṣr [Alfarabi] as *imâmiyyah*.[14] Averroës identifies this regime as an aristocracy, the third of Aristotle's four regime types (democracy, oligarchy, aristocracy, and monarchy) (*Rhetoric* 1365b30). In contrast, Plato uses the ancient Persian regime as an exemplar of monarchy. As we saw above, however, the monarch who ruled this regime was so free of envy that he allowed his counsellors to be "rulers" with him. His regime in fact was an aristocracy, and Averroës describes it as such.

According to Averroës, there are two forms of aristocracy: one in which both the rulers' actions and opinions accord with the demands of the theoretical sciences (whether they are simply true is another matter); and another, namely, the ancient Persian regime, in which merely their actions are virtuous. The former kind of aristocracy is reminiscent of the regime in the *Republic*. Consequently, Averroës describes monarchy in much the same way the Athenian describes the contemporary Persian monarchy in the *Laws*: It is not rule with an eye to virtue but to the exclusive glorification of the monarch. Ironically, Alfarabi's emphasis on the monarch's obtaining exclusive rule (disc. 3.13) is less reminiscent of the *imâmiyyah* ascribed to him by Averroës than it is of the contemporary Persian monarchy. One thing is certain: Alfarabi is further from striving to make his regime in the *Summary* into the politically impossible best regime described in the *Republic* than he is from striving to make it into an *imâmiyyah* in which virtuous actions reign supreme.

Let us look more closely at Alfarabi's nearly total silence on Athenian democracy. Taking advantage of the fact that the Athenian chose the Persian expedition against the Greeks as the occasion for singing the praises of ancient Athens, Alfarabi barely hints at the transition from the Athenian's discussion of the decay of ancient Persia to that of ancient Athens (disc. 3.14). He never mentions Athens or its regime divided into four classes. At most he alludes to Athens: He mentions how some people in attacking others struck them with something terrible and in doing so changed them from enemies to friends. He identifies the Persians as the attackers but never identifies the attacked as the Athenians. Alfarabi seems to disapprove of the Athenian friendship, derived from fear of their attackers (699c4), because he speaks of "prevent[ing] harm and corruption from affecting the law in that manner [*min tilka al-jihah*]."

Similarly, Alfarabi does not praise the fear of the laws that enslaved the Athenians to them (disc. 3.15)–which the Athenian praises both directly (699c7-8) and indirectly (701a6-c7). In a summary by a member of a monotheistic community of a work on divine law, it is surprising to see such silence about the need to be enslaved to law.[15] It may be that his community (precisely as a monotheistic community) has no need to be encouraged to enslave itself to the law more than it already does.[16] Perhaps it even has a need to be discouraged from enslaving itself. Thus, he repeatedly praises the legislator who can achieve the acceptance of the traditions he legislates in "the way of freedom": The city whose legislator must have recourse to "the way of slavery and coercion . . . is destined to ruin and corruption." Unfortunately, as we saw earlier, law proper makes use of just such slavery and coercion, and consequently, the city ruled by law inevitably decays (disc. 3.1).

During his summary of the Athenian's discussion of Persian monarchy and Athenian democracy, Alfarabi nearly everywhere favors monarchy over democracy. The regime in the *Summary*, however, cannot be confused with the best regime, in which philosophy rules. According to Averroës and Ibn Bâjjah, for Alfarabi the ancient Persian regime is a model for the rule of human beings capable of virtuous action, if not of thought. Although Alfarabi's standard here is the ancient Persian monarchy, there is some evidence that his regime falls far short even of this.

2. *The titles to rule*

In the *Summary*, the monarchic rule of human beings capable of virtuous action is the standard. By virtue of what title or titles, however, do the rulers of this regime rule? Though a full description of the rulers of Alfarabi's regime will not be given until the third part, we can already begin to answer this question.

In chapter 3, Plato's natural right theory was distinguished from that of Callicles and from natural law theory. As we saw, Plato's account in the *Laws* asserted a difference between "natural equality" (referred to in the previous section as "monarchic equality") and the equality of the lot ("democratic equality"). "Monarchic equality" gives equal things to equal people–and unequal things to unequal people–in accordance with the demands of the intellect; "democratic equality" gives equal things to all in accordance with the demands of the stronger, who happen to be the many. In the *Republic*'s best city, the claim of the intellect to rule is absolute and thus stands as the lone title to rule.[17] In the second-best city of the *Laws*, a compromise is reached between the highest claim to rule (intellect, or rather prudence), and the lowest claim to rule (strength). The result of this compromise is the predominance of certain intermediate titles to rule in this city. For instance, age is one of (and an aspect of another of) the intermediate titles to rule (690a4 and 9). Although wealth is an intermediate kind of title to rule, it is not admitted initially as a title (690a–d, 696b, 715b9–d).[18] (Perhaps the Athenian retains some hope that the colony might be ruled somewhat more by intellect, but by omitting the claim of wealth initially, he can make more apparent just how intense is the opposition between intellect and strength.) Eventually, however, he is compelled to admit wealth (744a10 ff.).

In contrast, Alfarabi chooses to omit any mention of the four property classes and the privileged access to office that this system is ultimately intended to offer to the wealthy (disc. 5.18[c]).[19] The question is whether Alfarabi's omission points in the direction of "democratic equality" or "monarchic equality."

The role of wealth as a title to rule is quite ambiguous. Of course, it is inferior to intellect as a title. It is less clear that it is inferior to strength, however—despite its exclusion from and strength's inclusion in the list of "worthy" (*axiôma*) titles to rule (690a ff.). Although wealth is not the title to rule that the strength of the many poor is, it is a title of the few rich. Through their wealth, the few are able both to train themselves more intensely and arm themselves better than the poor—not to mention that they can hire foreign mercenaries. Pindar argues that (physical) strength is *the* natural title to rule, while the Athenian argues that intellect or rather prudence is the most natural title (690b7–c4). Pindar's assertion derives from a confusion between what emerges earlier in the genesis of regimes (and what thus becomes customary) and what is natural.[20] Wealth, like intellect, emerges as a title later in the genesis of regimes than does physical strength. It is doubtful, however, that this makes wealth any less worthy. Despite wealth's inferiority to intellect, it provides a counterweight to physical strength that tends in the direction of intellect. The rich few are not the philosophic few, but the former imitate the latter more than do the poor many—if in nothing else than in education (cf. 700c5–8). From the point of view of the second-best city, the wealth of the few (as a title to rule of strength) acts as a counterweight to the physical strength of the many. From the point of view of the best city, however, the inclusion of wealth would signify a failure to live up to the demands of intellect. The Athenian is compelled to admit wealth when he realizes how profoundly the title to rule of physical strength compromises the title of intellect.

Alfarabi omits any mention of the property classes or wealth as a title to rule when he tries to conceal the difference between the colony (which is a second-best city) and the best city (disc. 5.18).[21] Perhaps this is another way to conceal how far his regime deviates from the virtuous city. However this may be, in other passages wealth and trade play an even more important role in

Alfarabi's regime than in Plato's city, as we will see in the last section of this chapter. In other words, with respect to the role of wealth Alfarabi's second-best regime proves to be more, not less, distant from the virtuous city than is Plato's second-best city.

3. *The ruling offices*

The offices in Alfarabi's second-best regime incline toward the monarchic "mother of regimes." As the divergence between the Athenian's contemporary Persia and his ancient Persia makes amply evident, however, the inclination toward monarchy is compatible both with virtuous and vicious rule. More importantly, monarchy was perhaps Alfarabi's sole option when envisioning the rule of a sizable regime. Presumably, he favors ancient Persia's virtuous rule over the later Persia's vicious rule. Whether he can stick closely to the model of the former is far less certain than that his regime and in particular his ruling offices will tend towards monarchy rather than democracy.

On two occasions in the *Summary,* Alfarabi lists names of ruling offices whose pedigree is neither clearly monarchic nor democratic (disc. 6.6, 6.10). It is possible that he chose names that approximate, as closely as was possible in the Arabic terminology that was in use during his time, the names for democratic offices. The names he uses, however, are not unlike the names he uses in another context to refer to monarchic offices, and in one case the name is identical.[22]

One indirect indication of the kind of ruling offices Alfarabi has in mind appears in his summary of bk. 6. In bk. 6 the Athenian repeatedly discusses election procedures. Alfarabi is almost totally silent about them.[23] Second, the Athenian discusses what is to be done when, in the course of electing rulers, one of the citizens determines that someone has not been nominated who would be better than those who have already been: The name should be added to the list of nominees (755d1-6 and cf. 756b4-7). In his summary of this passage, Alfarabi merely indicates that the better ruler should be appointed in the place of the worse (disc. 6.5). Appointment is, of course, not democratic but monarchic. Third, according to the Athenian, holding office is itself an honor (744b8). In a different context, Alfarabi presents an elaborate account of the honors awarded to rulers (disc. 6.6) that has no parallel in the *Laws* (cf. disc. 6.5 and 6.7 with 755d6-57d7).[24] Above all, he adds one form of honor, money, that the Athenian never identifies (at least not explicitly) as an honor. More specifically, he singles out "warriors" (*ahl al-ḥarb*) as the recipients of this honor. The Athenian makes no mention of the city's providing "warriors" with money, because in the *Laws* all citizens are warriors of one sort or another. It almost goes without saying that although paid warriors are more compatible with a monarchic than a democratic regime, they are not compatible with the monarchy (or aristocracy) of the best regime described in the *Republic*.[25]

4. *The regime's size*

The ancient Greek political philosophers were renowned for the strict spatial and population limits they placed on their best as well as their second-best regimes. An adherence to such limits was simply not practicable for Alfarabi. As a member of a community in which a large empire was the ideal, he could hardly expect to achieve much, particularly in the way of practical results, by exhorting his fellow citizens to reestablish the ancient Greek polis. Nonetheless, he acknowledges in the *Virtuous City* that even a large empire cannot truly achieve the virtue envisioned by the ancients unless each component of that empire is a virtuous city. Alfarabi in the *Summary*, as Plato in the *Laws*, lowers both his expectations and his demands. He does not speak of his regime as if it were composed of virtuous cities. As we have noted, his regime, although sometimes referred to as if it were a city, does not possess clearly defined borders. Yet Alfarabi levels such a stinging criticism of the monotheistic aspiration to world rule that we must infer that his regime is intended to have some limits.

On no occasion does Alfarabi mention the limits to the territory that the Athenian mentions,[26] nor does Alfarabi mention the internal divisions of the territory into the twelve parts that the Athenian mentions. Furthermore, although Alfarabi mentions strangers in the course of his summary of the difference between the "bodily discipline" (punishments) given to the citizens and those given to strangers (disc. 5.6), he does not mention strangers in conjunction with the distribution of wealth or in any way in connection with the limits of the territory, as does the Athenian. In other words, he accommodates his *Summary* to his community's understanding of what it takes to be the virtuous city: Islam does not distinguish between citizen and stranger but between a member of the faith (a protected person of the Book) and an opponent of the faith. But despite these concessions to the beliefs of his community, Alfarabi does not concede all ground to the unlimited aspirations of the Law.

The first occasion on which Alfarabi omits any mention of territorial limits is in the same paragraph in which he omits any mention of the property divisions or the title to rule of wealth (disc. 5.18[c]). His omission of territorial limits is merely the first element of a larger silence on the passage running from 745b3 to 747e13, except for 746e–47d. This passage falls into three parts: 745b3–e3, 745e4–46e, and 747d–e13. The first is a description of the limits of the territory and its parts. The second is a discussion of the need to allow a city in its actualization in deed to fall short of one's plans for it in speech.[27] And the third alludes to the differences between the kinds of citizens one will have, depending upon the kind of territory in which one locates one's city.[28] The third part can be considered a continuation of the discussion of the limits of the territory in the first.

In the first part that Alfarabi omits, the Athenian discusses the need to locate the city in the center of the territory (a center whose location one could not determine in a nation without clear borders); the division of the city into twelve parts (how can one divide a nation without clear limits into parts?); and finally, the giving of a particular god to each of the twelve parts (Alfarabi's silence about such details about the gods is readily understandable in this context).[29] In the third part that Alfarabi omits, the Athenian continues his discussion by indicating that different locations are conducive to "better [or] worse human beings" or, as Alfarabi says elsewhere, different "natural dispositions" (*ṭibâʿ*) (disc. 2.1[c]). Alfarabi's silence about borders and national differences here bespeaks the absence of clear limitations on his regime's size.

Alfarabi departs from the Athenian in another case not by an omission but by one noteworthy addition and one noteworthy substitution. The Athenian asserts that because the colony is going to avoid the pursuit of a maritime empire, the need for legislation and for occupations will decrease by half (842c). He lists both the occupations that the city will be able to dispense with and those it will not. In summarizing this passage, Alfarabi only cites the list of occupations to be retained by the city but with some modifications. The Athenian lists the following kinds of workers as engaged in occupations to be retained by the city: "farmers, herdsmen, beekeepers, and those who guard [*phulaktêriois*] such things and take care [*epistatais*] of the tools" (842d7). Alfarabi lists: "workers [*faʿalah*], artisans, farmers and frontier settlers [*sukkân al-aṭrâf*]." He adds "artisans" here because he must include artisans among citizens—he does not distinguish between citizens and strangers.[30] He also substitutes "frontier settlers" for the Athenian's "those who guard such things." The Athenian's city needs guards to protect its herdsmen who graze their sheep near its well-defined borders; Alfarabi's city needs "frontier settlers" whose purpose it is to "live" (*sakan*) at the edge of a "city" without well-defined borders.

The other passage in which Alfarabi omits any mention of the division of the city into twelve parts is the same passage in which he avoids any distinction between stranger and citizen. The Athenian describes how the city should first divide its food into twelve parts (847e7) and then each of these twelve parts into three parts for the "free men" (*eleutherois*), the "domestic servants" (or slaves, *oiketais*), and the artisans and strangers (848a ff.). Not only is Alfarabi silent about the first division into twelve parts, but he changes the three classes of recipients to the "citizens themselves" (*ahl al-madînah anfusuhum*), the slaves, and the animals (disc. 8.11). Note in this connection that he does not speak of "free men" but of citizens.[31] He makes no distinction within his class of citizens between free men and artisans because free men may very well be artisans.[32] In addition, he replaces "strangers" with "animals." In a later passage, he will similarly omit any mention of the statutes concerning the "resident alien" (*metoikion*) (cf. disc. 8.13 with 850a8 ff.). Thus, Alfarabi includes under the rubric of citizen at least the Athenian's free man, artisan, and stranger. Above all, Alfarabi does not recognize the distinction between citizen and stranger and all that this implies about the regime's limited size.[33]

One further observation in connection with his inclusion of artisans within the citizen body: He adds a discussion of the proper handling of money that has no parallel in the *Laws*, at least in the immediate vicinity (cf. disc. 6.9 with 758a5). On the contrary, it has a much closer parallel with a discussion in *Nicomachean Ethics* 1119b20-22a17.[34] Although Alfarabi's discussion of the handling of money is relatively uninnovative, he applies it to the rulers' distribution of "stipends" (*arzâq*) to the citizens. In the context of the *Ethics*, such an application would not have been particularly surprising; however, the mere suggestion that "stipends" or money should be distributed to the citizens runs contrary to the Athenian's attacks on money (see, for instance, 742a). This is consistent, however, with Alfarabi's inclusion of artisans within the citizenry and his decision to have warriors paid for their services.

A final example of Alfarabi's silence about his regime's territorial limits (cf. disc. 8.12-13 with 848d) concerns the division of the regime. After he discusses the distribution of food, the Athenian discusses the division of the city into twelve parts in connection with the internal organization of each of the parts or villages, in particular where the temple and marketplace should be located in each village. Whereas Alfarabi does not hesitate to mention the temples or sites for worship and the gods worshiped therein, he avoids mentioning the city's division into twelve parts.

The omissions, the substitution, and the additions discussed above all corroborate that Alfarabi's regime is not the limited ancient polis but perhaps even an association of the inhabited world.

Passages that qualify the apparent unlimitedness of Alfarabi's regime cast doubt on the possibility that Alfarabi envisions a second-best *association of the inhabited world*. Shortly after his summary of the Athenian's discussion of the various occupations to be included in the colony as the result of its renunciation of aspirations to maritime empire (842d7), Alfarabi begins to summarize a discussion of boundaries (cf. disc. 8.7 and 8.8 with 842e7-44d4). He continues to omit any mention of the Athenian's references to the borders between cities (842e12-43a9), not to mention between neighbors. Nonetheless, he alludes to the Athenian's reference to the gods to whom one makes oaths to ensure the maintenance of boundaries. Alfarabi does not mention the gods explicitly, but he mentions the need to prevent changing "temples [*hayâkil*] and esteemed places [*mawâḍi' mubajallah*] on earth [*arḍ*] because changing them will corrupt people's hearts [*qulûb*]." In light of his repeated omissions of the Athenian's references to the territorial limits of the colony, it is noteworthy that Alfarabi uses the term "temples" (*hayâkil*) rather than "mosques" (*masâjid*). (Contrast the use of "mosques" in disc. 5.14.) Perhaps here Alfarabi is broadening his view beyond the limits of his regime to include "the earth" (*al-arḍ*) as a whole. Indeed, the whole of his summary of the discussion of boundaries looks to the whole earth, as is made especially clear by his reference to "governors at sea and rulers on land" (disc. 8.8). By speaking of temples rather than mosques, does Alfarabi mean to imply the existence of a multiplicity of religions? In addition, his discussion of boundaries focuses on the obvious impediments to rule over the whole earth, at least such rule by one governor. (I will return to give a more complete account of his view of rule over the whole earth later when I discuss the limitations of law.)

In addition to the hint regarding a multiplicity of temples, there is a harsh and direct critique of the aspiration to an association of the inhabited world. This critique takes place in the context of Alfarabi's summary of the Athenian's inquiry into the leading cause of the failure of the Dorian league—especially its aspiration to form a league of sufficiently great size to be able to fulfill its hopes for world empire (cf. disc. 3.4-6 with 682e6-87e10, esp. 684e10 ff.). The Athenian takes advantage of the opportunity offered by this inquiry to criticize the league's aspirations.[35] Alfarabi transforms this critique of the Dorian league's aspiration to world empire into a critique of a law that aspires to world empire.

First, the Athenian describes the failure of the three cities, Argos, Messene, and Sparta, to form a successful alliance or league (685a-86c4). The three cities had a contingency plan to ally in pairs if any one of the cities stepped out of line, either with respect to other members of the alliance or citizens of their own city or their own kings (684a3-b13). Rather than inquire, as Megillus wishes he would, into why the league failed, the Athenian turns to consider what was wrong with its aspiration to achieve world rule (686c5). One might have expected Alfarabi (as a member of a monotheistic community) to transform the league into an irresistible imperial force in world politics. On the contrary, he maintains the criticism and makes it more direct. Rather than begin by describing the failure of three cities to form a successful alliance, he describes a successful alliance between two or more kings (of different cities) in conquering one city. Alfarabi uses this alliance as a vivid example of the negative result of the aspiration to world rule. In contrast, the Athenian merely makes an abstract argument about what is wrong about this aspiration—an argument, by the way, that does not seem to persuade Megillus (see 686c5-88d, especially the turn away from this argument at 688c6 to resume Megillus's preferred inquiry into why the league failed). Alfarabi not only intensifies the Athenian's critique, he redirects it: He does not just describe the successful alliance of cities but of cities that accept the "divine law" (*al-nâmûs al-ilâhî*).[36] Their intention in attacking the one city is to impose the divine law on it. Most striking of all, the result of this imposition is not the redemption but the "corruption" (*fasâd*) of this city.

The Athenian traces the desire to establish the Dorian league to that human desire to "have things happen in accordance with the commands of one's own soul—preferably all things, but if not that, then at least the human things" (687c5-7). Human beings become enamored of great things that offer the prospect of fulfilling this desire (686d). But, as Alfarabi cautions, one should not judge the worth of a desire for something (in this case, *a law*) by the mere fact that human beings "approve" (*istiḥsân*) of it, because oftentimes people approve of something that is not "good in itself" (*nafsuhu khayr*) (disc. 3.5). He implies that the proper viewpoint from which to judge the goodness of something is not to determine whether it is impressive in size (such as a wonderful ship—or a law with political claims extending over the entire earth) or possesses unlimited power to supply one's bodily wants (such as riches and wealth), but rather whether it is "conducive to happiness" (*sa'âdah*). The proper judge of what is conducive to happiness is "intellect" (*'aql*) (disc. 3.5-6). We should judge the worth of a law by how well it accords with intellect rather than how well it satisfies our desire to have all things occur as we would wish.

This desire not only inclines human beings to be receptive to regimes and laws that promise to deliver such control, but inclines them to prayer. Thus, Alfarabi is justified in identifying the "divine law" as the law that inspires cities to unite to subdue other cities only to subject those cities to corruption. This desire is an aspect of that disease of the soul whose cure is one of the aims of the philosophically revised law. Both Alfarabi and Plato believe this desire is irrational. The implications of this judgment are not particularly striking for Plato; however, they are rather striking for Alfarabi as a member of a monotheistic community. If the desire to have all things happen as we would wish is irrational, then the monotheistic aspiration to extend the Law's rule over the entire world is irrational. From the existence of the critique of divine law's aspiration to world rule, we may infer that although Alfarabi's second-best regime is larger than is the strictly limited polis of the Greeks, it is smaller than an association of the entire inhabited world.[37]

In conclusion, because Alfarabi envisions a second-best regime that is larger than the classical polis and because political associations larger than the city are not conducive to democratic (or republican) rule, it is to be expected that Alfarabi's regime would incline in the direction of monarchy. The question is what kind of monarchy. Now, Alfarabi shows a decided preference for the ancient Persian as opposed to the ancient Athenian regime. (Contrary to the initial impression he gives, the Athenian also shares this preference.) Averroës and Ibn Bâjjah helped to clarify that Alfarabi's ancient Persian regime, although tending more toward monarchy than democracy, is not synonymous with the best regime. Consequently, in using the ancient Persian monarchy as a model, Alfarabi does not aspire to establish the best regime. Moreover, in crucial respects his monarchy resembles the extreme contemporary Persian monarchy more than the ancient Persian monarchy. I showed in section 2 that the greater role Alfarabi affords wealth as a title to rule is ample evidence that his regime does not draw more closely to the best regime. In section 3, I also argued that his treatment of ruling offices favors monarchy. The greater size of his regime, rather than an aspiration toward philosophic rule, dictates their monarchic character. In section 4, I remarked that he, unlike the Athenian, includes artisans among the citizens of his regime. The latter excludes artisans because of the illiberal influence they can have on citizens.[38] Alfarabi's inclusion of artisans, although compatible with monarchic rule, is not compatible with virtuous monarchic rule. It is highly compatible, however, with a large regime. Although Alfarabi's regime is not confined to the strict limits of the Athenian's city, it does have limits. Alfarabi signals his disapproval of a world regime through his transformation of the Athenian's critique of the Dorian league's aspiration to world empire into a critique of a law's aspiration to such empire. Although Alfarabi's second-best regime is larger than the ancient polis, it is also not an association of the inhabited world or, worse yet, a homogeneous world nation or state.

The more I fill out the picture of Alfarabi's second-best "city" the more clear it becomes that it cannot be confused with any best city–indeed, it appears to fall short even of Plato's second-best. Could this be because Alfarabi has simply drawn the conclusions for his own community that he must draw in light of the caveat that predominates throughout the *Laws*, i.e., that the city be conceived in accordance with what is politically possible at a given time and in a given place? Although what constitutes a second-best regime varies in accordance with the conditions that limit what is politically possible at any given time and in any given place, perhaps beneath this variability lies something constant, namely, the foundations of law. Even if the political conditions vary–and thus the suitable second-best regime varies–the understanding of the disease of the human soul and of the whole nature of souls that guides the laying down of law may remain constant.

6
War as a Purpose of the Second-Best Regime

It has often been said that one of the characteristics that most distinguishes ancient from modern political philosophers is their concern for the virtue of each citizen, as opposed to the ability of the city as a whole to fight foreign foes. Indeed, Socrates' lack of concern with foreign foes in the *Republic* has about it an air of unreality.[1] This lack is to be expected, however, because the *Republic* is about the best city simply, not about the best politically possible city; the best city is ruled by and therefore looks to the highest virtue, intellect; and intellect's purpose is knowledge, not contention or war (disc. 1.9). Intellect's purpose is at odds with the city's martial purpose.[2] The city's highest purpose is in a sense at odds with or beyond the city.

Close to the opening of the *Laws*, Kleinias makes an argument that continues to be disputed and shapes the dramatic action throughout the rest of the book. He says all cities are naturally in a state of war with one another (626a). Despite the Athenian's initial rejection of this view, he eventually and subtly concedes ground to it. The city must compromise its highest purpose to be politically possible: It must renounce the rule of intellect. With this renunciation, the city's purpose of fighting wars is inevitably rehabilitated.[3] In discourse 3, Alfarabi shows that the origin of war is the "clannishness" (*'aṣabiyyah*) of the pre-political kin group. Clans eventually unite to form political alliances. No matter how large their alliance becomes, its objective remains the same: the prosecution of war. By discourse 6, war's rehabilitation as a purpose or cause of the city has gone so far that Alfarabi is willing to assert that "wars constitute one of the greatest causes [*asbâb*] of cities" (disc. 6.4).[4]

Finally, I will discuss how the law that rules in lieu of intellect rules with an eye to preventing war among allies, or, in the words of the earliest description of law, with an eye to promoting reconciliation among the competing kin groups or families or clans out of which the city is constituted (628a). Although the law aims at reconciliation among the members of the alliance and thus at the opposite of war (disc. 3.3), this reconciliation is merely an intermediate purpose. The law's ultimate purpose is unification for waging war. As we saw in chapter 5, spreading the rule of the one law by force of arms leads to the corruption of the conquered city. As I will show in the next chapter, this corruption occurs because one law is not appropriate to all regions of the earth.

War's centrality in Alfarabi's *Summary* bears witness once again to how great the distance is between the city ruled by written law and the city ruled by intellect. The more the city diverges from the purpose of pursuing intellect, the more it requires the assistance of *kalâm* to achieve its purpose. As I will show in the third part, an important role of the philosophic *mutakallim* is to persuade the citizens to wage war and, should it prove necessary, to lay down their lives for their city.

1. The denigration of war as a purpose of the city

Although near the opening of the *Laws* the Athenian denigrates war as an end of the city, Alfarabi from the very first raises doubts about whether Plato really denies that war is an important end. Kleinias prepares the Athenian's denigration of war by saying not merely that "the lawgiver of the Cretans established all our customs, public and private, with a view to [*apoblepôn*] war" but that he did so because without victory in war none of the good things is "beneficial" (*ophelos*) (626b). Thus, Kleinias tacitly acknowledges that he views war not as an end in itself but as existing for the sake of the preservation of the goods–in particular, those goods the Athenian calls the "human goods" (health, beauty, strength, and wealth) (631c). This response to the Athenian's denigration of war, however, is not sufficient. There is an even higher end for the sake of which war exists as a means, even if only a very remote end. That higher end is the "divine goods" (prudence or intellect, moderation, courage, and justice). The city should aim above all at prudence or intellect.

Alfarabi also argues that war is not merely for the sake of the "human goods." To begin with, he argues that war is natural to human beings, in general, and to the Dorians, in particular (disc. 1.5). This could mean merely that human beings naturally fight over scarce resources. Indeed, on one occasion, Alfarabi affirms that human beings do not fight wars as ends in themselves but for the sake of peace or rather the preservation of one's own (human) goods (disc. 1.6 and cf. 629b). In other words, human beings fight wars out of necessity. Yet Alfarabi, in contrast to the Athenian, adds elsewhere that human beings fight wars not merely out of "necessity" (*ḍarûrah*) but also because of "appetite" (or desire, *shahwah*) and "preference" (*îthâr*) and because "it is a source of pleasure" (*tastalidhdh*) for them (cf. disc. 1.9[b] with 635a5-634b7). Even Kleinias, who argues that there exists an unacknowledged war of all cities against one another, does not go so far as to speak of taking pleasure in fighting wars. Why not?

As we saw in chapter 4, Kleinias is predisposed to hate tyranny (see, for instance, 711a8). His rejection of the tyrannical rule of the "worthy men" over "the worse"—not to mention the destruction of the worse by the worthy—in favor of the reconciliation achieved by law is one of the first signs that he is not willing to apply his theory of the war of all against all in a consistent manner (627e-28a4). He takes none of the pleasure in the prospect of tyranny or domination to which Alfarabi refers. In no small part his hatred of tyranny derives from his age. In contrast, the Athenian's model lawgiver desires the assistance of a tyrant who is young (709e8 ff.). To begin with, Kleinias, as an old man, lacks the irresponsibility (*anûpeuthunos*) that usually accompanies youth (691c8). Although the young tyrant is supposed to be naturally moderate, even he would still be stung by more intense desires than is Kleinias (666a5 ff.). In particular, he would be far more prone than Kleinias to possess in abundance that natural human desire to have "things happen in accordance with the commands of one's own soul— . . . at least the human things" (687c). Indeed, the young man's desire to be tyrant no doubt derives directly from this desire. In contrast, old age weakens Kleinias's desires. Furthermore, it makes him prone to defend the democratic or republican tradition in which he grew up. Thus, despite his devotion to the Dorian view that the end of the city is victory in war, Kleinias lacks that love of victory or pleasure in war that the young tyrant is prone to experience.

Apparently, because of the old age and the predisposition to favor republicanism of both of the Athenian's interlocutors, relatively little is said about a love of tyranny in the *Laws*. As we saw in chapter 4, unlike Kleinias, Alfarabi speaks candidly about the tyranny of the virtuous city as one that "conquers [*ghâlibah*] by virtue of truth and rightness" (disc. 1.6). The tyrant who rules the virtuous city, however, is not a lover of victory in war or even of tyranny. The virtuous city is ruled by the philosopher who loves truth and rightness or wisdom rather than victory in war by virtue of power.[5] Out of ignorance, lovers of tyranny pin their highest hopes on the fulfillment of that irrational desire to have all the human things occur as one would wish. No matter how misbegotten this hope may be, it appears that the love of tyranny—like the desire to protect the good things one has—is an important part of human beings' natural disposition to fight wars.

To see how Alfarabi develops his interpretation of war as a matter of pleasure as well as necessity, let us turn to the Athenian's description of the genesis of regimes (bk. 3). If Kleinias had been right in the opening of bk. 1 that the end of the city is victory in war, then one would expect the Athenian in the opening of bk. 3 to suggest that the city first emerged as a result of human beings' desire to secure allies against their enemies in the war of all against all. He, however, does not suggest this. Rather, cities do not emerge until the "single households or clans" (*mian oikêsin kai . . . genos*) descend from the mountain peaks to the foothills in order to establish "one common, large dwelling by erecting defensive walls of stone" (680d7, 681a3). The first purpose of these walls, and thus of cities, is defense not in war with human beings but against "wild beasts"! Kleinias gives only grudging assent to this argument (681a). He would surely have rejected it but for the fact that he had already gone along, however grudgingly, with the Athenian's argument that human beings are not naturally disposed to "the desire to have more [*pleonexia*] [and the] love of victory [*philonikia*]" (677b5–10).[6]

Alfarabi appears to reproduce the Athenian's account of the origin of the city and of fortresses, in particular (disc. 3.2[b]). At first, people made cities and fortresses to fend off "beasts, wild animals, and other harmful things." Only later did people wage wars against one another. The Athenian's purpose in making this argument is not difficult to fathom: To persuade his interlocutors that war is not the leading purpose of the city, he denies that the city first arose to provide protection against human enemies. (The Athenian is compelled to make such arguments because, to repeat an observation made earlier, his interlocutors tend to identify the first or the oldest with the most important.) By reporting the Athenian's argument, Alfarabi supports this rhetorical purpose. Shortly before this passage, however, Alfarabi describes a different scenario (disc. 3.2[a]). Originally, after the flood, "people regarded each other cheerfully," but when the population grew and "envy [*ḥasad*] gradually began to spread" people began to war with one another. Finally, the people were "impelled" (or compelled, *taḍṭarru*) to acquire the arts of war, among them the building of fortresses (and thus of cities), by their "need" (*ḥâjah*) for them. They needed fortresses to fight wars with one another. Fortresses were not first intended to fend off wild beasts. One does not need the arts of war to fight wild beasts, because they lack the guile that necessitates substantial development of these arts.

Was the "envy" people felt toward one another merely the inevitable envy that people feel toward those who have access to scarce resources that they lack? Or was it the result of their desire to have more and of love of victory? If we may trust Alfarabi's statements shortly after the discussion of envy, the arts first emerge for the sake of providing what is "necessary" (*ḍarûrah*) and only later for the sake of what is noble and fair (end of disc. 3.2[a]). The example he provides, however, raises doubts about the truth of his own statement. Do clothes really emerge first out of necessity or for the sake of the noble and the fair?[7] Whichever comes first, human beings do not fight wars merely for the sake of the human goods but also for the divine. To summarize, the city and fortresses first emerged to enable human beings to prosecute wars with one another rather than to protect themselves from wild beasts. Furthermore, the love of victory plays an important role in the emergence of war. The Athenian attempted to conceal this account of war from his interlocutors in an effort to counteract their tendency to view victory in war either as the sole or the highest end of the city.

2. *The rehabilitation of war as a purpose*

Although Alfarabi lends support to the claims of war from the beginning of discourse 1, the rehabilitation of war as a cause of the city only begins in earnest toward the end of discourse 3.2. Here he summarizes the Athenian's account of the emergence of legislation. According to the Athenian, it emerges because human beings from different clans or households come together, each bearing its own "customs" (*nomima*) (681c8) into the "one common, large dwelling," mentioned above. He acknowledges that something "compelled" (*anagkaion*) those living in the common dwelling to select men to legislate (681c7). He never identifies explicitly, however, what compels them to select legislators. According to Alfarabi, the "need [that] impelled them" (*taḍṭarru al-ḥâjah*) was that the existence of different clans with different customs led to "clannishness" (*'aṣabiyyah*). And the "struggle for victory" (or the struggle to dominate or tyrannize, *mughâlabah*) derives from clannishness (disc. 3.3). When people from diverse clans come together in a common dwelling, they must legislate to prevent strife among the different clans—strife about which the Athenian is practically silent.

Yet Alfarabi's recourse to the notion of "clannishness" is not without precedent in the *Laws*. We saw in the earliest characterization of law in the course of the Athenian's discussion of the three different kinds of judges that the law "reconciles" (*dialattô*) warring members of "a single divided family" (627e6). Even in the present discussion of the four stages of regime development, Plato hints at the less than gentle character of the relations between different clans. They come together into one common dwelling in the foothills during the second stage of regime development, which is the first stage in the development of the city or politics proper. In the first and sole pre-political stage, however, individual clans live in isolation on the mountain peaks. In his initial characterization of human beings in this stage, the Athenian describes them as happy to see and "full of good will" toward one another (678c5 ff. and 678e9 ff.). Later, when he classifies this stage as "dynasty" (*dunasteia*) (680b), he cites Homer in apparent confirmation. Homer's account, however, is incompatible with his. According to Megillus, in Homer's account human beings (or the Cyclopes) show not their good will but their "savagery" (*agriotês*) toward one another (680d4).[8] Thus, while appearing to denigrate war as an original cause of regime formation, Plato alludes to the "clannishness" that plays such a prominent part in Alfarabi's account of the origin of legislation (and of the city). Thus, the Athenian continues his rhetorical opposition to his interlocutors' tendency to exalt war as the sole or highest end of the city—all the while alluding to its central role in giving rise to politics.

The desire to fight or dominate, which is the essence of "clannishness" (*'aṣabiyyah*), gives rise to the city by first leading clans to fight one another, which in turn leads each clan to seek allies with whom to fight their enemies. Originally, the city is a war alliance. But such alliances are inherently fragile. Allies who have pooled their desire to dominate in order to fight a common enemy have merely temporarily unified their clans. Especially when their common enemy has been subdued, each clan is likely to reassert its own *'aṣabiyyah* even against its former allies—if for no other reason than the close proximity of most allies. Their drawing together into a fortified common dwelling does not eliminate the differences between the clans. Something else is needed, namely, law. One essential purpose of legislation is to prevent the temporary alliance from decaying into a "civil war," fueled by the independent *'aṣabiyyah* of each clan.[9]

3. *The relation between war and law*

As we saw in the previous section, law provides a great boon to human beings: it reconciles warring clans so that they can unite to form a city. Yet law itself seems to have the end of fighting other cities. It eliminates strife—but for the sake of forming a more effective alliance for war. It eliminates strife among clans within a city—but not between cities. Thus, Alfarabi suggests that the "struggle for victory that stems from clannishness" gives rise to war between cities (disc. 3.3). Insofar as law's purpose is the elimination of strife, war between cities runs contrary to its purpose. Yet its purpose was to establish peace for the sake of more effective alliance formation.

Alfarabi goes on to discuss a further manifestation of this internal inconsistency of law: The "divine law" (*al-nâmûs al-ilâhî*) (not to mention Islam's *sharî'ah*) commands the prosecution of wars whose ultimate purpose is the elimination of war (disc. 3.4). The war is fought to convert those (pagans) who are willing to the one faith and to destroy those who are unwilling so that the whole world might live under one law. The peacemaking purpose of the law expresses itself ultimately in a paradoxical push to fight the war that will end all war. One wonders what the purpose of the law will become once it has achieved its purpose of eliminating strife. In other words, once it has accomplished its intermediate purpose of eliminating domestic strife, what will come of its ultimate purpose of facilitating foreign war? More immediately and less fantastically, one must also wonder, as Alfarabi does (disc. 3.4), whether the divine law achieves its purpose of eliminating strife at the expense of corrupting those cities it absorbs. As we shall see in the next chapter, the extension of one law over different regions gives rise to the corruption of those regions for which the law was not originally designed.

The law expresses its wish to be intellect (*Minos*) by its aspiration to world rule. Intellect is truly cosmopolitan; thus law aspires to be truly cosmopolitan. Unfortunately, the law aspires to control or dominate the unfolding of all human events—unlike intellect, which merely aspires to know the whole. Furthermore, the things of the intellect can truly be held in common; the scarce resources of the cities, however, cannot be. If the law ruled intellects rather than bodies, perhaps it could rule without force. But the law, like the ignorant slave doctor, is limited to issuing commands. The law merely says, "Do this!" or "Do that!" not "Do this because. . . ." The law does not attempt to persuade, let alone to reason. The Athenian must inject persuasion (poetic or imaginative arguments) into the rule of law before law can even come close to fulfilling its wish to be intellect. Even then, the link between the body and the imagination being what it is, law may be incapable of raising its sights above the citizens' physical well-being. As I will show in the third part, the poetic art of persuasion must gain a certain distance from law—enough distance to be able to engage in a critique of it—for the ascent to intellect to begin in earnest.

7
Legal Innovation: Law as an Imitation of Intellect

In chapter 3, I reviewed the modern scholarship that portrays Plato as a natural law theorist. This scholarship treats the account of the order underlying the whole given in bk. 10 as if it were the metaphysical foundation of law. In the first part, I explained that, according to Alfarabi, Plato is not a natural law theorist because for him the foundations of law are not metaphysical but psychological.

According to natural *law* theorists, the metaphysical order of the natural whole provides the ground for human actions—or the political order derives from the metaphysical order. Just as the arrangement of natural things is orderly or lawful, so are human affairs orderly or lawful. Because the "lawfulness" of the natural things does not admit of exceptions, there should be permanent principles or laws of human action such as those found in the second table of the Decalogue that at least in principle admit of no exceptions.[1] Furthermore, all people should be naturally predisposed to obey such laws because they are contained in the human soul as "conscience."[2]

Rather than derive such principles of human action from the natural order of the whole, the natural *right* theorist focuses directly on the human soul—on its inherent disorder and how to rectify it. As I have said, Plato (as a natural right theorist) is far less sanguine about the possibility of acquiring the kind of metaphysical knowledge that could serve as a foundation of law. More importantly, even if such knowledge could be acquired, the discontinuity between the human things and the natural things, mentioned earlier, precludes the possibility of deriving the political order from the metaphysical order. Of course, the natural right theorist is not wholly silent about metaphysics. On the contrary, this theorist engages in an inquiry into the limitations of the commonly accepted metaphysical accounts. Their limitations, however, become apparent less from any failure to provide a ground for natural phenomena than from their failure to meet the human needs they claim to meet. For example, the anthropomorphic gods of traditional Greek religion cannot fulfill the insatiable desire for domination of the Dorian league. Now, the natural *law* theorist seeks to replace the traditional metaphysical accounts with a superior–indeed, the final–scientific account. Accordingly, a Christian natural law theorist might propose a superior metaphysical account whose purpose would be to enable a league akin to the Dorian (or better yet the Roman) to achieve a Christian kingdom of the inhabited world. In contrast, the natural *right* theorist, rather than focusing on providing the definitive metaphysical account, focuses, for example, on how the traditional metaphysical accounts foster the desire for domination. Furthermore, this analyst attempts to determine how this desire fits into the soul's economy, for instance, whether it is rational–and if it is irrational, whether perhaps it is a distorted version of a more rational desire.

One of the fundamental propositions of this book is that all forms of political life rest on beliefs, if not necessarily religious beliefs. If this is correct, then analyzing how the traditional metaphysical accounts fail to meet human needs is tantamount to analyzing how political life succeeds or fails to meet human needs. As I will show, one of the central tasks of the natural right theorist is to compare how the various ways of life succeed or fail at this. The extent to which a way of life succeeds determines its relative rank. Ultimately, the most rational way of life will prove to be the most successful.

Through the inquiry into the soul, the natural right theorist seeks to know the permanent hierarchy of ends of human life–rather than the natural law theorist's permanent principles or laws of action. This hierarchy of ends is the hierarchy of the various ways of life. Different ways of life emerge in human society in part as the result of a search for the proper cure for the "disease" of the human soul. The most salient feature of the soul's disease is the unlimitedness of its desires. Because of their unlimitedness, laws or customs of some kind are required to prevent them from destroying communal life.

The human soul is in need of a supplement. The law provides the supplement required by the body politic as a whole, but it does not necessarily provide the individual soul's complete cure. This cure is the acquisition of intellect. The human potential for acquiring intellect grows out of the naïve human awareness of the whole–this awareness of the whole lies at the root of the desire to know it. Human beings, however, experience a sense of weakness before the whole because of our peculiar weakness at birth, the evident enormity of the whole, and our ignorance of its underlying order. Our sense of weakness gives rise to terror (791a).[3] In response to this terror, human beings strive for mastery or power over all things, whether it be through unlimited political conquest or through the projection of (metaphysical) myths upon the whole. The only proper cure for this defect is its transformation into the greatest of human assets, namely, by redirecting the naïve human desire to have all things occur as one would wish in the direction of the more attainable (and in a sense more fundamental) desire to acquire knowledge of the whole.[4]

The Platonic understanding of a permanent human nature does not require the existence in every place and time of human beings, namely, the philosophers, who both recognize the superiority of the cure provided by intellect to that of law and are able to achieve it. For example, a pre-political community such as that of the *dunasteia* cannot provide the leisure or a sufficient development of the arts and sciences to achieve it. Rather, the existence of a permanent human nature requires the existence of an upper limit (philosophy, which will be adumbrated in chapters 9 and 10) and a lower limit (submission to law out of shame, which will be described in chapters 8 and 9) on the range of possible cures. Just as the upper limit need not exist in all communities, neither need the lower.[5]

The possible range of ends is permanent, despite the fact that all ends may not be equally achievable in every place and time. In addition, the means of achieving these various ends will necessarily vary from time to time and place to place. Thus, according to the natural right theorist, insofar as political action is a means to the achievement of the highest end, the appropriate actions are bound to vary rather than to be permanent. And insofar as laws dictate which actions are appropriate and which are inappropriate, it would be most fitting if laws could vary in accordance with changes of time and place. As I suggested in chapter 4, only the rule of intellect unconstrained by written law is capable of providing laws that change in full accordance with changing times and places. In lieu of the rule of unconstrained intellect, human beings must rest satisfied with the rule of written laws and of subphilosophic citizen-legislators who are capable of innovating on them.

1. Changes of place: Differing natural dispositions and customs

One of the greatest advantages of written over unwritten and uncodified law is that it can command the obedience of different people in different places and times. This strength, however, may also be its greatest weakness. Alfarabi presents two accounts of the extension of the rule of one (written) law over the inhabitants of different regions (disc. 2.1[c–e] and disc. 8.7–8)–in addition to the account he gives of the corrupting effect of an alliance of cities conquering another city in the name of divine law (disc. 3.4–5). He is far more sanguine in the former than in the latter (and in disc. 3.4–5) about the prospects for extending the rule of one law over many regions. Ultimately, he tips the balance against such rule. He opposes it because law, although it can imitate intellect, falls far short of it and therefore should limit the extent of its rule.

Before I explain Alfarabi's first account of the extension of one law over many regions (disc. 2.1[c]), it is useful to describe the context of the discussion in the *Laws* that he is summarizing. The Athenian discusses musical performances and who is best able to judge their worth. According to the many, the pleasure of the crowd is the proper judge of which musical forms are the best or the most appropriate (657e). The Athenian proposes an imaginary competition among the different kinds of musical forms to illustrate the difficulties inherent in this view. Because different groups within the community–people of different ages, sexes, and upbringing–prefer different kinds of musical performances, the judges of such performances come into conflict over which kind is the best. The way to resolve this conflict is to establish one group's view as authoritative. It is only natural that when the Athenian, an old man, discusses laws with two other old men that they should all agree that old men of good lineage should be the judges of what is appropriate (658e). Here I should add, however, that the old men are suitable judges because they, like the law, receive the most respect as the representatives of the inherited tradition and because the old are naturally more moderate than are the young (see 659e and 666a ff.).

In his summary of this passage, Alfarabi transforms the discussion of establishing an authoritative opinion as to what musical forms are appropriate within what appears to be a specific city into a discussion of establishing the authority of one law over the inhabitants of every "region" (*buq'ah*) (disc. 2.1[c]). Apparently, the difference between the pleasures of young and old, male and female, and well-bred and ill-bred is analogous to the difference between the pleasures of the inhabitants of different regions. Thus, just as it is appropriate that agreement as to what kind of musical performance is to be preferred should be established in accordance with the authoritative opinion of the old men, so is it appropriate that agreement between diverse regions should be established by the "skilled [*ḥâdhiq*] legislator." This legislator is skilled because he is able to draw people toward "goodness and happiness" by means of "charm" (*mubhij*) or the promise of pleasure (660a and 667c). Because inhabitants of different regions, like the old and the young, have different "natural dispositions" (*ṭibâ'*) (as well as moral habits), they do not find the same things to be pleasant or painful. But how far does the analogy between differences in age or sex as compared with "region" go? The term Mahdi has rendered "region," *buq'ah*, need not refer to a large area. Perhaps if one discusses larger regions such as "climatic regions" (*aqâlîm*)–which Alfarabi does discuss in discourse 8.8–differences in "natural disposition" become even greater.[6] Although it is most certainly a sign of the skill of a legislator that he can charm people of different regions to have the same understanding of goodness and happiness, "charm" alone is not sufficient. Alfarabi adds that the skilled legislator is also the one who can "control" (*yaghlib*)[7] and "compel" (*yaqhar*) people to accept the same law by means of a certain kind of music and other "conventional statutes" (*aḥkâm al-sunan*) in spite of the differences in their natural dispositions. That the skilled legislator must have recourse to force reminds us that the law homogenizes the natural dispositions of people of different ages and sexes, not to mention different regions (or even more so, different climatic regions) at a price.

Alfarabi goes on to explain that the legislator and those who apply his law must "control [*yaḍbiṭ*] the many different human affairs in every respect and in all their details so that none of these human affairs will escape them" (disc. 2.1[d]).[8] If the legislator and the rulers who apply the law do not attend to all the details of human affairs, they will cease to be consonant with the law. Not only must the legislator attend to every detail, but he must also "address every group [*ṭâ'ifah*] with what is closer to their comprehension and intellects" (disc. 2.1[e]). We begin to grasp the magnitude of the difficulty confronting the legislator. How is the legislator supposed to adjust *written* laws so that they address the different "comprehension and intellects" of the inhabitants of different "regions," not to mention different climates, with respect to every detail of human life? In his *Attainment of Happiness*, Alfarabi describes a supreme ruler or prince who is ruler and legislator in one. This supreme ruler is comparable to the philosopher-king in the *Republic*. He is capable of inquiring into "all *or most* nations" (my italics) in order to determine how to apply his law.[9] Although he writes down some of his laws, many of them are unwritten. Unlike the legislator in the *Summary*, he is not restricted to written laws. Freed from the limitations of such laws, it is not inconceivable that he might rule over "all or most nations."[10]

Now let us turn to Alfarabi's second and less sanguine account of extending the rule of one law over all regions (disc. 8.7-8). In chapter 5, when I briefly touched on this passage, I explained that Alfarabi appears to describe a city or regime without clearly delimited boundaries. It is a regime that needs "frontier settlers" rather than "guards" (842e), that measures itself in terms of the entire "earth" (*al-arḍ*) (disc. 8.7), and whose governors are in some way analogous to governors who rule not merely a particular city but "at sea and on land" (disc. 8.8). This regime would strive to preserve "temples and venerated places" not merely "mosques and venerated places." In other words, the regime Alfarabi has in mind would not have as its purpose imposing its divine law on other cities. It seems to be conceived in full cognizance of the corrupting effects of such imposition.

The legislator "teaches governors [*aṣḥâb al-siyâsât*] and judges" how to administer each different "group" (*ṭâ'ifah*) (disc. 8.7).[11] This legislator, unlike the prince in the *Attainment*, is incapable of ruling "all or most nations" directly by himself. For "a single governor [*sâ'is*] and administrator [*mudabbir*] will not know the usages, rules, and habits of each inhabitant of all the [climatic] regions [*aqâlîm*]" (disc. 8.8). Each governor may be skilled in ruling one "group" (*ṭâ'ifah*) and the inhabitants of a particular "country" (*bilad*), but he cannot know how to rule other groups with their own usages, rules, and habits. One could infer from Alfarabi's two main assertions–that the legislator must teach governors and judges how to rule "each group" so that people will follow "his way" and that one governor and administrator cannot rule all of the climatic regions–that he means to imply that the legislator should teach a great enough multiplicity of governors to rule every climatic region in the world. But one thing is certain: Alfarabi never says that. At most he affirms the wisdom of the legislator's teaching a multiplicity of governors to rule a multiplicity of "groups" who inhabit an area of indeterminate extent. Note that there is no indication that these groups cooperate freely, as do the virtuous cities and nations in the virtuous association of the inhabited world. Although Alfarabi may advocate compelling groups or clans to form an association in order to form a viable city (disc. 3.2[c]), his condemnation of alliances whose purpose is to impose their divine law on other cities (disc. 3.4) is proof enough that he would not condone the legislator's compelling different cities to embrace his law. He never suggests that these "groups" are equivalent in extent to cities, let alone nations.[12] On the rare occasions on which he speaks of a multiplicity of cities and who rules them, he always speaks of a multiplicity of legislators (see disc. 7.11, 13, and 14)–thus implying that the legislator presently under discussion rules only one city. Another thing is certain: Alfarabi refuses to condone the aspiration of the monotheistic religions to extend the rule of a single, homogeneous divine law over the whole earth.

In between his remark that "the legislator must teach the governors and judges how to administer each group" and his remark that "a single governor and administrator will not know the usages, rules, and habits of each inhabitant of all the [climatic] regions," Alfarabi launches perhaps his most scathing criticism of the rule of written law in the form of a very peculiar analogy between the rule of legislators and the rule of beekeepers over bees.[13] To begin with, the analogy draws our attention to the despotic–or enslaving–character of the law. Here inhabitants of the city ruled by written law are like bees in a beehive (disc. 8.7), and bees make honey not for their own consumption but for the consumption of their rulers, namely, their beekeepers. The inhabitants of the hive are either like free people or like slaves. The free people are treated as are evil people: In other words, they are punished. Perhaps they have no desire to make honey for the rulers.[14] The slaves are treated like vagabonds: In other words, they prefer not to work. Since the rulers want honey, the slaves are driven to work lest they act like their true selves, namely, vagabonds.[15] The tyrannical implications of the analogy between the rule of legislators of written law and the rule of beekeepers over beehives raises serious doubts about the wisdom of extending the rule of one written law over the whole earth. What if the free people, who are treated like evil people by the legislator, are incapable of escaping the city when the legislator threatens them with the ultimate punishment? To answer this question, one need only remember what would have happened to the abstemious ascetic if he had not been able to escape from his city.

2. *Changes of time: Conservation and innovation*

Not only is one code of written law inappropriate for every region or place, but also written law resists the changes that time necessitates. Alfarabi considers the problem of legal innovation to be so central to his *Summary* that he makes discourse 7 into a summary of and expansion upon the Athenian's discussion of innovation and conservation of customs (796e6-804c)–only one of the many subjects discussed in bk. 7. Why are innovation and conservation so pressing that they justify Alfarabi's neglect of the Athenian's discussion of the family and private matters?[16] The monotheistic law of the former's community presents new impediments to innovation that did not exist for the latter. The divine Law's authority in the monotheistic communities dwarfs the divine law's authority in Plato's.[17] The greater authority of the former derives inevitably from the greater authority that is attributed to the one God in the monotheistic communities than is attributed, for instance, to Zeus by the Cretan (624a3).[18] Insofar as the one God is the source of prophecy and the Prophet is the transmitter of the divine Law, it is inevitable that the greater authority of the source should redound to His dispensation, the divine Law.

Before we consider Alfarabi's discussion of innovation in discourse 7, however, let us return to an earlier account in the *Laws* of why conservation of laws is desirable. The account of the Egyptians' conservation of their traditions concerning music, as it so happens, immediately precedes the discussion of determining which musical performances are appropriate (656d ff.).[19] This discussion of Egyptian conservation is, at least in part, a response to the poets' use of their own pleasures–which need not be equivalent to those of the many–as guides to innovation in musical traditions (disc. 2.1[b]). Of course, Kleinias, as a Cretan with little experience with poetry, is all too ready to support any measure restricting the choice of poets (680c3-6). As I will show in chapter 10, pleasure is not a dependable guide to what is appropriate. In particular, people, including poets, are pleased by variety and change. When judging whether a musical tradition should be conserved or innovated on, however, we should tend not in the direction of change but in the direction of Egypt's never-changing traditions, because the law will possess no authority whatsoever if it is constantly changing (798b).

Despite the fact that pleasure is a poor guide to innovation, Alfarabi develops an argument for the necessity of innovation. As we have noted, law has an inherent tendency to decay over time (676c and disc. 3.1). Its loss of authority over time, however, is not the only source of its decay. Another is the inability of written law to change with the changing conditions that differences or the passage of time bring. (That law must change is true even because, or perhaps especially because, laws must be made with an eye to the same or permanent ends: Changing conditions necessitate that one employ different means to achieve the same ends.) Consequently–and in direct contradiction to the threat to law that loss of authority poses–the greater a law's authority, the greater is its resistance to change. In this respect, then, the more authoritative the law is, the more subject it is to decay. Because of the greater authoritativeness of the divine Law in his community, Alfarabi transforms the corrupting influence of time on the law into a distinct kind of prelude, i.e., the "natural [*ṭabī'iyyah*] prelude," not found in the Platonic text (cf. disc. 4.16 with 721e5).

On a few noteworthy occasions, Alfarabi highlights for the attentive reader the differences in what things are deemed appropriate in his A.D. tenth-century Muslim community and the Athenian's fifth-century (B.C.) community. For instance, when the Athenian describes how objectionable "everyone [*pas*] as he gets more elderly" finds singing (665e), Alfarabi describes how objectionable flute playing and dancing are to old men (disc. 2.4). It appears that singing, as opposed to flute playing, was not objectionable or a source of shame for old men in his community.[20] In another instance, in describing the different ways that Greek communities from Plato's time made use of wine, Alfarabi mentions that one group shunned wine "even in the case of necessity" (disc. 2.9). In fact, the furthest the Athenian goes toward describing a historical community that makes no use of wine is to describe a hypothetical community that in fact makes a substantial use of wine (673e4-74c6). The divine Law of Alfarabi's own community, however, is known for striving to avoid making use of wine even in cases of necessity. Why do laws vary so much from (Plato's) time to (Alfarabi's) time? As Alfarabi says, this is because "the law is given with a view to the requirements of an existing situation [or condition, *ḥâl*]." Legal innovation is needed to adjust the law to suit the changed conditions of different times. Only legal innovation can reverse or rather slow the corruption that is inherent in written law's petrified character.[21]

Keeping the factors necessitating both legal conservation and innovation completed in mind, let us turn to Alfarabi's summary of the Athenian's discussion of conservation and innovation of games and music (cf. disc. 7.1-11 with 796e6-804c). Because the act of legislating a law is itself a form of innovation, Alfarabi's first three paragraphs are devoted to describing how the legislators can innovate in "the matter of hymns" (*amr al-tadhâkir*) in the way that is least likely to lead to the citizens' rejection of them.[22] Alfarabi will describe three different approaches (disc. 7.2 and 7.3). He prefaces this discussion, however, with the observation that hymns need to be established by the legislators so that they will be "referred to" *(marji')* by the citizens not just during the lifetime of the legislators but after they have passed away. Unfortunately, the line of legislators or excellent legislators tends to be interrupted.[23] In lieu of a continuous line of such legislators, hymns need to be established and, according to the Athenian, left unchanged (799a4–b12). Is it possible that if the line of excellent legislators could be continued, such unchanging hymns would not be needed?

Alfarabi's three different approaches to the introduction of hymns are an elaboration of the Athenian's two different approaches (799c4–e8). The Athenian describes the two extreme approaches; Alfarabi simply adds an approach that is a mean between them. In the preceding passage, the Athenian described an innovation (796e6–99c4). It was to make all children's games unchanging: the innovation of absolute conservation–with the exception of changing that which is bad. Only at the end of his description of this paradoxical innovation does he begin to raise doubts about it (799c4). His interlocutor Kleinias, as might be expected of a Cretan legal conservative, eagerly embraces this innovation (797d4–7). He does so merely because this particular innovation agrees with his own habits. Innovation as such is not bad; it troubles us when it happens to run contrary to our own habits. For the average Athenian who is used to constant innovation in matters of music, the suggestion that all hymns be left unchanged would no doubt be an objectionable innovation. As if to reveal to Kleinias the reaction of the average Athenian (who is a young man, as compared with a conservative such as Kleinias) to the innovation of absolute conservation, the Athenian Stranger describes the reaction of "every young man" (799c4). If someone were all of a sudden to mandate this, every young man would object to that to which he is unaccustomed. This is the sudden kind of innovation Alfarabi has in mind when he speaks of innovation in the matter of hymns "when the legislators begin to reveal their plans" (disc. 7.2). As if to emphasize how strongly "every young man" would object to the innovation of absolute conservation, the Athenian suggests that they skip ahead to the end of the legislation lest they be prevented from completing it. Similarly, Alfarabi describes the opposite extreme to innovating at the beginning of the laws as introducing innovations "collectively at the end" (*jumlatan fī âkhir*). Innovations introduced in this manner would be prepared for by the legislation itself. Indeed, in each particular case they would be viewed as the natural result of the preceding process of legislation. Such innovations would hardly be perceived as innovations. The mean between these two extreme forms of innovation, introducing it in the beginning and at the end, is introducing it "piecemeal" (*shay'an ba'da shay'*).

Alfarabi goes on to describe the relative desirability of these three different approaches to innovation (disc. 7.3). As the objections of "every young man" indicate, the first extreme, introducing innovations in the matter of hymns at the beginning, is undesirable because they are rejected as "counterfeit" (*muzayyaf*). Furthermore, their rejection necessitates that one have recourse to the moderate approach of introducing piecemeal changes. That which is introduced "gradually" (*qalīlan qalīlan*) or in a piecemeal manner is deemed fair and noble simply because its introduction is imperceptible. That which is introduced all at once in the beginning is too directly confrontational. Yet an innovation whose introduction is imperceptible is nonetheless an innovation. Finally, hymns that are introduced at the end of legislation are the "noblest of all" because the laws are ordered in such a way as to prepare the way for their acceptance. In such a case, the law itself stands as a guarantor of their acceptance. Thus, hymns introduced at the end have been provided with the most effective precautions.

Up to this point, the Athenian's discussion about innovation has concerned, at first, merely children's games, and second, merely hymns. Eventually, however, the distinction between the discussion of innovation in these lesser matters and the discussion of the law itself becomes hazy. The Athenian raises the possibility that songs should be treated as if they were "laws"[24]–in other words, as if they were inviolable and unchangeable (799e10). If the discussion about innovation in musical matters translates directly into a discussion about legal innovation, then just as innovation in musical matters is deemed fair and noble according to how imperceptible it is, so would legal innovation. Insofar as it is an innovation that citizens need to "learn and work hard to memorize," it is perceptible and presumably objectionable. On the other hand, a legal innovation that "citizens already know" is imperceptible and barely deserves the name "innovation" (*mustabda'ah*) (disc. 7.6).

In light of this similarity between matters of music and matters of law, it is not surprising that Alfarabi suggests that people be left free to inquire into the meaning of the "laws" (disc. 7.4). Are not poets constantly engaged in discussing the multiplicity of meanings contained in music (viz., poetry)? And if so, why should they not be engaged in the "discussion" (*kalâm*)[25] of the "rich [or multiplicity of, *jammah*] meanings" in the "laws," or, as Alfarabi calls them, the "sayings [*aqâwīl*] of some ancient legislators" (disc. 7. 5)? Despite the Athenian's almost imperceptible transition from musical matters to legal matters, there is an obvious objection to be raised to the poets' inquiry into the multiplicity of meanings contained in the laws or the sayings of the legislators. As Alfarabi himself notes earlier in the *Summary*, the "one who lays down traditions should only defend the one thing that is useful to him" (disc. 4.12; cf. 719a4–d4). In contrast, the poet and the "discussant" (*mutakallim*) may say one thing as well as its contrary. If there are contradictions in the law (unlike poetry or *kalâm*), they are antithetical to the purpose of the law. Chapter 10 will explain what fruit is borne of this difference between poetry and law. In chapter 9, I will discuss what Alfarabi here characterizes as the Athenian's digression (*'adl*) from his proper subject of innovation (cf. disc. 7.7–10 with 800b5–

804c).[26] He digresses to criticize the poets' indulgence in tragic music for religious purposes. In the course of the digression, he advocates an innovation (and in this respect imitates the poets) banning all publicly sanctioned indulgence in dispiriting emotions (and in this respect diverges from the poets).

From Alfarabi's summary of the Athenian's rather indirect discussion of legal innovation,[27] let us turn to Alfarabi's far bolder independent discussion of it (disc. 7.11–14). With an eye to making innovations imperceptible and thus acceptable, he asserts that later legislators should not repudiate (*yankar*) matters legislated by their predecessors, or rather he implies that later legislators should not appear to repudiate them (disc. 7.11). Therefore, if "necessity" (*ḍarûrah*) dictates that previous laws be "changed" (*taghyîr*), then they should (claim to) repudiate the "alteration" (*tabdîl*) and the "distortion" (*taḥrîf*) by the citizens of the laws, traditions, and usages introduced by the previous legislators. A way of making innovation imperceptible is to persuade citizens that it only appears to run contrary to the laws laid down by one's predecessors. All reformation should appear to be restoration. If a legislator openly asserts that he is replacing the laws of his predecessors, he not only raises doubts about all of the other laws they legislated but, in so doing, also raises doubts about the authority of his own innovation, which can derive only from their authority.

Having discussed the relation of contemporary legislators to their predecessors, Alfarabi turns to the relation of contemporary to future legislators (disc. 7.12–13). On the one hand, a legislator should not raise doubts about the authority of his own legislation by raising the expectation of the citizens, especially those who lack sophistication (*ghayr al-muḥtanikîn*), about the coming of another legislator in the future. Why should the citizens obey a law that they know will be changed in the future? The citizens will shift their obedience toward the law that is to be brought by the future legislator in the expectation that his law will be final and therefore authoritative. With an eye to establishing just such respect for the authoritativeness of the *present* traditions of the Law (*shir'ah*), Alfarabi eventually concludes his discussion of legal innovation with the assertion that some of the traditions do not "change" (*tataghayyar*) or "alter" (*tatabaddal*) and they are called "natural" (*ṭabî'iyyah*) (disc. 7.14).

On the other hand, the legislator should not claim that it is impossible for him to have any "successor" (or, literally, legislator coming after him, *yakun ba-'dahu . . . ṣaḥib nâmûs*). Indeed, it appears to be inevitable that he will have a successor if the law is to be sustained. Consequently, to deny that he will have a successor raises doubts about the credibility of his own legislation. And to raise doubts about his own legislation is to raise doubts about the foundation of past legislation upon which his successor will anchor his legislation. Finally, because his own legislation is only the last in a long line of predecessors for his successor, what applies to his own law applies to the laws laid down by all his predecessors as well. Thus, for a legislator to deny the possibility that he will have a successor leads to the undermining of his successor's law, his own law, and the laws laid down by his predecessors.

To avoid the pitfalls of either confirming or denying that anyone will succeed him, the legislator must "steer a middle course" (*yajriy . . . ṭarîqan wasṭan*). Just as the legislator should portray himself as the restorer of the original intent when he reforms the laws of his predecessors, so should the legislator portray his successor as the restorer of his law. He should claim that his successor will defend him and restore those parts of his law that have been obliterated by "the passage of time" (*ṭul al-zamân*) (cf. 769c5). As a mere restorer of the original intent, the successor should be presented as a lesser likeness of his predecessor. Note that Alfarabi does not say that the successor will *be* merely the defender of his predecessor but rather that the legislator "should declare" (*yuṣarriḥ*) that his successor will be of such a kind: The successor may in fact not be a lesser likeness. The legislator is compelled to declare this because whether he tells the whole truth by confirming that he may have an innovative successor or tells a complete untruth by denying it, he will undermine obedience to the law.

Just as Alfarabi exhorts the legislator to steer a middle course between denying and confirming that he will have a successor, Alfarabi himself steers a middle course between denying and confirming that laws or rather traditions should change. As I mentioned earlier, Alfarabi asserts that there are some traditions called "natural" that do not change or alter. If Alfarabi were not to make such an assertion, then it is difficult to see why anyone, especially those who lack sophistication, would obey any of the traditions. To possess any authority, the traditions must appear to possess at least an anchor in what does not change. The traditions "relating to kinsmen, ingratitude for favors, and other things" that Alfarabi offers as examples of "natural" traditions are certain minimal laws to which citizens must in general be obedient if political life is to be possible. That such laws may be necessary for even the crudest form of political life to exist does not make them natural to human beings (or mean that they are engraved in conscience); it merely makes them necessary in general for political life.[28]

According to Plato and Alfarabi, unlike living intellect, written law resists the demands of different places and times. The rule of one written law over the whole earth would lead to the corruption of the cities over which its rule had been extended by force. Alfarabi implies such a critique of the revealed religions in other of his writings when he allows for the possibility of a multiplicity of virtuous cities and even more so when he allows for a multiplicity of virtuous religions. He levels his harshest critique of the monotheistic Laws' aspirations to world rule, however, in the *Summary*. Although, to speak figuratively, the written law wants to remain the same—indeed, to be viewed as "natural"—the conditions that change over time and that therefore give rise to a change of habits within any given human community make it imperative that there be innovation on written law. To keep a community oriented toward the same ends, the law must be altered to respond to changed habits. Because Alfarabi and Plato are natural right theorists rather than natural law theorists, they recognize the need not only for legal conservation but also for innovation.

Having arrived at the end of the second part, let us assess in what ways the rule of law has been drawn closer to the rule of intellect and in what ways the gulf between them remains unbridgeable. The rule of law may be made to imitate the rule of intellect by providing ways for law to undergo modification over the course of time. Since modifying law puts its authority or power to rule in doubt, however, the legislator must undertake innovation in as concealed a manner as possible. With respect to differences of place, the rule of law approximates most closely to the rule of intellect when its rule is restricted to a limited area. Finally, the rule of law cannot be made to imitate the rule of intellect with respect to its concern for individuals. The law always applies to groups: for instance, rulers and ruled; men and women; children, young men, middle-aged men, and old men; and slaves and citizens. Not only is the law unable to pay attention to the exceptional individual, but one of its leading purposes is to produce a homogeneity among different kinds of individuals. Without a certain amount of homogeneity political life would be impossible.

Law as such cannot provide the medical treatment of the individual soul. As I will demonstrate in the third part, however, by attaching preludes to some laws, Plato and Alfarabi provide a means of access to the medical treatment of the soul, if not the treatment itself. The preludes to the laws rather than the laws proper educate souls in good breeding. According to Alfarabi, good breeding fosters intellect, whose acquisition is the medical treatment of the soul. The law proper cannot cure the individual soul.

Try as we might to bridge the gap between the rule of (written) law and the rule of intellect, our efforts have proven only modestly successful. In fact, we have barely achieved any success yet. The philosophic *mutakallim* will lead the way in bridging the gap by laying down preludes. The art of *kalâm* proves indispensable not only for persuading human beings to obey the law but also for offering us a narrow avenue to the rational way of life.

III.
Shame, Indignation, and Inquiry

8
The Rule of Law and Good Breeding

Who or what rules the second-best regime? As I have suggested already in chapter 4, the intellect does not. I also suggested that the titles to rule that predominate in this regime are a compromise between intellect and bodily strength. Are not the gods and law contenders for the role of ruler, however? The gods may play a part in *legislation*. But because the Athenian describes the best city as the city ruled by gods or children of gods (739e)—and the (tyrannic, nonlegal) rule of Kronos as the rule of a god over daimons, who possess intellect and who in turn rule over human beings who may or may not possess intellect (713a3–d)—the second-best regime would seem not to be *ruled* by the gods. As for law, it rules to the extent that human beings obey it. Traditionally, the success of the law depended upon the citizens' fear of what the gods might do to them if they disobeyed it. Plato goes to great lengths to weaken this fear. Although the Athenian Stranger speaks favorably about the ancient Athenian enslavement to the laws and to the gods (699b9–d3 and 701c),[1] when it comes time for him to prove that the gods are provident in bk. 10—a providence about which Alfarabi is silent insofar as he is silent about bk. 10—he makes no mention of fear of the gods in his *arguments* defending their providence (899d8–903b) and only very scant mention of fearful things in Hades in his *myth* defending it (903b–905d3, see especially 905a9). As the opening of bk. 6 makes amply evident, in lieu of the gods' rule, law can rule only with the assistance of good human rulers.

Because the good human rulers of the second-best regime are not philosopher-kings, they do not possess intellect but some imitation of it. These rulers are worthy of the honor of ruling because they possess what Alfarabi calls "good breeding." The phrase "good breeding" is a translation of the Arabic term *adab* (sing.) which Mahdi has consistently rendered simply as "breeding." I have chosen "good breeding" to avoid misleading the reader into thinking that Alfarabi is referring to eugenics of the sort found in the *Republic*, a potential problem in a study in which such frequent reference is made to that work. *Adab* is a rather complex word, but its general meaning can be grasped by contrasting it with *'ilm*, "knowledge" or "science." Both *adab* and *'ilm* are the product of education–but the former of moral and the latter of intellectual education.

"Good breeding" is the term that Alfarabi uses to designate what the Athenian means by the consonance between the pleasures and pains of decent human beings and their opinions of which pleasures and pains are just (disc. 3). Note that the consonance involves not *knowledge* of but *opinion* of which pleasures and pains are just. Not the intellect but something less than intellect rules in conjunction with law.

The role of "good breeding" reaches its peak in two of the central discourses of the *Summary*: discourses 5 and 6. Strauss has observed that in discourse 6 "there does not occur a single mention of the following themes: God, gods, revealed law and the other life." Furthermore, he has noted that it is the only discourse in which the term "substance" (actually "substances," *jawâhir*) appears.[2] The "substances" in question are of human beings rather than gods. Only human beings of the proper "substance" should be chosen to legislate and rule in the second-best regime.

In the *Book of Letters*, Alfarabi defines the term *jawhar*, substance. One of the popular meanings of "substance" is "good breeding" (*adab*). Thus, it appears likely that when Alfarabi speaks of the substance of human beings in the *Summary* he is speaking of their "breeding." Further, he suggests that, according to the popular understanding of "good breeding," human beings possess it if their lineage is good.[3] Thus, *adab* is not purely a matter of education. As in the traditional, aristocratic English view of "good breeding," *adab* depends to some extent on one's lineage. One is likely to receive a good education if one is of good lineage, but, of course, neither lineage nor education can make up for a bad nature. Nonetheless, as the absence of eugenics from the *Laws* indicates, the city or regime that is politically possible must find a way to compensate for or overlook such natures. Awarding citizens honors in accordance with the goodness of their breeding must stand in for eugenics.

1. *Prudence and good breeding*

Because human beings of "good breeding" must rule in conjunction with law, one of law's purposes, perhaps the highest, is to inculcate good breeding (disc. 3.7). In chapter 1, I argued that a knowledge of the disease of the soul and of the whole nature of souls is the foundation of law. Consequently, one can deduce fitting laws on the basis of such knowledge of political psychology (and of the peculiar conditions of one's time and place). Because fitting laws give rise to good breeding,[4] Alfarabi can say that the cure for the natural illness of the human soul is to provide it with the "character traits [*âdâb* (pl.)] promoted by the divine regime" (disc. 3.11). (It almost goes without saying that Alfarabi's "divine regime" is not ruled directly by gods or God, as is the Athenian's best regime, but rather by divine Law. In what sense this Law is divine, I will explain in the course of this chapter.) Yet law can achieve only a partial cure by means of "good breeding." If the law could inculcate knowledge or intellect, it could achieve a complete cure of the soul. Again, "good breeding" is merely the best imitation of intellect the law can inculcate.

The descent of "good breeding" from intellect is prepared early in the *Laws* by a discussion of the divine and the human goods (631c). The context of this discussion is an attempt to determine the purpose of legislation. The Athenian has already prepared his interlocutors to admit that the laws should look not only to the virtue of courage, which is so useful both in the aggrandizement and the defense of the city, but to all of the virtues. The Athenian identifies four human and four divine goods. In descending order of worth, the human goods are health, beauty, bodily strength, and wealth; the divine goods are prudence, moderation, justice, and courage. When describing moderation, the Athenian recapitulates the highest divine good, calling it "intelligence" (or intellect, *nous*) rather than "prudence." Is "intellect" equivalent to "prudence"? Later, when prudence becomes little more than the highest expression of "good breeding," We will be able to answer this question with a definitive: No. At present let us see how Alfarabi interprets this modifying recapitulation.

To begin with, Alfarabi states boldly one of this recapitulation's implications. The highest virtue, "intellect," is above the "four moral virtues" (*al-faḍâ'il al-khulqiyyah al-arba'ah*) (disc. 1.7). After presenting this interpretation, Alfarabi digresses or rather leaps ahead to discuss those imitation legislators who do not legislate with an eye to the true goods–a discussion not undertaken by the Athenian until 632d. By means of this digression, Alfarabi diverts the reader's attention from the line of thought linking what precedes it with what follows it. Then, he returns to the two lists of goods. Although he calls the goods "virtues" (*faḍâ'il*), at first glance he seems to reproduce the Athenian's morally edifying suggestion that whoever possesses the divine goods (i.e., the four moral virtues) also possesses the human goods–although the reverse need not be the case. Upon closer inspection, however, he casts doubt at least on whether he means to reproduce the Athenian's distinction between the two kinds of goods. To begin with, his list of human virtues is not the same as the Athenian's list of human goods. More interesting than his moving around the elements of the list is his substitution of one element: He substitutes "knowledge" (*'ilm*), the object of "intellect," for "health." If we connect his inclusion of knowledge in the list of the merely human virtues with his earlier assertion that intellect is higher than the four moral virtues, then he must intend to include the four moral virtues among the human virtues. Thus, he denies the distinction between the two kinds of goods. He reinforces this denial by concluding his list of human virtues with the vague phrase "and so forth" (*ghayr dhâlika*) and by noting that they are "enumerated in the books on ethics." Insofar as none of the four "virtues" he explicitly mentions are the proper subject of the "books on ethics" (*kutub al-akhlâq*), the "and so forth" must refer to the four moral virtues. Far from being elevated as divine, the moral virtues seem to trail after the other virtues almost as an afterthought. One thing is certain: Alfarabi brings all of the goods or virtues down to earth.[5]

If all of the goods the Athenian mentions are actually human, then what did Alfarabi mean when he seemed to echo his assertion that if one possesses the divine goods (the moral virtues), one will possess the human goods—although the reverse need not be the case? Alfarabi goes on to clarify that he was not merely echoing him. The human virtues are not different from the divine. When one possesses the human virtues in accordance with the law (the divine regime, see disc. 3.11), these virtues become divine. Thus, if one possesses the divine virtues, one must possess the human virtues because the divine are merely the human possessed in a certain manner, that is, in accordance with the law. But if one possesses the human virtues, one need not possess the divine virtues, because one can possess the human without the law (see disc. 9.7.) Thus, while appearing to confirm the Athenian's morally edifying suggestion that if one possesses the moral virtues (divine goods) one will necessarily possess the worldly goods (human goods), Alfarabi departs from it.

Insofar as prudence is one of the four moral virtues, it cannot be equated simply with intellect. Intellect is above the moral virtues. Insofar as knowledge, the object of intellect, is merely human, the moral virtues are most certainly merely human. But one may be tempted to call the moral virtues, especially prudence, divine, because they, unlike intellect, guide human action in accordance with opinions. Although knowledge is clearly superior to opinion, the latter partakes of the divine insofar as it is generally received as if from on high.

Good breeding, which entails the possession of certain opinions, is, as I said above, the cure for the illness of the divine regime. Indeed, good breeding rules the divine or second-best regime. Thus, opinion, not intellect, rules this regime. Opinion is substituted for knowledge. To understand some of the effects of this substitution, let us turn to the Athenian's metaphor for the perfect citizen (643e8): the divine puppet (644d8). Contrary to what one might think, this citizen is not synonymous with the perfect human being (653b).[6] The latter cannot dispense with intellect. Before the Athenian resorts to the image of the divine puppet, he offers an account of the perfect citizen that neither Kleinias nor Megillus can follow. Here, there is an identity or harmony of "calculation" (*logismos*), the "common opinion of the city," and the "law." The citizen of this city, it appears, would be the same as the perfect human being. In this city the "law" that rules is calculation. It hears out the imprudent counsel of pleasure and pain, which elicits expectations of future pleasure and pain, but it deliberates and lays down the law—in spite of these frequently misleading expectations. The inability of his interlocutors to follow the Athenian represents dramatically the impossibility that the ruler-lawgivers of Magnesia—among whom his interlocutors are by no means the worst part—should be such perfect human beings.

The Athenian must resort to the metaphor of the divine puppet if his interlocutors are to follow him. Certain "private individuals" (*idiôtês* [Gr.] or *al-rajul al-wâḥid* [Ar.]) can sit in judgment over their own fate and pull their own cord of calculation in opposition to the pull of the many cords of the passions (cf. disc. 1.20 with 644e–45a and 645b4). As this metaphor implies, however, most are destined to have some other, possibly divine, being manipulate their passions. According to the Athenian, the perfect citizen, as opposed to the perfect human being or private individual, must follow the "reasoning [*logos*]" that the city takes over from "the gods or from this [private individual] knower of these things, and then set[s] up the reasoning as the law for itself and for its relations with other cities." Alfarabi, in contrast, not only emphasizes the defectiveness of the so-called perfect citizen who must rely on the reasoning adopted by the city, but he also makes no mention of the citizen body receiving its "truth" from the gods; rather, the citizen body receives it from "their lawgivers, from those who follow the latter's footsteps, from those who speak the truth about their laws, and from those who are good [*akhyâr*] and righteous [*ṣâliḥîn*]." Of course, the "good and righteous" are not the same as the "good and virtuous [*afâḍil*]" (cf. disc. 1.20 with 9.7). And those "who speak the truth about their laws" need not be capable of pulling their own cord of calculation. The divine thing that sits in judgment over the imprudent counselors, pleasure and pain, is not a god and certainly not calculation but rather the opinion that law inculcates.

Let us turn to the definition of the perfect human being's education, which will serve as the model to be *imitated* in the final definition of prudence as good breeding (653b ff.).[7] Perfect human beings, while still children, must be taught by the law what pleasures to love and what pains to hate so that when they become mature their loves and hatreds will be consonant with what their "reason" (*logos*) dictates. If these are not consonant, they will be impeded in acquiring, as the Athenian says, "prudence and true opinions . . . and all the good things that go with them," namely, what Alfarabi calls "intelligence [*ḥilm*][8] and the sciences." Alfarabi implies that citizens who are merely capable of a citizen's perfection are like children, even as adults, insofar as they are beginners in knowledge who must rely on the dictates of the law (rather than their own reason) to "know" which pleasures to love and pains to hate (disc. 2.1). As we will see, in the soul of perfect citizens, possessed of good breeding, a consonance exists between their opinions of (rather than any reasoning about) what pleasures and pains are appropriate and the pleasures and pains they actually experience.

In his interpretation of this passage, Alfarabi suggests that what one loves and hates are natural things that are based on and have their origins in pleasures and pains (disc. 2.1). In other words, one loves things that cause pleasure and hates things that cause pain. But legislation or "education [or rather, discipline, *ta'dîb*][9] and training" intercede to "straighten out" (*taqawwam*) the loves and hatreds originating from the pleasures and pains of the human being as a child. The pleasures and pains of human beings give rise to loves and hatreds that are "crooked" or perhaps "sick." In chapters 5 through 7, we have seen that the highest manifestation of this sickness is the desire to have all things (or at least the human things) happen as our soul commands. Childhood "discipline and training" inculcates an understanding of what pleasures are noble and what pleasures are base as the means of straightening out the natural desires. In bk. 2 the opposition between the things human beings find naturally pleasurable and the things they deem noble is dramatized by a dispute between the artistically capable poet, whose sole guide in composing poetry is natural pleasure, and the noble citizen, whose guide is the noble (see 654c6 ff. and 666e-70a3 and disc. 2.5-6). I will return to this dispute in chapter 10. For the present let us simply observe its resolution.

Alfarabi describes Plato's resolution of this dispute as a form of "relativism" (*iḍâfah*) (cf. disc. 2.2 with 660d12-61e5). Those things that were defined as the "human goods" (health, beauty, bodily strength, and wealth; 631c) are really only good for "good people." For "evil and unjust people, however, they are not good and do not lead to happiness." In other words, the noble is the pleasant life and the base the unpleasant life. Both the Athenian's interlocutor here, Kleinias, and Alfarabi's Plato deny that such a thesis is demonstrable (661e6 ff.; disc. 2.3). Nonetheless, the Athenian is able to persuade Kleinias of the necessity of inculcating such "relativism" among the young (663e). Without its inculcation the young will not be willing to act justly. Without subjecting the natural loves and hatreds of the young to such a "straightening out" the city would be impossible. The disharmony between the claims of the individual's private nature and of the city first becomes evident in the positing of this fundamental opinion.[10]

Finally, let us turn to the passage in which the Athenian identifies "prudence" with what Alfarabi calls "good breeding" (688a-89e4, disc. 3.7-8). The general context in which this identification takes place is a discussion of the ignorant faith human beings put in their own regime's ability to fulfill by means of military conquest (or divine intervention) the human desire to have all things or at least the human things happen "in accordance with the commands of one's own soul." The more immediate context is the Athenian's recapitulation of the need to look to the whole of virtue rather than to victory in war alone as the end of legislation (688a3 ff.). Just as Alfarabi will identify prudence with good breeding in this context, so the Athenian here recalls that first occasion on which he identified "prudence" and "intelligence" in the course of exhorting his interlocutors to look to the whole of virtue rather than war (631a4 ff.). On the present occasion the Athenian appears to be encouraging his interlocutors to look even higher to the "leader of all virtue," namely, "prudence, and intelligence, and opinion" (*phronêsis . . . kai nous kai doxa*). Of course, the striking addition introduced to the pair "prudence and intelligence" is "opinion." Thus, while appearing to aim even higher than he had on the earlier occasion, the Athenian is modifying the "leader of all virtue" in such a way that it is not as elevated as it was in the discussion of the divine and human goods (631c). Yet here "intelligence" as the central of three terms draws the primary notice of the reader. Just how far the "leader of all virtue" has descended from its earlier height is not yet clear.

Only when "prudence"—or rather "lack of intelligence" or "ignorance"—is itself defined does it become clear just how far "prudence" has descended from its original position of being on a footing with "intelligence." The "greatest sort of ignorance" is when "someone doesn't like, but rather hates, what in his opinion [*doxa*] is noble or good, and likes and welcomes what in his opinion is wicked and unjust" (689a6). Who is this "someone"? Because the "opinion" this individual holds about which pleasures are noble is "according to reason" (*kata logon*) (689a8), one is led to believe initially that the individual in question is the "private individual" or the "perfect human being" rather than the citizen. The city, however, is not composed of "private individuals" but rather of citizens. When the majority of the citizens "refuse to obey the rulers and the laws" this is what is called "lack of intelligence" in the case of a city (689b4). Who or what are the "rulers"? According to the Athenian, the "natural rulers" are not "prudence, and intelligence, and opinion" but rather "knowledge [literally, knowledges], or opinions, or reason" (*epistêmais ê doxais ê logô*). A number of things should be noticed about the differences between this recapitulation of the "leader of all virtue" or the "natural rulers" and the previous recapitulation (688b3) discussed in the previous paragraph. First, "opinion" (or rather, "opinions") now takes center stage rather than "intelligence" or knowledge. Second, the disjunctive *ê* rather than the conjunctive *kai* relates the terms of this list, thus raising the possibility that one of the terms in the list, most likely the middle term, is more truly the "natural ruler" of the city than the others. Third, a multiplicity has entered into "opinion," making it "opinions" (as well as into "knowledge," making it "knowledges").[11] As we will see shortly, the inherent multiplicity of opinions gives rise to another problem of consonance (in addition to the problem of the consonance between one's opinions about what pleasures and pains are noble and one's actual experiencing of pleasure and pain), namely, the consonance among different individuals' opinions about which pleasures and pains are just or noble.

In his interpretation of the passage just discussed, Alfarabi identifies the consonance between the citizens' opinions about what pleasures and pains are noble and their actual experiences of pleasures and pains as "good breeding" (disc. 3.7). Without good breeding human beings find pleasure in "evil things" (*shurûr*). Insofar as the law contains the authoritative opinion as to what is evil and what is good, what is noble and what is base, it is the source of good breeding. It is in this sense that the law is the "fount and origin" of the good things. The law gives the citizens the opinions they possess about what pleasures are noble and what pleasures are base. First, the law gives rise to good breeding. Then good breeding in turn "fosters" (*tûrith* [form 4 of *warith*]) intellect. The law does not directly cause intellect–it does so only indirectly, by way of good breeding. Furthermore, as we will see, only the highest aspect of the law, the preludes, causes good breeding.

According to Alfarabi, good breeding does not become part of the "natural dispositions" (*ṭibâʿ*) of all the citizens but should at least be possessed by "the rulers of cities and their counterparts [*amâthil*]" (cf. disc. 3.8 with 689c8 ff. and disc. 3.10–12 below). Those who possess good breeding are those the Athenian calls the "prudent ones" (689d5). According to the Athenian, these prudent ones possess the required consonance between the pleasures and pains they experience and those they believe to be noble. Alfarabi adds that the authoritative "harmony" (or consonance, *ijtimâʿ*), the harmony that should be deemed wise, is not the harmony within the soul of each individual ruler but the harmony among the "testimonies of those who have [good] breeding."[12] The inherent multiplicity of opinions, despite the "natural" tendency toward unity of opinion within any community, may lead to disharmony among the various understandings of good breeding. This potential for disharmony should be counteracted by establishing a harmony among the testimonies of those who have good breeding.

As I explained in chapter 5, section 2, the rule of the second-best regime is a compromise between the competing claims of intellect and physical strength. Immediately after establishing his proper definition of prudence as what Alfarabi calls "good breeding," the Athenian discusses the seven worthy titles to rule, and the lower limit remains physical strength; however, the upper limit is prudence as good breeding rather than as intellect. According to Alfarabi, the upper limit is "virtue" (*faḍîlah*) (disc. 3.9). Because "prudence" is clearly the highest of the Athenian's seven titles to rule, there is reason to assume that here Alfarabi means by "virtue" what the Athenian means by "prudence,"[13] that is, good breeding. If this is so, it lends weight to my earlier suggestions that the virtuous city alluded to in discourse 5. 13 is not *the* virtuous city but the second-best city, which is ruled at most by good breeding.

2. *Shame, law, and honoring the body*

Having begun with good breeding–in effect, the virtue or morality of the citizens who rule–let us consider the virtue or morality of the ruled.[14] Although the morality of the rulers must place limits on the fulfillment of the desire to have all things happen as one would wish, i.e., for domination, the morality of the ruled must place limits on the pursuit of bodily desires. Indeed, the bulk of morality, and even more so of law, is directed toward the latter limitations. As mentioned, Plato indicates his view that the law proper concerns the body by remaining silent on the soul in the *Crito*, his dialogue devoted to the question what is law. Although it is characteristic of law proper (*nomos*) that it does not treat the soul, the Athenian in the *Laws*, by adding preludes to the laws, reformulates law so that it can be said accurately to treat the soul. In digressing to discuss the morality of the ruled, I digress to discuss the law proper, the immediate concern of which is the body. There is more than one sense in which the law is concerned with the body. Obviously, it punishes the body. In addition, however, it uses opinion or moral suasion to place restraints on the bodily desires of the ruled. Thus, even when the law addresses the soul by way of opinion, it does so for the sake of restraining the body. Furthermore, the opinions espoused by the law possess moral suasion precisely because they are backed up by the threat of physical punishment. Consequently, Alfarabi, following the Athenian, refers to this morality of the ruled with the phrase "honoring the body" (cf. disc. 5.4-6, esp. 5.4 and 5.5; with 728d5-29c6).

According to Alfarabi, "the way to honor the body is to follow moral discipline [*ta'dîb khulqî*]." This moral discipline consists in following "commendable and agreeable habits [*'âdât*] and ways of life in agreement with traditions [*sunan*]" (disc. 5.4). (Alfarabi uses "tradition" throughout the *Summary* as more or less equivalent to "law" [*nâmûs*].)[15] At the end of the passage that Alfarabi interprets as bearing on honoring the body, the Athenian says, "In turning to these next matters we must speak not of law, but rather of how praise and blame can educate each of them . . ." (730b6). Thus, he clearly distinguishes the law's concern with honoring the body from the (preludes') task of praising and blaming (or honoring the) souls.

How does "moral discipline" lead one to honor the body properly? To answer this question it is useful to see that the recipients of moral discipline are children and ignorant adults (disc. 5.5). Earlier, Alfarabi stated that when Plato mentions children he means not just children but all beginners, including beginners in knowledge or the ignorant (disc. 2.1).

What Alfarabi says about the ignorant adult is also based on what the Athenian says about the example that the elderly should set for the young (729b ff.). The Athenian includes in his account of honoring the body the fitting uses of money and property. His discussion of the case of children's inheritance of property from their parents is the occasion for a digression on the most important inheritance the old can give the young, "an abundance of awe." In the course of this digression, the Athenian launches into something of a tirade against the elderly who make a habit of condemning the shameless behavior of the young all the while that they indulge in shameless behavior themselves. The best way to admonish the young is to set a good example (729c4). The Athenian's tirade is directed against the ignorant adult whose behavior is defective in the same sense that a child's behavior is inevitably defective. Such adults are not merely lacking in good breeding; they have suffered from a deficient "moral discipline": They lack sufficient awe or shame.

In the course of our attempt to understand Alfarabi's application of "moral discipline" to ignorant adults and children, we have happened upon an explanation as to why this discipline results in the appropriate honoring of the body. Physical punishment or the threat of it is the source of that moral discipline we call awe or shame. Children and ignorant adults are moral insofar as they fear physical punishment.[16] Above all, the ruled obey out of awe or shame the laws' opinion about what pleasures are noble and what base. To better understand the morality of the ruled, let us take a closer look at the Athenian's account of awe or shame at the end of bk. 1.

I have described awe as the fear of physical punishment. There are two kinds of fear which the Athenian goes so far as to call "nearly opposite" (*schedon enantia*): fear of evils and fear of opinion (646e4). Awe (or shame) is a form of fear of opinion. In what sense then are fear of evils and fear of opinion "nearly opposite"? The best example illustrating this "near opposition" is war (647b4 ff.). When the Athenian discusses war, however, he chooses to discuss only shame, the more complex and confusing of the two fears. Furthermore, his discussion is at first misleading. Although he discusses how shame procures victory and safety in war, he seems to describe only part of how it does so. He suggests that shame, or rather fear of shame, prevents the soldier from doing vile things to his friends. He seems to say nothing, however, about shame encouraging the soldier with respect to the enemy. Instead, he speaks merely of boldness as the crucial ingredient in victory over the enemy. According to the Athenian's previous definition of it, boldness, as opposed to fear, is the expectation of pleasure (644d). He appears to be completely silent about the form of shame most apposite to the problem of procuring victory over enemies.

The form of shame that procures victory over enemies is, somewhat surprisingly, the same shame that prevents the soldier from doing vile things to friends, such as abandoning them on the battlefield. Such an abandonment may testify either to a weak bond of friendship or to a calculation as to the worth of risking one's own life to save the life of one's friend. What is the shame that prevents "friends" from doing this to one another? The soldier fears either the opinion of his community or of his friends (or both) should he fail his friends on the battlefield. (As the Athenian says at 647a5, the fear of opinion opposes not only pleasures but sufferings *and fears*.) Such fear of opinion or shame is "nearly opposite" to the fear of evil that sends the soldier headlong in flight from the battlefield; shame keeps the soldier on the battlefield and perhaps even makes him seem bold. The fear of the opinion of one's community or of one's friends that keeps the soldier on the battlefield is not truly the opposite of the fear of evils, however. Rather, the soldier filled with shame or awe fears the evil that may result from opposing this opinion. Presumably the basis for the fear of such an evil is the childhood experience of physical punishment.

In his summary of the Athenian's discussion of awe or shame, Alfarabi presents a critique of the shame that characterizes the morality of the ruled (disc. 1.22). Through a discussion of this critique of shame, perhaps it will become more readily apparent why the ascent must be made from the "moral discipline" constructed for the sake of the ruled to the good breeding constructed for the sake of the rulers.

Alfarabi's critique takes the form of a discussion of three virtuous "moral habits" (*akhlâq*) and their opposites: "modesty" (or, rather, shame, *ḥayâ'*), "having a good opinion of people" (*al-ẓann al-jamîl bi-l-nâs*), and "caution" (*ḥidhr* or *ḥadhar*). The first and third moral habits are closely related in two ways. (1) Both at least appear to be considered independently of whether they are possessed in relation to friends or enemies. (The second moral habit, in contrast, is solely understood as depending upon whether it is possessed in relation to friends or in relation to enemies.) (2) Both have some similar effects. Shame and caution can both restrain (immoral) action. Shame when excessive leads to inaction on inappropriate occasions and so does caution. What then is the difference between shame and caution? (One almost wonders if the difference would have been noticeable if Alfarabi had not interposed the second virtuous moral habit.) Caution is a policy of restraint in the face of potential dangers. Shame is a highly derivative fear of evil. It is the fear, for instance, not of the evil of death on the battlefield but of the bad opinion of one's community (which in turn is derived from a less realistic–what the moderns might call "superstitious"–fear of the continued efficacy of earlier punishments). In contrast, caution is or results from a direct and reasonable fear of evils such as of death on the battlefield.

Finally, contrary to appearances, both shame and caution are virtuous moral habits only in relation either to friends or to enemies. Shame is virtuous, or at least not vicious, when it prevents us from harming our friends (for instance, by abandoning them); however, it is vicious whenever it counsels withholding attack on one's enemies. Conversely, caution is vicious if it prevents us from harming our friends–because that we should need to be so prevented implies the intention to do so on a future occasion–however, it can be virtuous if it prevents an attack on one's enemies at the wrong moment.

This brief critique of shame at least raises the possibility that caution may be part of a more reasonable understanding of the virtues than is shame. Let us begin to turn toward the morality of honoring the soul in the hope that we might find such a more reasonable account of the virtues.

Alfarabi's Plato asserts that the traditions for honoring the soul are the same for "strangers [*ghurabâ'*], kinsmen [*aqârib*], and citizens [*ahl al-madînah*]" but the traditions for honoring the body are different for "strangers and kinsmen" (disc. 5.6). Presumably, the "kinsmen" referred to are the kinsmen of the citizens. Certainly, the citizens are those who inflict punishments on their kinsmen, the strangers, and the ruled, because the citizens rule, rather than the ignorant adults discussed in the previous paragraph.[17] In the passage being summarized by Alfarabi, the Athenian is never explicit about how the physical punishment of strangers should differ from that of citizens (729e4-30b). He does, however, warn against taking undue advantage of strangers because, despite their relative weakness in living apart from their own city, the gods will surely avenge them. Alfarabi is silent about the willingness of the gods to avenge strangers. One should not infer from the Athenian's exhortation to gentleness toward strangers that they are to be punished less severely. On the contrary, strangers are to be treated like children and ignorant adults–that is, physically punished–because they are, as a rule, merely merchants or artisans (764b4 ff.).[18] In contrast, citizens who break the law–for instance, citizens who violate the laws of the marketplace–are only to be fined. Although it is apparent why the strangers are to receive a different "moral discipline," it is not so readily apparent why the traditions concerning honoring the soul should be the same for the citizens and the strangers. Perhaps they should be because, despite the fact that the ignorant (and the strangers), unlike the citizens of good breeding, fear the opinions inculcated by law, the opinions they *fear* are the same as the opinions that the citizens of good breeding *honor*: They are the opinions laid down by the city in the preludes to the law. As we saw earlier, the city should stand united in its opinion of what pleasures and pains are noble or just (disc. 3.8). Despite this unity, the citizens and the ignorant, the rulers and the ruled, stand in a different relation to the law's opinion.

3. *Good breeding, praise and blame, and honoring the soul*

"Caution" is absent from Alfarabi's account of honoring the soul (disc. 5.7-9). (Perhaps "caution" is characteristic of an even higher morality or way of life than the life of "good breeding.") However this may be, indignation is at least more noble than shame. Indignation characterizes what may be the first true morality in the *Laws* and the *Summary*. Only after "indignation" (*ḥamiyyah*) has been mentioned can "moral habit" (*akhlâq*) be mentioned (cf. disc. 5.7 with 5.9). In discourse 5, prior to the mention of "indignation," even the "moral virtues" are referred to merely as "habits" (*'âdât*) or the product of "habituation" (*i'tiyâd*). As we saw in the morality of shame, "habits" (*'âdât*) can just as easily be for the sake of honoring the body as honoring the soul. Only after indignation is mentioned, however, does the soul become the focus of discussion. (Note the extraordinary frequency with which Alfarabi refers to the soul after the reference to "indignation" [disc. 5.7].) It is almost as if the soul were constituted of "high-minded[ness] or . . . natural strong indignation" (*anafah wa-ḥamiyyah ṭabî'iyyah qawiyyah*).

To understand what the morality of "indignation" (*ḥamiyyah*) or, as the Athenian calls it, "spiritedness" (*thumos*) (731b2) is, we must turn momentarily to Alfarabi's interpretation of the Athenian's account of honoring the soul and spiritedness. The Athenian discusses first the willingness of the spirited "man" (*anêr*) to punish others and only later his willingness to direct spiritedness toward himself (cf. 731b3–d9 with 731d10–32b6). This man is not only willing but eager to punish those he deems unjust, "in no way easing up on punishment" (731b7). Although Alfarabi mentions the need to practice habits "in every situation, and together with all groups" if one is to truly cultivate them, he does not say this specifically about indignation. Above all, he is silent about the need for the "great man in the city" to assist the magistrates in punishing the unjust (730d5–8) and the need for the spirited man to begin by punishing others, rather than himself. This silence may be a way of emphasizing a crucial caveat of the Athenian's call to the spirited man to vent his rage on the unjust: He should do so only against the incurably unjust (731d5–7). Following Socrates, the Athenian affirms that everyone who is unjust–including the incurably unjust–is so involuntarily. Alfarabi is silent about the need for the spirited man to vent his rage against the incurably unjust, because to punish even a person like this is in a sense unjust. Before we have even seen spiritedness or indignation at work on the spirited man's own soul, we are already able to detect a flaw and a kind of unreasonableness about spiritedness that makes it hardly superior to shame.[19]

Let us turn to how the spirited "human being" (*anthrôpos*) directs his or her spiritedness toward him or herself (731d10 ff.).[20] According to the Athenian, justice is in need of our spiritedness in an alliance against our souls. He never specifies toward what unjust thing in the soul this spiritedness should be directed. According to Alfarabi, indignation "restrain[s] [one's] beloved soul from appetites [*shahawât*] that are a source of pleasure to [one]." Here it is useful to recall the tension between the natural desires of the child and the opinions about what is just that are indispensable to the maintenance of the city.

Spirited human beings who restrain their souls with their own spiritedness are not as independent of the opinion of the city as they might appear at first.

How is the morality of "indignation" or "spiritedness" different from and similar to the morality of "shame"? The most obvious similarity is that both the morality of indignation and the morality of shame depend in some way on the opinion of the community. Nonetheless, each depends on this opinion in a different way. The morality of shame is constituted by a *fear* of opinion but a fear of opinion, that is, in the final analysis, a highly derivative fear of evil, i.e., the fear of the evil of physical punishment. Ashamed human beings fear the consequences of their departure from generally accepted opinion. In contrast, the morality of indignation is constituted by an *honoring* of opinion. Indignant human beings honor their community's opinion of what is just. They do not honor, not to mention fear, the consequences of disobeying this opinion. They honor the just above their own pleasures. They derive some pleasure, however, from their consequent sense of self-worth. Nevertheless, they do not look first and foremost to their own pleasure but rather to what is "just and good and noble" (732a). It almost goes without saying that honoring opinion is far less craven than fearing the consequences of disobeying it.

Let us return to the *Summary* for further clarification of the distinction between the morality of shame and the morality of indignation. Alfarabi identifies the person who honors the soul by making use of his strong natural indignation as the person who possesses good breeding. Such a person keeps a tight rein on expressions of emotion (cf. disc. 5.8 and 732c). This person is clearly one of the rulers rather than the ruled, such people (rulers) command "their subordinates" (literally, the one who follows them, *man yalîhim* [from *waliy*]) to imitate their restrained behavior.

Discourse 5.9 is especially noteworthy because in it Alfarabi reverses his usual policy of being more reticent about the gods and God than the Athenian.[21] Strikingly, Alfarabi mentions the gods when discussing the proper way to honor the soul, a discussion which is directed at the rulers.[22] In contrast, he made no mention of the gods or God when discussing the proper way to honor the body, which is directed at the ruled. I have shown that among the ruled, fear of opinion or shame plays the central role. Yet Alfarabi did not rely upon the fear of the gods as a supplement to their training in honoring the body. Apparently, the ignorant should not be encouraged to fear the gods more than they already do. Of course, Alfarabi does not exhort those of good breeding, the rulers, to fear the gods; he exhorts them to derive hope from belief in them. They need hope to acquire the appropriate "character traits" (*âdâb*). Acquiring good breeding is painful because it entails resisting pleasures in the name of what is just. To overcome such pain, rulers require that their suffering should not be in vain. Only the most unreasonable kind of god would withhold support for such a worthy cause.

An apparent contradiction emerges between Alfarabi's and the Athenian's assessment of the spirited person's life of moderation. After a long and involved calculus of pleasure and pain has been traced out by the Athenian, he asserts that the moderate life (indeed, the life of all of the moral virtues, except justice) is more pleasant than the unrestrained life (734d ff.). Here the Athenian seems to be echoing, yet with far greater certainty, the argument he made earlier about the life of pleasure that was laid down as the fundamental assumption of legislation (663e; Alfarabi's relativism). Contrary to this, Alfarabi simply and clearly affirms that the virtuous life or the "way of life of choice" (*sîrah ikhtiyâriyyah*) of the spirited man is the life in which pain is chosen over pleasure.

I began this chapter by tracing the descent of prudence from its initial identification with intellect to its final identification with good breeding. I showed that good breeding has the highest title to rule in the second-best regime. To better understand it, I inquired into the differences between this virtue or morality of the rulers and the virtue or morality of the ruled. Thus, I proceeded to compare the morality of the ruled, as the morality of shame, with the morality of the rulers, as the morality of indignation. The former showed itself to be far more craven, if not less reasonable, than the latter. I should add here that even if the morality of indignation is not more reasonable or internally consistent than the morality of shame, it is more conducive to reasonableness. People who honor their bodies by fearing public opinion have little or no disdain for their own physical wants. Despite their willingness to bow to the authority of public opinion, they remain at the beck and call of their physical wants. They are less able to attend to the voice of intellect (or, rather, of calculation) within themselves than are spirited human beings who have a certain amount of disdain for their physical wants. This is of course a crucial reason why the spirited human being is more suited to rule.

Nevertheless, the morality of indignation or the spirited way of life has its limitations. Its most obvious limitation, its irrationality, is evident in its wholehearted deferral to the fundamental assumption of legislation that the the noble life is the pleasant life. On the contrary, the noble life is filled with the forgoing of pleasures out of a desire to honor the law's opinion of what is just and noble. The spirited human being endures pain out of a conviction that the noble life must somehow receive divine recompense. It should be emphasized, however, that all decent political orders rely upon the existence of rulers who are willing to forgo certain pleasures in the name of public service. As we will see in chapters 9 and 10, this irrationality, along with others in the morality of indignation will give rise to the search for another morality or way of life.

9
Pleasure and Indignation

The morality of indignation, as we have seen, is synonymous with what Alfarabi describes as the "way of life of choice" (disc. 5.9). And this way of life is characterized by the choice of the painful over the pleasurable. Thus, the spirited human being's morality of indignation is, in a sense, characterized by pain. Indignation itself, however, is not pain. Indeed, indignation or anger is a response to pain, just as love is the desire for certain pleasures. When certain desires "that are a source of pleasure to" indignant human beings (disc. 5.7) contradict their understanding of what pleasures are just and noble, then these desires become a source of pain to them. Consequently, they react with indignation toward them. Is the pleasure accompanying inquiry into the law one of those pleasures to which they respond with indignation? If so, the rulers of Plato's city and Alfarabi's regime who are spirited, indignant human beings may be fated not to inquire into the law and thus not to be capable of rational innovation.

To determine whether indignation opposes the desire to inquire, we need to consider Alfarabi's interpretation of the role of pleasure and indignation in the *Laws*. Their roles are clarified in the context of the Athenian's discussions of festivals and wine drinking. Festivals, as occasions on which one imbibes wine, are occasions for pleasure and enjoyment. The Athenian makes a substantial innovation on traditional festivals by introducing the cultivation of indignation through war games. His purpose is to transform festivals from an occasion on which citizens indulge in weeping and are filled with shame at the sight of tragic dramas into an occasion on which their martial virtue and indignation are roused.

As we saw in the previous chapter, shame plays a role similar to that played by indignation: both resist one's desire for pleasures. Because shame is more primitive than indignation, the Athenian treats the relation between shame and pleasure in bk. 1, prior to his treatment of the relation between indignation and pleasure. He argues there that wine drinking is useful for cultivating moderation (or, rather, shame). At the end of bk. 1 and the beginning of bk. 2, the Athenian replaces this formulation with the assertion that wine drinking safeguards education. It does so by counteracting rather than cultivating shame. Because at least Megillus understands moderation as shame, however, the Athenian is initially compelled to argue that it is useful for cultivating moderation as shame. Contrary to Megillus's own self-understanding, to become truly moderate he must be made less filled with shame. True moderation is only possible where education is possible. And education is impossible without at least the temporary suspension of shame. Of course, without an educated inquiry into law, legal innovation is impossible.

In bk. 1, shame not only sanctions the restrictions on pleasure imposed by the law, i.e., makes one moderate, but also serves the martial purpose of the law. Dorian courage, like Dorian moderation, stems from shame. By bk. 7, the Athenian has undertaken to replace the courage based on shame with one based on indignation. He criticizes the tragic music of the poets, which accompanies sacrifices at festivals, and supplants it with a spirited music. By eliminating tragic music and the shame and humility to which it gives rise, the Athenian increases the self-reliance of the rulers.

The greater self-reliance of these human beings would seem to facilitate their inquiry into law. Yet their honoring of the law's opinion about what pleasures are just and noble would seem to undermine their desire to inquire into the laws' goodness. Furthermore, wine drinking loosens the constraints set on inquiry by shame, while war games intensify the indignation of spirited human beings. Does wine drinking similarly loosen the constraints that indignation places on inquiry enough to enable the indignant to inquire into the law? Or does wine drinking intensify indignation?

1. *Divinizing pleasure or undermining shame*

In bk. 1, the Athenian attempts to develop the argument that wine drinking is useful for cultivating or educating in moderation (645d–49d3) as well as for revealing the nature of the ruled to the sober ruler of the drinking party (649d4–50b10). Alfarabi also mentions the latter role for wine drinking (disc. 1. 23); however, he never mentions the former (disc. 1.21–23). His omission could be readily interpreted as expressing his view as a Muslim that wine drinking could not possibly be conducive to moderation—contrary to the blasphemous view of the pagan, Plato. I will show, however, that Alfarabi's view is only apparently pious and that it conveys Plato's own view, as opposed to the view expressed by the Athenian.

Both Alfarabi and the Athenian discuss wine drinking by means of analogies (cf. disc. 1.21 with 645d–46e2). The Athenian attempts to draw an analogy between cultivating moderation by means of drinking wine and cultivating physical well-being by undergoing the "suffering or pain" (*algêdôn*) of ingesting drugs and physical exercise (646d11). Alfarabi, however, makes no mention of wine drinking in this connection. Rather, he draws an analogy between bearing the "toil and discomfort commanded by the legislator" and ingesting "distasteful" (or painful, *karîhah*) drugs. In other words, obedience to the laws rather than participation in wine-drinking parties is analogous to taking painful drugs. Perhaps obeying the laws that limit one's indulgence in pleasure would be more conducive to moderation than wine drinking. Of course, Dorian laws do precisely this.[1] Perhaps Dorian laws and laws like them, however, do this too well. Furthermore, perhaps abstinence from wine renders Dorians insensitive to the most sublime (intellectual) pleasures and thus conduces to their excessive preoccupation with the simplest and most intense (sexual) pleasures.

In the course of defending the analogy between cultivating moderation and cultivating physical well-being, the Athenian chooses to identify "moderation" with "shame" or "awe." He does so because at least Megillus understands moderation as shame. In addition, the Athenian identifies "moderation" as a kind of "courage" (633d). In sum, he describes both "courage" and "moderation" as different forms of shame (647b4–8). Although Megillus had proudly defended the Dorian view of moderation as a form of courage, he did so with the conviction that courage as he experiences it is a fearlessness in the face of danger (633d). As we saw in the previous chapter, however, shame is a highly derivative form of fear of evil. Consequently, courage as a form of shame hardly deserves to be characterized as fearlessness.

The Dorian condemnation of wine drinking—and in particular Megillus's disgust at it (637b)—appears in a new light: It results from a shame-induced adherence to custom.[2] Needless to say, Dorian custom does not encourage shame-filled restraint in regard to all pleasures. Indeed, it is renowned for condoning homosexual relations. More problematically, the pleasures that it condones may be interfered with by the pleasures it condemns. For instance, although it condones homosexual relations, it condemns wine drinking, one of whose effects is to loosen constraints on sexual activity (637b1–5). The Dorian legislator must have shunned wine drinking not because it is conducive to an increased indulgence in pleasures per se, as Megillus seems to think, but because it is conducive to certain pleasures. Indeed, if sexual pleasure were this legislation's only worry, it might have condoned wine drinking.

As we have seen, the Dorians' abstinence from wine is not conducive to their true moderation. To convince them that wine drinking is conducive to moderation, the Athenian must convince them that it is conducive to moderation as they understand it, namely, as shame. Thus, the Athenian is compelled to argue that wine drinking is useful for cultivating shame, even if it is not true, because such a belief would be conducive to the true moderation of Megillus. Unfortunately for him, Megillus's lack of education precludes him from a more straightforward means of access to moderation.

Having established that Dorian courage and moderation are both rooted in shame, the Athenian then draws an analogy between cultivating courage (as shame) by frequently subjecting oneself to the fear of pain and death and cultivating moderation (as shame) by frequently subjecting oneself to the temptation to act immoderately (647c7–49d3). Alfarabi is wholly silent on this analogy (see disc. 1.22 and 1.23). He thus leads the reader to wonder whether there is not something spurious about it. Is moderation really cultivated by repeatedly subjecting oneself to the temptation to act immoderately as courage is cultivated by facing fearful situations? Because moderation as shame and courage as shame are "analogous" in the loose sense that they are both forms of shame, one is easily led to believe that producing these two forms of shame must occur in an analogous manner.

Although moderation and courage may be understood as two different forms of shame, they are produced quite differently. The shame or fear of disrepute that one feels when confronted with pain and death on the battlefield, even the mock battlefield (831a4–12), is more real and is given more effective support by other feelings than is the shame or fear of disrepute one feels in confronting pleasures that one desires. It is lent support by the constant urgings of one's comrades that one should stand one's ground, if for no other reason than that they also fear their own deaths. Furthermore, assuming that one's fear of disrepute is capable of keeping one on the battlefield, one's eagerness to fight is also supported by one's own fear of death. In contrast, the wine-drinking party does not conduce to one's fear of disrepute because one's comrades are also drunk. Unlike the comrades on the battlefield, all of whom are to some extent drunk with fear, the comrades at the drinking party have no fear of death should one of their comrades cave in to the pleasures deemed shameful by the city. Of course, none of the members of the drinking party fears his own death should he cave into his desires. To make his argument more persuasive, the Athenian abstracts from the battlefield by arguing that wine drinking acts as a fictional fear drug would (647e ff.; contrast Alfarabi's silence on this drug, disc. 1.22–23). By abstracting from the battlefield, the Athenian can abstract from the aspects of it just mentioned that make it, unlike the drinking party, an arena for the cultivation of shame.

Although the various ways in which shame reinforces its hold over the comrades on the battlefield are absent at the drinking party, one might expect the party's sober ruler to play a role akin to the comrades in spurring on the drunks to feel shame when they indulge their desires. Would not the sober ruler severely scold the drinkers when they act drunk rather than sober? The sober ruler, however, is not subject to the opinions or prejudices of any group, especially not to those of the drunks. Such a ruler, unlike comrades on a battlefield, would demand that the drinkers act in accordance with true moderation, avoiding both immoderate pleasure seeking and insensitivity to pleasure. Unlike Megillus, the sober ruler does not mistake insensitivity to pleasure for true moderation. As the sober ruler of this dialogue, the Athenian steers his interlocutors, whom in effect he rules, away from abstinence toward true moderation. By portraying drinking as if it could facilitate the cultivation of moderation as shame, the Athenian undermines the constraints that shame places on Megillus—thus making him more moderate, if not shame-filled.

Early in the *Summary*, Alfarabi suggested that festivals and that wine drinking make pleasures divine (disc. 1.12). One might have thought at the time that he meant that they make pleasures divine by limiting their fulfillment,[3] even though he emphasized that festivals are divine "because they involve pleasure to which all men are naturally inclined." One need only contrast the positive tone of Alfarabi's assessment of festivals and wine drinking with Megillus's diatribe against them (636e5-37b8) (which Alfarabi is "reporting") to know that Alfarabi's views are not synonymous with Dorian, not to mention Muslim, views on festivals and wine drinking. By the opening of discourse 2, Alfarabi makes it unambiguously clear that festivals and the wine drinking that accompany them are divine because they provide an occasion that departs from the norm in which laws restrict indulgence in pleasures. A good law sets aside festivals as occasions on which people can "pursue pleasures" (disc. 2.1). In other words, a good law accommodates people's natural need for pleasures by periodically and temporarily suspending itself.

Because wine drinking and festivals are useful for divinizing pleasure or facilitating people's indulgence in pleasure rather than for cultivating moderation as shame, by the beginning of bk. 2 the Athenian discontinues arguing that wine is useful for cultivating moderation. Indeed, Alfarabi never suggested even in discourse 1 that wine was useful for cultivating moderation (as shame). The Athenian, however, continues to argue—as did Alfarabi in discourse 1.23—that wine is useful for revealing people's natures and (in addition) as a "safeguard for this education" (653a3).[4] What the Athenian calls a "safeguard for this education" Alfarabi speaks of as divinizing pleasure. Wine drinking safeguards education by suspending the constraints the law usually places on the pursuit of certain desires.

We recall that Dorian custom forbids wine drinking but permits homosexual relations. Evidently, it did not forbid the former because it thought it would give rise to the latter–otherwise it would not have permitted the latter. Megillus assumes that Dorian custom forbids wine drinking because in general it seems to promote a noble disdain for pleasures. The Dorian legislator, however, forbids most wine drinking not to prevent the pursuit of pleasures per se but to prevent the pursuit of certain pleasures–above all, the pleasures of inquiry and most importantly of inquiry into the law. Because shame is the means by which law rules human beings, wine or some other opponent of shame such as the intoxicating speech of the Athenian Stranger is needed to make possible inquiry into it. Education about the law can occur only when the law, which demands unquestioning obedience, suspends itself or leaves itself open to question. The Dorian law (and other laws like it) is not a good law because it does not allow for its own temporary and periodic suspension. It almost goes without saying that where inquiry into the law is impossible, so is intelligent legal innovation.

2. *The critique of tragic music as a critique of shame*

By criticizing tragic music, the Athenian intends to make citizens perform spirited instead of tragic music, especially during sacrifices at religious festivals. By means of this transformation, he supplants humility or shame with spirit or indignation. Although Alfarabi at first appears to diverge from his intention, upon closer inspection, it becomes apparent that he must cultivate both humility and indignation–the former among the ruled, the latter among the rulers–because a gap exists in his regime between rulers and ruled that does not exist in the Athenian's city. What is their purpose in supplanting shame with indignation among the rulers? Although indignation is as useful for resisting one's own desires as shame, indignation has the advantage of, at the same time, increasing self-reliance. It would seem that self-reliance is indispensable for rulers. Does it, however, enable the indignant human being to inquire into the laws and in turn to innovate on them? We will have to wait until the next section to answer this last question.

Alfarabi treats the critique of tragic music (800b5–804c) as a digression from the general subject matter of bk. 7, namely, *how* to innovate. This critique of the poets is in simpler terms an account of *what* innovations need to be made. Thus, Alfarabi says that Plato "digressed [*'adal*] to mention the classes of things that should be set down in these books" (disc. 7.7). Because the first of the two paragraphs of Alfarabi's summary of the critique of the poets diverges so fully from Plato's text, I will first describe Plato's text and then Alfarabi's interpretation (cf. disc. 7.7–8 with 800b5–801d11).

The passage in the *Laws* (summarized in disc. 7.7) falls into two parts: a description of the kind of tragic music that should not be heard at sacrifices (or only rarely) and the laying down of three laws outlining what kinds of music should be heard on such occasions. The Athenian begins the first part by painting a picture of a sacrifice at which a kinsman, probably a younger kinsman, "breaks out in a total blasphemy" (800c). Having touched on his fellow aged legislators' hatred of insubordination and impiety as on a raw nerve, the Athenian asks them whether a father would view such behavior with religious unease. Most likely a father himself, Kleinias says he would. To the surprise of his interlocutors, the Athenian proceeds to describe this behavior on the part of younger kinsmen as the norm rather than as the exception. Sacrifices, especially at festivals, are regularly accompanied by music composed by poets in a competition to see who can make the citizens "weep the most" (800d6). It appears likely that the Athenian is describing those festivals at which tragedians competed for the victory prize (see 828c3). Unlike historians of Greek literature and perhaps unlike his own contemporaries, Plato focuses the reader's attention on the act of sacrificing, rather than the performance of tragedies, as the centerpiece of such festivals. With such an emphasis on the sacrifice, their religious import comes into the foreground.

Why does the Athenian suggest that a sacrifice at a religious festival should not be accompanied by a (mournful) tragedy or tragic chorus?[5] Sacrifices are offered to the gods in mournful atonement for past misconduct and fear of deserved future punishment.[6] According to the third theological thesis in bk. 10, the gods should not be viewed as capable of being swayed by sacrifices to favor those who are unjust. In tragedy, because the hero is fated to act unjustly, he is presented as deserving some favor or rather, as Thomas Pangle puts it, some "divine compassion or regret".[7] In consoling human suffering, the tragic poets increase human reliance upon some form of divine intervention. By forbidding that sacrifices should be accompanied by tragic choruses, the Athenian hopes to increase human self-reliance.

Not only do such tragic choruses increase our reliance upon the gods, but also in a less direct manner they interfere with the need of human beings to rule themselves. As the Athenian explains in connection with a different discussion, tragedy affirms shamefulness, especially the shamefulness of certain illegal actions (838c ff.). By undercutting tragic indulgence at sacrifices, he weakens the claim of shame on the citizens of his city. As I will show, in bk. 8 indignation is cultivated sufficiently to answer for any weakening of shame that might occur as a result of the modification of traditional music. But whereas shame precludes all inquiry into law, indignation may not be so completely opposed to inquiry.

Rather than dispense with tragic choruses altogether, the Athenian admits them in connection with funeral processions. When it comes to what at least appears to most human beings to be the greatest human suffering, namely, death, he includes that consolation which he excluded from every other event in the lives of human beings. Perhaps he includes it here because, unlike other events, in the face of the loss of loved ones human beings are wholly incapable of action.

In the second part of the passage summarized in disc. 7.7, the Athenian lays down three laws outlining the kind of music that is to take the place of the outlawed tragic chorus. The first law briefly commands that the songs to be used in lieu of the "very mournful [*goôdestatais*] harmoniae" (800d3) must be "auspicious" (*euphêmia*) (800e11). The second law is that the poets should pray to the gods. Perhaps he believes that the tragic choruses do not constitute proper prayer. The third law leads precisely to such a conclusion: the poets need to be commanded to pray to the gods, because at present their prayers are for evil things. Just as no one can be said to be evil voluntarily (731c4 and 860d), so no one can be said to pray (voluntarily) for evil things. Such prayers, as the result of ignorance, are in effect not prayers at all (cf. 688c). Having touched on all of the parts of the passage summarized in discourse 7.7, let us now turn to Alfarabi's summary of this passage.

In some respects Alfarabi does not diverge from the Athenian. First, it is noteworthy that in this paragraph Alfarabi only mentions two things: presenting "statutes" (*aḥkâm*) in a fair manner and presenting exhortations to sorrow and humility. He only mentions the contrast between the fair and what the Athenian calls the mournful. Thus, he limits himself to summarizing the first part of the Platonic passage, the critique of the tragic poets, and the first of the three laws in the second part, the law concerning "auspicious" speech. In remaining silent on the last two of the three laws, Alfarabi remains silent about prayer to the gods. Thus, Alfarabi points to and perhaps enhances Plato's intention to reduce human reliance on divine intervention. As I will show later in this section, Alfarabi maintains his silence about the gods into his summary of the next Platonic passage (disc. 7.8).

Although Alfarabi follows the Athenian in speaking of something fair and of humility, he diverges from him in acknowledging ungrudgingly the need to use "exhortations . . . to humility [*khasha'û*] and sorrow [*ḥazanû*]" (disc. 7.7). He does not admit such exhortations as something to be mentioned only on the occasion of funerals. Thus, he seems to drop the Athenian's critique of the poets. Does he admit "humility and sorrow" because he is under the influence of one of the revealed religions–humility being a virtue of revealed religion rather than of pagan religion?

There are reasons for doubting that Alfarabi has gone so far in diverging from the Athenian (and Plato). In several other passages, he has deviated from the Athenian in ways that undercut the latter's own occasional emphasis on humility and different forms of abasement. First, when summarizing a passage in which the Athenian praises humility (*tapeinos*), he goes only so far as to condemn arrogance (*qiḥah*) (cf. disc. 4.9 with 716a5). Second, when summarizing the Athenian's praise of honoring the soul, he not only praises honoring the soul but adds that "contempt [*ihânah*] of the soul is base" (cf. disc. 5.1 with 726a ff.). Third, when the Athenian praises cultivating a body that is in the mean between health and illness, he is not only silent about striving for such a mean but also characterizes the "healthy" as the "fat" body (cf. disc. 5.4 with 728e1–7). Finally and above all, Alfarabi does not echo the Athenian's praise of enslavement to law (cf. disc. 3.14 with 699c ff.).

Alfarabi does not mean to celebrate "humility" and even "compassion" (*riqqah*) as virtues. In a regime, however, that tends toward the monarchic rather than the democratic, the ruled ("the citizens" [*ahl al-madînah*])[8]–despite Alfarabi's intention not to encourage them to enslave themselves to the Law any more than they already have–may need to be encouraged to submit to their rulers with humility. Such humility would be of dubious value in the Athenian's city. His city inclines toward democracy: All of its citizens, albeit to lesser or greater degrees, participate in rule. Alfarabi speaks of exhortations to humility without any reference to sacrifices or to the gods or God. Perhaps this humility is to be held by the ruled with respect to the rulers. As mentioned above, he makes no explicit reference to the gods in summarizing the Athenian's revision of the popular hymns, prayers, and encomia sung to the gods and prayers and encomia sung to daimons, heroes, and human beings (disc. 7.7 with 801e ff.). Not only is Alfarabi silent about the gods, but he is even silent about the semidivine beings, the daimons and heroes. Even the human beings he mentions do not seem to be worshiped as dead, divine human individuals. They are merely abstract "peoples" (*unâs*) lauded, rather than prayed to, in "parables" (*amthâl*). Imitation is intended to replace prayer. Most strikingly, Alfarabi adds to parables about peoples parables about "beasts" (*bahâ'im*). The divine extreme is withdrawn and replaced by the beastly extreme. For whom could parables about beasts be instructive? Surely not for the rulers. Perhaps, after all, we were correct in supposing that Alfarabi admits "exhortations to humility and sorrow" as fair for the ruled. However this may be, it is at least clear that even the rulers are not to take their bearings from divine, deceased human beings or other divine beings but rather from mere mortals.

Still, we may have spoken too hastily about the absence of the gods. The parables are concerned not just with human beings and beasts but with "strange matters" (*gharâ'ib*). Insofar as all of the "songs and dances" discussed throughout the Platonic passage summarized in discourse 7.8 (801e–803e4) are ultimately directed toward the gods (803e3), there is every reason to believe that the "strange matters" are the divine matters. Of course, by giving the divine the vague designation "strange matters," Alfarabi leaves it altogether unclear what beings are described in the parables about these matters. One is hard put to know how to imitate "strange matters." At the same time, he speaks more boldly than he possibly could if he were not vague in referring to the divine. These "strange matters" are a source of fascination to the "unsophisticated as well as the majority of people" precisely because they are "unintelligible" (*mâ gharaba 'an 'uqûlihim*). Although their unintelligibility disqualifies them as matters of interest to the "sophisticated"–among whom not only philosophers but rulers can be counted (disc. 2.1[c] and 2.4)–it also, whether intentionally so conceived or not, contributes to the "continued existence of the law." People are not fascinated by the law itself but by the stories about strange matters that are interwoven with it. In the case of divine laws, such stories concern the gods or God. Because they are unintelligible, people are taken up with attempting to "extract" (*istikhrâj*) meaning from them. It is possible that if people, namely, the ruled, were not so engaged with these strange matters, they would not obey the law. Still Alfarabi does not exhort the ruled or the unsophisticated to obey the law or the gods or God out of humility before these "strange matters." He merely describes the fascination of the unsophisticated with them.

In contrast, the obedience of the rulers to the law will not result from their being taken up with the activity of extracting meanings from these strange matters, let alone from humility before them, but rather from their desire to acquire good breeding and an indignant disdain for illiberal pleasures (disc. 3.8–10, 3.12–13, and 5.9). An obedience to the law that is inspired by the desire to acquire good breeding is less an obedience to specific laws than to what one understands to be the law's opinion about what pleasures and pains are just and noble. If spirited human beings can be persuaded that some of their city's laws are not in harmony with good breeding, they will allow for their replacement (see 635a9). Yet they are not likely to find the assertion acceptable that the overarching purpose of their city's laws is not good. Thus, the Athenian presents his criticism of the purpose of Cretan and Spartan laws as if it were merely a criticism of Kleinias's and Megillus's misunderstanding of the purpose of their own laws (630d2 ff. and see disc. 7.11). Above all, spirited human beings are not predisposed to question but rather to agree with their law's opinion concerning what pleasures and pains are noble and just. Must they, if they are to question their law's opinions at all, be led to do so by someone who is not essentially spirited, namely a philosophic human being such as the Athenian Stranger? Can they engage in an inquiry into their city's beliefs without engaging in a casuistic defense of them? Or must they follow the fate of the popular *mutakallimûn* who defend their city's beliefs at any cost? (See, for example, Kleinias's spirited inquiry into the divine in bk. 10 [887b ff.])

The casuistic defense of the law, by precluding genuine inquiry into the law, precludes genuine innovation. Without such innovation the power of the law to rule is doomed to decay. Does the possibility of true inquiry into laws, and thus of true innovation on them, depend upon the presence of the philosopher?

3. *War games and drinking parties: Pleasure and indignation*

As mentioned above, wine drinking and festivals loosen the constraints imposed by shame. The Dorian lawgiver prohibits wine drinking for fear that it might undermine the shame that guarantees obedience to, and prevents innovation on, the law. Perhaps the Athenian intends wine drinking to undermine indignation in a similar manner. At the same time that he advocates it, however, he introduces war games. Far from undermining indignation, war games contribute to its intensification.

Just as in bk. 7 the Athenian revised the choruses and musical contests to accord with a less tragic and more spirited understanding of human life, so he adds not only gymnastic contests but war games in bk. 8. Eventually, he poses the question as to why his revised "choral activity and contests [*choreia kai agonia*] are almost in no way practiced" in the cities at present (831b6). After revealing to Kleinias that the reason for the absence of such choruses and contests is not, as he is inclined to assume, the rule of the democratic faction, he offers two reasons: (1) the citizens' preoccupation with their private well-being, in particular with moneymaking (831c4 ff.), and (2) the interest of rulers in preventing the ruled from acquiring (military) means of self-protection and self-aggrandizement (832c ff.). Through an analysis of the opening passage of bk. 8 on festivals, I intend to show that there is a further reason that such choruses and contests are generally not practiced: the wine drinking that occurs, at least at Athenian festivals, works at cross-purposes to some extent with spirited choruses and martial contests. This is only to be expected in light of indignation's role as an opponent of the desire for pleasures. Yet does not wine overcome indignation's opposition to the desire to inquire at festivals, much as it overcomes shame? Or is its opposition only enhanced by partaking of wine? Or, to mention the only other possibility, is indignation left unaffected? If indignation's opposition to inquiry cannot be overcome, then the question will have to be raised whether the indignant human beings who rule Magnesia are not in need of the guidance of someone who is not essentially indignant.

In some ways, wine drinking and war games work at cross-purposes. The most obvious way is captured in the slogan of the 1960s student movement: "Make love, not war." It is not by chance that this antiwar movement also championed the use of intoxicants. Wine drinking is most conducive to the pursuit of pleasures, among which love and sexual pleasure may be counted. In contrast, war games are occasions on which anger and indignation find their expression. As I noted earlier, of course, anger and indignation are expressed in response to pain. Not only are they expressed, but they are experienced as a result even of the kind of mock injuries, not to mention the actual injuries (831a4), that occur during such games. Thus, wine drinking and war games would seem to be opposed to one another as are love and hate, and pleasure and pain. And although they are not intended by the Athenian to occur at the same time, they are intended to occur at the same festivals. Unless some way is found to harmonize the hatred stirred up by war games with the love stirred up by wine drinking, the different aspects of such festivals would seem bound to work at cross-purposes.

Alfarabi begins his interpretation of the opening of bk. 8 (cf. disc. 8.1–7 with 828a–842b) by linking the present treatment of festivals to the earlier treatment in bk. 2. According to him, Plato describes a wonderful advantage in the opening of bk. 8 "other than" (*siwâ*) the advantage alluded to in the "beginning of the book" (*awwal al-kitâb*). I take "the beginning of the book" here to be not the very beginning of the *Laws*, as one might expect from Alfarabi's use of *kitâb*, but the beginning of bk. 2. As we saw in the previous section, the Athenian's understanding of wine drinking as a safeguard for education in bk. 2 is in effect the correction of his assertion throughout bk. 1 that it is useful for cultivating moderation (as shame). Festivals and wine drinking safeguard education by providing an occasion on which people may pursue pleasures free from the usual legal restraints (cf. disc. 2.1 with 653d). The advantage described in bk. 8, however, is that festivals provide an occasion for exalting the gods and restoring their renown. If Alfarabi were not so reticent about the gods throughout his *Summary*, one might expect him to assert at least that the advantage here is a greater advantage than that in bk. 2. Perhaps mentioning an advantage first, however, somehow privileges it over one mentioned later. And perhaps safeguarding education through the temporary suspension of the law is a greater advantage of festivities than exalting the gods.

Further doubts are raised about the rank of the advantage of exalting the gods by Alfarabi's very next assertion that "exalting and esteeming the gods exalts the traditions and the laws" (disc. 8.1). The worth of the present advantage is in its usefulness as a means to the end of exalting the traditions and laws. Of course, the advantage possessed by a means is inferior to the advantage possessed by an end. Thus, from all points of view, what would appear to the casual observer to be the primary advantage of religious festivals, exalting the gods, turns out to be a secondary advantage. Alfarabi's characterization of the gods' exaltation brings to mind the observation that the philosophic *mutakallim* looks above all to the well-being of the political community when inquiring into the roots of the law. Is the well-being of the political community more fully served by the festival's effect of suspending the law—thus making innovation possible—or by exalting the law? As we saw earlier, Alfarabi is not averse to juxtaposing such apparently contradictory purposes (disc. 7.13). The need to both conserve and innovate necessitates such juxtapositions. Although it is uncertain which advantage is greater–exalting the laws or suspending them to make possible legal innovation–it is certain that each of these is greater than exalting the gods. Alfarabi contributes to this undercutting of the gods' exaltation by omitting the Athenian's command that there should be a sacrifice for each day of the year "so that there will always be at least one magistrate performing a sacrifice" (cf. disc. 8.1 with 828b).

As has been his custom in discourses 6 and 7, Alfarabi passes over in silence the provision made by the Athenian for separate festivals for women. Then he mentions the distinction between the two primary classes (*ṣinfân*) of gods: the heavenly ([Ar.] *al-samâwiyyât,* [Gr.] *ouranioi*) and the earthly (*al-arḍiyyât, chthonioi*) (disc. 8.2). According to the Athenian, warlike human beings are disposed to abhor Pluto, the leading *chthonios* and the ruler of Hades, but they "should honor" (*timêteon*) him (828d3). Alfarabi observes that Plato does not suggest that these gods be worshiped but merely that they be "esteemed or honored" (*tubajjal*). It is readily understandable that warlike human beings, who are more likely than others to face death–or to paraphrase the Athenian's euphemism, dissolution of body and soul–cannot bring themselves to worship the god who oversees their descent into Hades. They prepare themselves during war games to perform acts of great valor whose utility for the city is obvious but for themselves is less so (disc. 8.2, end).

Without any break, Alfarabi goes on to summarize the Athenian's description of the war games. The discussion of war games follows as inevitably upon the discussion of the appropriate sacrifices to be offered to the different classes of gods as war games will follow sacrifices at these festivals (829b8). These sacrifices are to be accompanied by the revised choruses and musical contests described in bk. 7. Seen in this context, the Athenian's criticisms of the poets' tragic choruses make even more sense. How could warlike human beings be expected to participate in war games after hearing disheartening tragic music? No doubt such music reached its highest pitch traditionally in conjunction with the worship of the *chthonioi*. Not only wine drinking but the fear of death conspires to undermine the Athenian's introduction of war games into the religious festivals.

If the sacrifices at (religious) festivals are accompanied by spirited choruses, then it will be possible, as Alfarabi suggests, for the "youth" (*aḥdâth*) of the city to turn from sacrifices to occupy themselves with "combat" (*jihâd*) in a "cheerful" (*hashâshah*) state of mind (disc. 8.2). Indeed, holding war games at festivals is intended to make of combat itself a more cheerful affair. Before going on to describe the war games themselves, the Athenian emphasizes that there will be prizes for the victors, including poems of praise and blame (829c). A discussion of battle, which necessarily has painful associations, must be sweetened by anticipation of the fruits of victory. Following suit, Alfarabi goes so far as to omit a summary of the Athenian's description of the war games.[9] Alfarabi seems to have taken to heart the Athenian's adage that war itself has never been of any educational use (803d5–8).

The Athenian cannot turn to discuss war games without first discussing warriors' states of mind prior to and following battle. According to Alfarabi, although the music accompanying the sacrifices may instill "cheerfulness" in the youths, they are not a source of "pleasure" (*ladhdhah*). Little can be a source of pleasure in preparation (even) for (mock) battle. We may feel cheerfulness–in other words, be filled with the hope of overcoming future obstacles–in preparation for battle, but we cannot feel pleasure. The pleasure in "adhering to the tradition" that commands taking part in combat comes only in hearing songs of praise in the wake of mock battle. Needless to say, only the victors experience the pleasure of being praised. The pleasure of the victors is pleasure in domination. "Adherence to the tradition" that commands waging war, however, results not only from the songs of praise but also those of blame. The victors out of a love of victory and the losers out of shame adhere to this tradition. Shame, it seems, has not retreated fully from the battlefield. Songs of praise contribute to the cultivation of indignation by associating pleasure with the painful exertions of battle. Here pleasure and indignation are allies. Yet it is not indignation that lends support to the desire for pleasures, but rather the desire for pleasures that lends support to indignation.

According to Alfarabi, the songs of praise that follow the war games are intended not only to associate pleasure with battle (or, rather, with victory), but also to give rise to an "eagerness" (*ḥirṣ*) to acquire the virtues[10] (see also 829c5). Earlier, in his moment of expansiveness about the gods, he argued that the rulers turned to the gods for hope in overcoming the obstacles to acquiring good breeding (disc. 5.9). Similarly, in the present discussion the gods appear prior to battle, in the sacrifices that precede the war games, but not after it (disc. 8.2). In the latter case, one needs only songs of praise and blame to stimulate the "indignation" that was also used earlier to spur human beings on to acquire good breeding (disc. 5.7–9). The anger that is inevitably stirred up by war games is guided by songs of praise and blame through the degrees of spiritedness from "eagerness" through "heart" (*qalb*) to "indignation" (*ḥamiyyah*).

Almost as if he has forgotten himself, Alfarabi concludes his summary of the Athenian's description of the war games, or rather of the activities surrounding them, with the assertion that they are useful in preparing the youth for wars. There is something just in his almost total neglect of the subject of war games proper. As such they are ultimately of use only to the city. Then he turns to summarize only the first of the two impediments to the use of festivals for the cultivation of martial virtue: the citizens' excessive devotion to moneymaking (cf. disc. 8.3 with 831c4 ff.). Perhaps it is to be expected that he would omit the Athenian's second impediment: Rulers wish to prevent the ruled from acquiring the means of overthrowing them (832c ff.). The Athenian identifies this impediment because the city he is describing is supposed to be a true "regime," i.e., a mixed regime (see 712e9 ff.). Alfarabi is silent about it because his regime tends toward monarchy rather than the mean between democracy and monarchy. Consequently, its rulers must be concerned about the ruled acquiring the means of overthrowing them. The monarchic character will also affect his description of the first impediment to the cultivation of martial virtue, the love of wealth.

According to the Athenian, the love of wealth prevents citizens "in the cities nowadays" from undertaking the practices necessary for the proper cultivation of martial virtue (831b5). At first, one assumes that this love prevents the acquisition of martial virtue in general: The desire for pleasures interferes with indignation. By distracting citizens from communal duty, it turns them into private individuals (see 705a4). The Athenian's list of the kinds of human beings it turns citizens into, however, suggests that when coupled with courage it produces not only criminals, including temple robbers, but "warriors" (*polemikous*) (832a). Although the Athenian makes noteworthy provisions for preventing the love of wealth from entering the citizen body—for instance, by excluding artisans from citizenship and restricting the use of money (846d and 742a)—he includes certain loopholes that allow it to remain somewhat active. For instance, he weakens implied restrictions on trade he made earlier in the dialogue by adding modifications later (cf. 742a2-5 and 849c7 with 915e).

Having gone from assuming that the love of wealth opposes courage and indignation to recognizing that they can be allies at least for military purposes, we are now in a position to look closely at Alfarabi's summary of this passage. Rather than argue, as the Athenian does, that his city will not include artisans among the citizens and thus it will be free from the infection of the love of wealth, he argues on that artisans will be citizens in his regime and thus it will be so infected. As I explained in chapter 5, because a monarchic regime does not rely heavily upon the virtue of all its citizens, since all do not participate in rule, it is possible for it to give artisans citizenship. Alfarabi integrates artisans to the extent that he envisions their presence even at festivals, a moment of great vulnerability for the regime—albeit they are there merely as slaughterers of sacrifices and decorators of the city. The artisans' mere presence at the festivals, however, does not enable them to acquire the benefit provided by the festivals, namely, the enhancement of the virtues and in particular of moderation. "They become unscrupulous" (literally, their consciences become corrupt, *infasadat ḍamâ'iruhum*) (disc. 8.3). Perhaps the confluence of the love of wealth and courage poses a danger not to courage but to moderation (see 836a2). Although the Athenian allows for some minor loopholes through which trade and the love of wealth may enter his city, the harm that this love does to the moderation (of the courageous in particular) may account for his overwhelming rhetorical opposition to commerce throughout the *Laws*.

Alfarabi attempts to limit the harm that the love of wealth can do to his regime by restricting the number of citizens who may become artisans. Citizens are to be issued permits to practice an art only if they have "bad natural disposition[s]." Only such citizens will be attracted to the arts by the legislator's description of them because it will only mention their base aspects. Yet there are noble aspects to the arts (see disc. 2.5-6 and chapter 10 below). What then does Alfarabi have in mind when he distinguishes good from bad natural dispositions? He probably means what the Athenian has in mind in distinguishing between the orderly and the courageous (831e4-32a3). The orderly are suited to the arts and commerce; the courageous are suited to the tasks of citizenship. If infected with the love of wealth, citizens may become good "warriors" but they are less likely to become good citizens because of their consequent lack of moderation (667a). Similarly, Alfarabi would not want those with good breeding who are bound to become rulers to be exposed to trade lest they become immoderate and even tyrannical. Yet, in view of the mutual support that the love of wealth and courage can offer one another, it would be useful to infect mere warriors with this love. In a departure from the Athenian, Alfarabi does precisely this by offering ample monetary compensation to the "warriors" (*ahl al-ḥarb*) (cf. disc. 6.6 with 755c ff.). In his regime, however, warriors are not necessarily identical with rulers (as they are in the Athenian's city). Similarly, he has no difficulty separating the warriors from the artisans, because warriors are not likely to be drawn away from their own financial honors to pursue the more moderate rewards of the artisans.

Once again we have found that desire for pleasure and indignation can lend support to one another. The desire for money can lend support to martial virtue and indignation. But this particular complementary relation was not quite what we had in mind. Rather we were in search of a case in which indignation gives its support to (or at least does not oppose) the desire for pleasure—in particular, desire for the pleasures of inquiry. Let us turn then to the Athenian's account of the erotic pleasures associated with festivals. Perhaps there we will be able to find this particular alliance of indignation with desire for the purposes of desire.

A strong hint as to whether indignation can be found in such an alliance with desire at festivals lies in the observation that indignation is absent from the whole discussion of erotic pleasures at festivals (cf. disc. 8.5-7 with 835c-842b). We have seen that indignation is in need of the assistance of desires for pleasure. For instance, martial virtue needs the assistance of pleasure to overcome the natural human resistance to confronting pain and death. Erotic desire, however, seems to derive no such support from indignation. On the contrary, the absence of indignation in this context no doubt contributes to the Athenian's fear that erotic desire will become uncontrollable (835d4).

Perhaps the success of the suspension of indignation during at least portions of these festivals is the reason for the unexpected fact that there is not a single mention of wine drinking during the Athenian's discussion of the erotic pleasures associated with festivals or in Alfarabi's summary of this passage (cf. disc. 8.5-7 with 835c-842c). Perhaps we are to assume its presence in light of the earlier discussions. Furthermore, there are explicit references to wine later in bk. 8 that preclude the possibility that the Athenian wishes to prohibit wine drinking altogether (845b8, 849d3). I cannot rule out the possibility, however, that the present silence about wine drinking is intended to moderate the freedom with which the Athenian expects the youths of this city to pursue at least some pleasures. Perhaps his weakening of the power of shame has had more far-reaching effects than we anticipated.

Wine drinking or no wine drinking, these festivals are not characterized merely by martial spirit and piety but also by intense erotic pleasures. Where do the desires for these pleasures lead? To the sort of dead end they lead to among the Dorians? The average shame-filled Dorian man avoids drink and, even more importantly, avoids speech (see 642a) but readily takes advantage of the concession to erotic desires offered by the example of Laius (836c3) and the myth of Ganymede (636d). Can regimes as martially oriented as the Athenian's city and Alfarabi's regime, by resting their martial virtue on indignation rather than shame, find a means of access to some higher fulfillment of erotic desires?

As Alfarabi explains, these festivals allow for so great a fulfillment of erotic desires that these desires become a preoccupation during nonfestival days. Indeed, the appetite of the young men and women who participate in the festivals is so stimulated as to lead also to a preoccupation with pleasures that are outside the "legal traditions" (*sunan nâmûsiyyah*) (disc. 8.5).

According to the Athenian, the legal traditions in the city they are founding should not follow the Dorian example. The Athenian argues in favor of a revision of Dorian erotic traditions on the basis of nature. To begin with, he argues that, human sexuality being analogous to animal sexuality, human beings should not indulge in homosexuality because animals do not (836c2). The Athenian acknowledges that this argument is not persuasive (836c10). The reason is readily apparent: If human beings were prevented by instinct from indulging in homosexual activities, one would not need a law to restrict them. Human erotic desires are not analogous to those of animals. They are not limited by instinct because human beings are capable of possessing intellect. The mere potential for possessing intellect guarantees an openness of human beings to the world that defies the constraints of instinct. Human desires are consequently not only potentially unlimited in extent—as we saw in the case of the

Dorian league—but also potentially unlimited in their objects. On what basis then can desires be labeled justifiably as legal or illegal?

If we are to trust Dorian legislation, perhaps we should label the more intense pleasures legal and the less illegal. For does it not prefer homosexuality to inquiry because the former is a more intense substitute for the latter? If Dorian legislation were based on an adequate self-understanding, however, it would become apparent to its legislators that in sanctioning homosexuality, they are not sanctioning the most intense pleasure. As the Athenian explains in his discussion of love and friendship in the context of festivals, the most intense pleasure is associated with the attraction of opposites and the most moderate with the attraction of likes (837b2). Unwittingly, Dorian legislators promote one, although not the highest, form of moderation. In contrast, the Athenian shows that the most moderate love of all is the love of like soul for like soul. (The love of like body for like body is possessed of a "terribleness" akin to that of the attraction of opposites.) As has been noted elsewhere, Socrates was the consummate example of such a lover of like souls: in this respect, at least, he was the most moderate of human beings.[11] His love of the best and the brightest is truly moderate because it is guided neither by shame nor indignation. Nor is it in need of wine as a stimulant.[12] Socrates as a man of "sophistication," as Alfarabi would say, is not subject to shame. His freedom from indignation is most evident in his persistent adherence to his own dictum that no one is voluntarily evil (a freedom from indignation that the Athenian Stranger evidently shares [731c1–3 and 860d]). In contrast, the rulers in the *Laws* have as their primary objective the indignant prosecution of all those whom the law deems guilty (730d–e and cf. 731c1–3 with 731d5–9). One cannot become moderate in Socrates' sense—and thus truly capable of inquiring into the law—without ceasing to be a spirited human being.

Although the Athenian failed to present a persuasive argument against the Dorian solution to the problem of erotic desire on the basis of natural instinct, he presents another more persuasive argument from nature. The most natural desire, he argues, is the most moderate one; in other words, he argues from virtue (836d). On the face of it, this argument looks like the somewhat ascetic argument of Megillus, who avoids pleasures because his shame before the law dictates that he avoid them. But Socrates' success in adhering to a moderate life contrasts with the evident failure of shame and the law to moderate erotic desire. To try to make the case for the legal restraint of erotic desire, the Athenian is compelled to appeal not only to shame (838c and 840b8) but also to the recently discredited argument from instinctual nature (cf. 840d6 with 836c9). As Alfarabi indicates, pleasures are so difficult to control from the point of view of the law because the law is incapable of determining a good criterion for distinguishing between legal and illegal pleasures (disc. 8.6–7). He goes on to suggest, in merely apparent contradiction of the Athenian, that the most obvious proof of this failure is the impossibility of successfully moderating with shame and law even the most popularly condemned erotic desires–incestuous desires (cf. disc. 8.7 with 838b6). Ultimately, the law is consigned to issuing an ambiguous "prayer" (*euchê*) that is so fraught with exceptions as to barely qualify as a prayer, let alone as a law.[13] The incompatibility of even the most enlightened law's understanding of moderation with Socrates' understanding of moderation is evinced by the law's prayer that his moderate kind of erotic desire be prohibited (841d7).

Assuming for the moment that such a thing is possible, the indignant human being must forgo indignation to be capable of inquiry. Although drunkenness was sufficient to suspend shame's rule over erotic desires, it is not clear that drunkenness has the same effect on indignation. When an indignant man becomes drunk he picks fights.[14] Despite the greater nobility of the indignant as compared with the shame-filled, this human type seems to be no closer to renouncing its opposition to inquiry into the law. Ultimately, the possibility of inquiry seems to rest upon the existence of a human being whose moderation does not depend upon either shame or indignation, i.e., the truly moderate lover of inquiry. The need for the philosopher to lead inquiry into the law has led certain readers of the *Laws* to assert that upon arriving at the end of this dialogue one must turn to the opening of the *Republic*.[15] This need not mean that Plato has left the city in the *Laws* without the means to inquire into the law without the guidance of a living philosopher. Plato has left behind this dialogue that may, by engaging its readers in an inquiry into law, suffice as a substitute for this philosopher. Yet if the city described in the *Laws* is to win in its battle against the decay that results from the immoveable character of law, it must approach the rule of intellect achieved in the *Republic*. Of course, even if rulers in the city in the *Laws* are able to read the *Republic*, that can hardly guarantee their success in resisting the decay inherent in law's rule.

10
Poetry and Inquiry into Law

The rule of law gives rise to at least two kinds of morality: the morality of shame and the morality of indignation. The morality of shame is a fear of the opinions or of the consequences of disobeying the opinions inculcated by the law concerning what pleasures and pains are just and noble; the morality of indignation is an honoring of these opinions. The law proper commands either obedience or respect; however, it does not engage its adherents in inquiry. In the first part of this book, I often mentioned the unique role played by the prelude as a means of access to the overarching purpose of the law. Although the prelude is subtly integrated into the law by the Athenian beginning at the end of bk. 4, it does not originate from law proper. The law itself does not make inquiry into the law possible. As I will show, the prelude has its origins in poetry.

Not only does the law command obedience, it commands the same thing of different people, even of different psychological types. The poet does not command. Rather he describes, and he describes different kinds of people differently (see disc. 4.12). Although the law is not the origin of inquiry into law, this does not mean that the law cannot permit inquiry into itself, as the Athenian demonstrates in laying down the Dorian law of laws (634e4).

In section 1, I will discuss the permissibility of inquiring into the law as it is discussed in bk. 1 and discourse 1. We saw earlier that the original question about who makes the law (the efficient cause) is ultimately answered by answering the question about what the purpose of the law (the final cause) is. Prior to any attempt to determine its purpose, one must gain access to it. To inquire into it, one must gain permission from it. Would any law permit inquiry into it if the express purpose were to fundamentally alter it? More than any other inquiry, the inquiry into its overarching purpose threatens to lead to its fundamental transformation. Thus, one can gain permission to inquire into the law only if one begins by affirming one's intention to uphold and defend it, rather than to inquire into its overarching purpose.

In section 2, I will take up again the search for the human type capable of genuine inquiry into the law. Alfarabi introduces an additional alternative to the shame-filled and indignant ways of life described in the previous two chapters, namely, the artisan's way of life. He contrasts the artisan's way of life with the superior of the two previous alternatives, namely, the indignant or courageous way of life. The Athenian lays the groundwork for this comparison when, in the course of one of his discussions of education, he draws an analogy between the arts proper and the so-called art of citizenship (643b4–44b5). In interpreting this analogy, Alfarabi shows that the education in citizenship is not really analogous to the education in the arts proper. Rather, in the political sphere, the education of the educator of legislators is analogous to the education in the arts (disc. 1.17–18). Although the educator of legislators is truly interested in coming to know the truth about the laws, the citizen, even the ruling citizen (or courageous human being), merely wants to be told what things the laws deem good and what bad. What had been the *analogy* between the education in the arts and in citizenship in discourse 1, resurfaces as the *disanalogy* between the artisan and the courageous human being in discourse 2. Courageous human beings affirm that only the pleasures and pains deemed just and noble by the law are genuine pleasures and pains. Artisans, observing the disagreements among themselves about what is pleasurable, acknowledge that different people have different pleasures (disc. 2.5–7).

Finally, in section 3, I will adumbrate the ascent from poetry through preludes, *kalâm*, and dialectic to science. I will describe the poetic origins of preludes, discuss the relation between poetry and *kalâm*, and return to the discussion that opened this book: the interdependence of *kalâm* and political science.

1. *The permissibility of inquiring into law*

Inquiry into the law is necessary if there is to be rational innovation on the law. Because the appearance of changeability casts doubt on its authoritativeness, however, the law resists innovation. More specifically, if the authors of the divine law are the gods or a god or God, innovation on the law is a form of blasphemy. One cannot begin inquiry into the law with the explicit purpose of modifying what is defective in it. One must begin, rather, with the explicit purpose of clarifying to oneself what is fine about it. In other words, one must begin with the explicit purpose of defending it. Who threatens the law, thus necessitating its defense? Are they merely harmless fools or thoughtful opponents? Not only are thoughtful opponents a greater danger, but they may be transformed into a greater asset than harmless fools. When they are persuaded that their opposition is likely to be harmful to themselves, they may become the most useful allies. They are not only better equipped to defend the law than its blindly loyal proponents but also may be in a better position to transform their own inquiry into it into a basis for innovation.

Very early on in the *Summary*, Alfarabi first raises the possibility that the laws may have their detractors (disc. 1.3). In the previous paragraph, he raised the justification for such detraction, only to dismiss it. Although the Athenian mentions more than one legislation (namely, the Spartan and Cretan legislations), Alfarabi denies that the mere fact that there is more than one law "detracts from the validity of" (literally, nullifies, *lâ tubṭil*) the different laws. Although this would not be a striking observation for the Athenian to make, it is for Alfarabi as a Muslim. That there is more than one law nullifies the various laws only if one demands of a law code that it have universal applicability.

Perhaps the nameless people who attempt to nullify the laws in discourse 1.3 are attempting to nullify it with the objection expressed in discourse 1.2. However this may be, the mere fact that people attempt to nullify them and argue they are "foolish" (*tasfîh*) is a sufficient ground for "examining" (*baḥth*) them. The apparent purpose of any such examination or inquiry is the defense of the law against its detractors. There is no evidence that such an inquiry is to be unbiased. Indeed, Alfarabi follows up the suggestion that it is right to examine the laws with the assertion that "the laws occupy a very high rank and that they are superior to all wise sayings." He appears to have decided in favor of the laws before any inquiry has taken place. As a matter of fact, he warns the reader later not to submit without inquiry to rhetoric such as we have just seen him offer in support of the law (disc. 1.17). Furthermore, he himself eventually contradicts the assertion that the laws are superior to all wise sayings (disc. 9.7).

Later in discourse 1, Alfarabi summarizes the argument that leads up to the Athenian's introduction of the Dorian law of laws (cf. disc. 1.9[c] with 634c–d). I have noted before that this law permits old men to inquire into the law. In the argument leading up to it, the Athenian suggests that the purpose of blaming things in each other's laws is to "see what is true and, at the same time, what is best" (634c9). This seems to mean that he and his interlocutor (Kleinias) should blame some laws to separate out the good from the bad. It does not seem to mean that the laws of any one of the discussion's participants are fundamentally flawed, i.e., that the lawgiver had the wrong overarching purpose in mind in legislating.

Alfarabi begins summarizing this passage by speaking vaguely of a running argument between the speaker and interlocutor. This argument, he says, may lead to "debasing and degrading certain noble and preferable things." Contrary to this possible result, the purpose of this argument is not to debase and degrade but to prove the excellence of these things through inquiry. We are not given a clue as to what these "noble and preferable things" are until he asserts that what preceded—which part of what preceded he does not specify—was presented as an "excuse" (*ma'dhirah*) for those who would condemn statutes of the law. Could the assertion that the purpose of inquiring into the law is to prove its excellence (viz., to defend the law) be an excuse for condemning some of its statutes? Previously, Alfarabi mentioned that the legislators use various means, including "base and noble matters," to enable citizens to acquire the virtues (cf. disc. 1.8 with 632b). Some of the means used by legislators (or some of the laws) can indeed be "noble matters" that would suffer degradation by being subject to inquiry. He concludes his description of this "excuse" by adding the caveat that it is fit only for those whose purpose is "examination" (*baḥth*) and "inquiry" (*naẓar*) rather than "contention or mischief." The assertion that one is defending the law is a useful pretext for inquiring into the law. Although he had appeared to be a devoted servant of the law earlier, Alfarabi himself used this very pretext to justify inquiring into the law (disc. 1.3).

Alfarabi refers to inquiry into the law as a subject Plato treated "tacitly" (*'urûḍ*) (disc. 1.9). In contrast, he refers to the fact that Plato "started to condemn" certain statutes of the law, presumably more explicitly than he had treated the subject of inquiry into it (cf. disc. 1.10 with 635b4). Of course, Alfarabi has already justified his (or Plato's) inquiry with the excuse that in condemning the law he is actually defending it. Without specifying which statutes Plato condemns, he returns to the general subject of inquiring into the law, in particular to the Dorian law of laws (634d8–e7). According to the Athenian, this law forbids all young people from inquiring into which laws "are finely made and which are not" but permits old men to make such inquiries so long as each makes the inquiry in the presence of another and a magistrate, and in the absence of any young person. Rather than merely recapitulate this law, Alfarabi summarizes its meaning. He asserts that those who "accept" such laws in spite of the fact that they know they are bad act like children or, worse yet, like ignorant people. The purpose of the "intelligent" (*'âqil*) person who "examines" (*yabḥath*) these statutes is not to defend the law but "to overcome his doubt and understand the truth about them."

After speaking far more boldly in discourse 1.10 than did the Athenian in the passage being summarized there, in discourse 1.11 Alfarabi beats a hasty retreat from truth-seeking inquiry into the law to pious defense of the law. Indeed, there is no parallel in Plato's text to his assertion that obedience to the law is difficult, whereas unfounded attacks are very easy. Perhaps his boldness in describing the purposes of inquiry in discourse 1.10 made it incumbent upon him to beat such a retreat in 1.11.

Let us conclude the analysis of the permissibility of inquiring into the law by turning to what may be Alfarabi's boldest statement in favor of inquiry (disc. 1.17). Here he summarizes the Athenian's interchange with his interlocutors about whether they will permit him to make a rather long and involved inquiry into the "small activity of getting drunk" (642a4; 641e2–43a2). As citizens of regimes known for the brevity and pithiness of their speeches, the interlocutors need to be prepared for the length of this inquiry. Although the interlocutors are gracious in accepting the prospect of listening to an extended discussion of a subject with which they lack familiarity, there is little doubt that if the Athenian intended to have the most clear-headed discussion possible, he would adjust his speeches to suit the habits of his interlocutors. To begin with, however, he speaks about a subject that is foreign to them. And although he denies that his purpose is to speak at length about a small subject, lest his interlocutors think that such an approach to inquiry characterizes Athenians in general (642a), he speaks at great enough length to intoxicate them.

Alfarabi begins summarizing this passage by noting that people doubt the sincerity with which a person praises things when that person is known for excellence in "dialectic" (*jadal*) and "discussion" (*kalâm*) and for copiousness of speech.[1] In contrast, the Athenian Stranger merely mentions Athenian loquacity: he says nothing about Athenian excellence in dialectic and *kalâm* (641e5–6). Alfarabi's additions lead one to wonder whether the Athenian's loquacity conceals a great deal of just such dialectic and *kalâm*. Eventually, Alfarabi affirms that doubts about the sincerity of such oratory of praise are justified. One should determine the genuineness or lack thereof of such praise by engaging in one's own inquiry with one's "intellect" (*'aql*). Thereafter Alfarabi himself praises the law. His praise is not "copious," yet it could exemplify his own excellence in dialectic and *kalâm*. He says, "In itself, the law is sublime and excellent; it is more excellent than anything said about it and in it." Thus, he begins with a fine piece of irony: The law is more excellent than anything said about it, such as Plato's *Laws* and Alfarabi's *Summary*. He ends by revealing his irony: Indeed, the law is so excellent that it is more excellent than anything in it. But what is the law other than what is in it? Insofar as successfully condemning something while appearing to praise it is a mark of excellence in dialectic and *kalâm*, Alfarabi's praise of law is a fine example of such excellence.

In summary, Alfarabi begins his discussion of the permissibility of inquiry into the law in discourse 1.3 by suggesting that certain unnamed persons with unidentified motivations attack the law. Because the law is under attack, it needs to be defended. One can successfully defend the law, however, only after having inquired into it. (Nevertheless, those who inquire into the law should never discuss the results of their inquiry without at the same time defending the law.) In discourse 1.9, Alfarabi explains that the claim that the purpose of inquiry into the law is the defense of the law is really an excuse for those who wish to condemn certain statutes of the law. It is a fitting excuse, however, only for those whose ultimate purpose is inquiry, i.e., inquiry into the goodness or the badness of the laws, rather than contention and mischief. Of course, one has every reason to condemn that which one determines is bad. In discourse 1.10, Alfarabi summarizes the Athenian's discussion of the Dorian law of laws. He transforms this discussion into a bold attack on those who are unwilling to condemn that which they know is bad. In discourse 1.11, he retreats from his bold attack by celebrating the exertions of those who obey the law and condemning unjustified attacks on the law. Finally, in discourse 1.17, he both warns the reader to doubt the sincerity of speakers who are excellent in dialectic and *kalâm* when they praise things and engages in some praise himself. Even while praising the law, he raises doubts about its excellence.

After following this circuitous route, I conclude that the law itself will permit inquiry into it only for those who are devoted to defending it. Those who are "keepers" of the laws, such as the popular *mutakallimûn*, would, if they were able, resist all attempts at innovation even by the thoughtful. Keepers of the law are resistant to changing it, both because they cannot imagine other laws being better and because they fear the decay of its authority. The former rationale is frequently unfounded; the latter is well-founded. As we saw, Alfarabi offers guidance as to how the law can be changed without losing its authority.

Having determined on what bases the law will and will not permit inquiry let us return to the question, Who is capable of genuine inquiry into the law?

2. *Artisans versus courageous men*

Neither the shame-filled nor the indignant way of life is conducive to genuine inquiry into or innovation on the laws. Although my comparison of these two ways of life was based on an extensive analysis of Alfarabi's interpretation of the *Laws*, this contrast itself is not a prominent Alfarabian theme. In this chapter, I will continue the search for the way of life conducive to inquiry with a prominent Alfarabian theme: the contrast between the courageous human being's and the artisan's way of life. As we saw in chapter 9, courage may be rooted in either shame or indignation. As it is discussed in Alfarabi's contrast between the artisan and the courageous human being, however, it is rooted in indignation. This courageous human being is the perfect citizen, who, filled with spirit, opposes all injustice. In bk. 5, this citizen is characterized as the city's willing (male) executioner (bk. 5. 730d7–8). Although the Athenian continually denigrates the artisan's way of life as it compares with this courageous man's way of life, Alfarabi explains that so far as the inquiry into the law is concerned, the artisan rather than the courageous man is the model. To begin with, the artisan lacks that insurmountable impediment to inquiry, the courageous man's indignation. The artisan that Alfarabi has in mind throughout this discussion is the poet. Poetry, rather than law proper, gives us access to the foundations of law.

The Athenian first defines education in relatively humble terms as education in the arts (643b4). Here education's purpose is to prepare young people for the activities they will undertake as adults. The young acquire education by playing at adult activities. In addition, young people must "learn any knowledge that is a necessary preliminary" to them (643c4). Furthermore, their desire must be drawn in the direction of these activities. The examples the Athenian draws from the arts are not the most impressive: farming and housebuilding (643b8–c), and carpentry and horseback riding (643c5–7).

In contrast, Alfarabi's summary of this passage could hardly paint a more glorious picture of the arts or rather of the art of arts (disc. 1.18). Alfarabi begins without any mention of art. He begins with the need to know the "truth" (literally, truths, *ḥaqâ'iq*) about the laws–and about their excellence–and the truth "of all things" (*jamî' al-ashyâ'*). In other words, he begins with the need to know the art of political philosophy and the art of philosophy. With this lofty purpose in view, he explains that one may acquire such knowledge only through "reasoning" (or logic, *manṭiq*) and through exercise in it. Stepping back from the lofty goal, he acknowledges that in obtaining exercise in reasoning or logic one's immediate purpose may not be inquiry into the truth of the law but at least this is one long-term purpose of it. Thus, he intends to hold up reasoning or logic as a paradigm of art. Only after such a lofty opening does Alfarabi mention briefly one or two of the four arts that are the sole examples the Athenian offers. With housebuilding or carpentry in mind, he mentions setting up doors and houses for play. All arts share in common the pursuit of truth, whether their area of inquiry is noble or not.

When the Athenian draws the analogy between the education in citizenship that he is going to describe and the education in artisanry that he has already described, he begins by making it clear that the education in the arts (specifically, trade and merchant shipping) is not the real education (643e1–9). In other words, he does not mean to draw an analogy between the lack of nobility of the education in the arts and the nobility of the education in citizenship (644a3–6).

In interpreting this next step in the Athenian's argument, Alfarabi draws our attention to a deeper disanalogy between the arts proper and the so-called art of citizenship. He subtly signals this disanalogy, and more specifically the disanalogy between the art of the political philosopher and the philosopher, on the one hand, and the so-called art of citizenship, on the other, with this opening to discourse 1.19: Plato then "turned (*'aṭaf*) to the legislator." (This is the only occasion on which Alfarabi uses this term, "to turn," to open a paragraph.)[2] The "legislator" (*ṣaḥib al-nâmûs*) here mentioned is a citizen-legislator such as

Kleinias, as opposed to the philosopher-legislator or political philosopher (the Athenian Stranger) or philosopher-king (celebrated in such works as Alfarabi's *Attainment of Happiness* and Plato's *Republic*). The citizen-legislator receives merely an education in citizenship. Kleinias demonstrates throughout the *Laws* the lack of training in political philosophy that is characteristic of such legislators. Their education in citizenship or virtue is, as Alfarabi explains, the result of a "training from childhood in political matters and reflection [*ta'ammul*] on their rightness [*ṣawâb*] and wrongness [*khaṭâ'*]." This education focuses "reflection" on what is right and wrong rather than on inquiry into the truth of the laws. Surely this "training" is not intended to be filled with critical inquiry, because it is undertaken in childhood. In contrast, Alfarabi makes no mention of childhood when describing the training in reasoning or logic that precedes the inquiry into the truth of the laws and of all things. Furthermore, he elaborates the purpose of the childhood training as enabling the individual to "control himself and face what confronts him with perseverance." This training does not have as its purpose inquiry but moral education. Indeed, it is nothing other than the education in good breeding that teaches indignant human beings what pleasures and pains they must deem noble and just.

The Athenian first refers to the opposition between the artisan and the courageous man, although not in these exact terms, in the course of elaborating his next definition of education—of the perfect human being (rather than citizen) (bk. 2. 653b ff.). This definition makes explicit the intention to train the soul to react to pains and pleasures as it should (653c). Music, the combination of song and dance, trains human beings about the proper loves and hatreds. The opposition between the artisan and the courageous man appears in the following manner: The Athenian asks Kleinias whether a man is better educated in music if he is able to convey adequately with his body and voice that which is understood to be "fine" (or noble, *kalon*) on each occasion, although he neither loves the "noble things" (*tois kalois*) nor hates the "ignoble things" (*ta mê kala*); or if he is not able to convey these things adequately, although he loves and hates what he should love and hate (654c6–d3). Evidently, the former man possesses excellent skill in the musical arts; the latter possesses an appreciation of the nobility of the noble. What is most striking is the apparent exclusivity of these two possessions. Although the Athenian had drawn an analogy between the education in the arts and the education in citizenship in bk. 1, Kleinias detects, as any thoughtful citizen would, just how great a disanalogy exists between them: He says simply that the difference between the two men is a "vast difference as regards education" (654d4). Although it is clear which education characterizes the perfect citizen already long before bk. 8, the Athenian makes this even clearer when he asserts that only men over fifty who have performed conspicuous and noble deeds and who may or may not "possess poetry and the Muse within themselves in an adequate way" should be allowed to compose the songs of praise and blame sung at festivals (829c8-d2). To be adequately educated as a citizen, one needs a sincere love of the noble rather than skill in music. To be adequately educated in the arts, even in poetry, one needs skill in music rather than a love of the noble. The poets' understanding of the art of music certainly makes greater demands on the intellect than the mere rote understanding possessed by some craftsmen. Nonetheless, the emphasis of both is the same; it is on understanding or knowledge about something rather than love of its nobility.

Eventually the Athenian presents the courageous man in a less than flattering light (666e-68b3). He describes the courageous man—exemplified by the citizens of Kleinias's Cretan city, Knossos—as a herd animal who fails to acquire the kind of education that would enable him to rule. He comes to possess only the fourth and lowest part of virtue: courage. Courage or strong indignation, although it may suffice as a motive for executing the unjust, is apparently insufficient for engaging in the highest aspects of rule. Needless to say, Knossos was a city and not a herd of animals. One is led to wonder just what aspects of rule they were lacking. Perhaps they act like herd animals because they lack the independence of thought necessary for legal innovation.

It may be the Athenian's intention, at least in this passage, to adumbrate a perfect citizen who is a cross between the poet and the courageous man. The contrast between the courageous (citizen) and the orderly (artisan), made as late as bk. 8 (831e4 ff. and cf. disc. 8.3), indicates he is less intent on replacing this opposition than on reformulating the purposes, of the courageous man.[3]

With these reservations in mind, let us turn to Alfarabi's summary of this passage (disc. 2.5-6). He begins his interpretation with the bald assertion of an opinion: "Pleasures vary with respect to different people, their conditions, natural dispositions, and moral habits." He attributes this opinion to Plato through his initial silence. It is apparent that he also attributes this opinion to artisans rather than to courageous men, because he adds that artisans expert in one kind of art have different pleasures (and a different understanding of what is proper, noble, and moderate) from those expert in another kind of art. The courageous, in contrast, follow the laws' guidance as to what pleasures are noble. Furthermore, artisans do not fall into disagreements over their differences, although they recognize their existence (disc. 2.6). Courageous men could hardly be expected to settle so peacefully their differences over what they deem noble.

Why are artisans, particularly poets, so even-tempered when it comes to differences over pleasure? According to the Athenian, pleasure is merely a kind of "charm" that accompanies more important characteristics of the imitations that imitative artists produce. Their most important characteristic is their accuracy or "correctness" (*orthotêta*) (cf. 667c1-7 with 668a). One "learns" (*mathêsis*) from the correctness of an imitation *what* the imitated thing is (cf. 667c5 with 668b5-9).

A criticism commonly leveled against poets is that they are concerned only with inducing pleasure in their audience (see 700d7). Inducing such pleasure, however, is merely a prerequisite to their having an audience. They are not concerned primarily with their own or their audiences' pleasure. In a sense, the courageous man possesses a greater concern with his own pleasure than the poets. He allows himself to enjoy only the pleasures deemed noble by his city, but his foremost concern is with his own pleasure. He deems the correctness of imitations of little consequence.

According to Alfarabi (and Plato), the poet is rightly concerned first and foremost with what things are (disc. 2.7). He shares this view with the person who possesses "perfect knowledge [*kâmil ma'rifah*] of a thing." Indeed, this priority is adhered to in all of the arts and sciences. Knowledge of what something is must precede one's knowledge of how "fair" (*ḥasan*) it is, not to mention how "fine" (*jûdah*) or "base" it is, because, for one thing, if one does not truly know what a thing is, then one does not know what is being identified as "fair" or as "base." The courageous man, although filled with worthy feelings, may not even have worthy feelings about the right thing.

The poet's knowledge of what things are, especially what human beings are, is more indispensable to the inquirer into the law than the courageous man's opinions about what pleasures and pains are noble and base. Furthermore, the poet possesses a more comprehensive knowledge of different (psychological) types of people. The courageous man does not know what other types exist because he does not inquire into other ways of life. And he does not inquire into them because he does not approve of them. The inquirer into the law must possess an understanding of all the different ways of life to be able to assess the way of life that law advocates.

In his first definition of education, the Athenian draws an analogy between the arts proper and the art of citizenship. Alfarabi makes apparent the difficulties with this analogy. He also shows that the true analogy to the arts proper is not citizenship but the art of reasoning or logic and the art of political philosophy. In his second definition of education, the Athenian begins to acknowledge this disanalogy more explicitly. Indeed, he opposes the artisan's way of life to the courageous man's. Although the indignant or courageous man is the exemplary citizen, he is not equipped to inquire into the law. The artisan, specifically the poet, is equipped at least to begin the inquiry into law because his leading concern is with what things are rather than with whether they are noble or base.

3. *Poetry,* kalâm, *dialectic, and political science*

The laying down of the law already signifies the choice of a way of life. The law does not command different things for different *individuals*. The law may command different things for different *kinds of people*–for instance, rulers and ruled, citizens and slaves, men and women, and young and old[4]–but the law has one way of life in view in all that it commands: the courageous man's. All of the laws for other kinds of people serve the promotion of this way of life. Neither the courageous man nor the law itself is capable of teaching the inquirer into the law what he needs to know, namely, why the courageous way of life is more desirable than any other way of life. But, the poet, who has access to other ways of life, can answer this question.

The citizen-legislator attempts to defend the law merely on the basis of his credentials as a courageous man. Although such defenders are sufficiently spirited, they lack the knowledge needed to provide the correct defense. Poetry provides (or at least begins to provide) the philosophic defender of the law, the philosophic *mutakallim*, with the needed knowledge. Consequently, a knowledge of the art of poetry is prerequisite to a knowledge of philosophic *kalâm*. (Although poetry provides the indispensable insight into the multiplicity of the ways of life, this does not mean that it provides insight into all of the possible ways of life. As we will see, the philosophic *mutakallim*, therefore, requires more than the art of poetry.)

That poetry, rather than the law itself, gives one a means of access to the foundations of law first becomes apparent almost immediately after the Athenian lays down the first general prelude to the laws (716a–18a7). He attempts to explain what effect his own prelude has on himself (719a5), and he dramatizes this effect by performing a dialogue between "the lawgiver" and some poets. He casts himself in the role of advocate of the poets and Kleinias in the role of lawgiver. I need hardly remind the reader that Kleinias is a citizen-legislator, not a philosopher-legislator.

In his summary of this passage, Alfarabi underlines the most salient point: Althought poets are free to describe different even contradictory ways of life, the lawgiver should "only defend [*yanṣur*] the one thing that is useful to him" (cf. disc. 4.12 with 719a4–d4). For the citizen-legislator Kleinias, the establishment and preservation of his city are the purposes he serves in laying down legislation for Magnesia. His portion of immortal fame depends upon his serving these purposes. For such a legislator, the means of achieving them is the formation of noble and courageous citizens. The one thing useful to him is the defense of this way of life or of the law that promotes it.

In contrast, poets are not constrained by the need to defend what is useful to them. Their highest purpose is to describe what is. Upon inspection of the human scene, they discover that different people have different, even contradictory, desires and pleasures. By no means do they restrict themselves to describing the courageous man. The Athenian supplies the following example in defense of the poets: According to the poet, the lawgiver prescribed only one size funeral for all citizens, namely, the "medium size" (*tên mesên*) (719d7).[5]

The poet, in contrast, is comfortable presenting stories in which he praises both the wealthy woman's plans for an elaborate funeral for herself and the poor man's plans for a skimpy funeral for himself. It is not merely unreasonable from the economic perspective that the law should demand the same size funeral of all citizens–many laws accommodate such differences.[6] It is also unreasonable from the perspective of the different and even conflicting needs of different kinds of people, thus, the difference between the two characters described by the poet is not merely economic but also a matter of gender.[7]

By means of this dialogue between a poet and the citizen-legislator, the Athenian succeeds in persuading Kleinias, the citizen-legislator, that he needs a supplement to the law, namely, the prelude. The prelude is poetic rather than legal in character. Although the law proper commands one way of life, the prelude will both defend the law (or engage in *kalâm*) and lead its thoughtful reader to speculate about this way of life as well as others (or engage in political philosophy). The law is made more flexible by the addition of the prelude.

Alfarabi attributes the task of laying down preludes that is inspired by poetry to the (philosophic) *mutakallim*. When he first mentioned the contrast between the poet and the legislator, he included the "disputant" (*mukhâṣim*) and the "discussant" (*mutakallim*) in the same class with the poet (disc. 4.12). Later, he distinguishes between the tasks of commanding the law and "talking about" (or rather discussing, *yatakallam*) it (disc. 4.13). Presumably, the person responsible for "discussing" the law would be one of the two human types "whom we [i.e., Alfarabi as opposed to Plato] enumerated" above, namely, the "discussant" or *mutakallim*.[8]

Just as the free doctor is the teacher of the slave doctor, so the philosophic *mutakallim* (Athenian Stranger) who composes preludes is the teacher of the citizen-legislator (Kleinias). The philosophic *mutakallim* is merely the highest aspect of the philosophic legislator. The philosophic legislator is both *mutakallim* and jurist. This legislator as jurist merely infers laws from the foundations he discovers as *mutakallim*. Thus, Alfarabi eventually draws the analogy between the free doctor and the slave doctor, on the one hand, and the (philosophic) legislator and the judge, on the other (disc. 4.14). The most problematic aspect of legislation is not laying down punishments but acquiring political science, the knowledge of the psychological roots or purposes of the law needed to guide this laying down. Furthermore, because of the danger the knowledge of the roots poses to the authority of law, it must never be communicated without the accompanying defense of law (or art of *kalâm*). With these insights into the analogy between the free doctor and the slave doctor, we are brought back to the discussion of preludes and philosophic *kalâm* in chapter 1.

Before concluding this chapter, a few questions need to be raised: What, if anything, is the difference between the insights of poetry and of political philosophy as insights into the soul? Why are the rhetorical and dialectical arguments employed by the philosophic *mutakallim* of a higher rank than the poetic arguments (to speak in accordance with Alfarabi's understanding of Aristotle's *Organon*)[9] used by the poet? According to Alfarabi's Plato, poetry lessens the need of most human beings for the law (disc. 9.7). It is superior to the law at inculcating "moral habits" (*akhlâq*). Alfarabi does not suggest that poetry is capable of inculcating other habits, such as intellectual virtues. Poetic argumentation is insufficient both for inculcating such virtues and for employing them. For this, one must make use of higher forms of speech than poetic argumentation, namely, rhetoric and dialectic. Dialectical speech in particular provides a means of resolving the contradictions between the various moralities or ways of life that poetry is merely able to describe.

True inquiry into law is made possible only by the intellectual virtues. As became apparent in the case of Socrates, the true acquisition of the intellectual virtues places the inquirer beyond the courageous man's indignation. Thus, Socrates could adhere strictly to the dictum that all men are evil involuntarily. If not he, then Plato's Athenian Stranger was capable of reconciling–to the extent it is possible–the indignation of the courageous man and the laws he defends with philosophic moderation.

The right to inquire into the law can be granted only by the law itself. Lest the law submit itself to its own fundamental transformation and thus to its own destruction, it permits only its advocates to inquire into it. True or rational advocacy, however, is not possible without previous inquiry. Who is capable of uncovering the law's purposes or roots? The citizen, who honors that which the law deems noble, is not naturally inclined to question its purpose. The poets possess an awareness of the differing views about what is pleasurable and what noble, and are consequently predisposed to question it. Yet they do not understand fully all of the ways of life, and in particular, the philosophic way of life. For instance, they incorrectly ascribe the philosophers' relative indifference to many bodily pleasures to asceticism rather than to the all-consuming character of their erotic pursuit of knowledge. Presumably, the philosophers are in a better position than poets to understand this way of life.[10] The poets' inevitable misunderstanding of it precludes them from providing an adequate resolution of the contradictions in human life that they represent so aptly.

The most explicit task of the philosophic *mutakallim* is the defense of the law. Because of the conflict between the way of life advocated by the law and the other ways of life, the law stands in need of defense. Any way of life that is not strictly rational can be defended only by arguments that are not strictly rational. Thus, the philosophic *mutakallim* must not only grasp law's purpose (political philosophy) but must also be a master of rhetorical speech (*kalâm*).

Conclusion

This book is divided into three parts. The main purpose of the first part was to show that neither Plato nor Alfarabi is a metaphysical dogmatist, as were the Neoplatonists and Christian natural law theorists. Indeed, what is frequently construed to be the metaphysical dogma of each thinker is in fact his art of *kalâm*. The main purpose of the second part was to draw attention to the gap between the rule of intellect and the rule of law, or between the best city and the second-best city. Even the best city must resort to religion or beliefs to rally the whole city toward its rational goal. The gap between the best city and the second-best city makes the need for a religion and an art of *kalâm* to defend that religion felt all the more strongly. Finally, the main purpose of the third part was to clarify how the art of *kalâm* provides the thoughtful human being with a potential point of entry into the life of reason, the prelude to the law. Although each prelude is placed before a law or before the laws as a whole, it does not originate from the law. At best the law sanctions the existence of preludes. We must turn to poetry, then to rhetoric, and eventually to dialectic to find the resources for the fitting preludes to the laws.

Although nineteenth-century German scholarship claimed to have freed itself from the tendency of the Renaissance to find Neoplatonic doctrine in the Platonic dialogues, it failed in the decisive respect: It continued to view Plato as a metaphysical dogmatist. This view of Plato has gained currency among postmodernists by way of Heidegger. Because Heidegger views Plato as a metaphysical dogmatist, he is able to establish Plato as the origin of the "history of metaphysics." A crucial purpose of this study has been to begin to show that

Plato is not the founder of metaphysics. Above all, I have tried to show that he does not ground his account of politics on metaphysical presuppositions.

Heidegger is right that Christian scholastics ground all of their inquiries on a presupposition about Being, namely, that because the highest being is the eternal God, Being is by definition permanent. In other words, their *metaphysica generalis* (inquiry into being *qua* being) is predetermined by their inquiry into *metaphysica specialis* (theology). And the highest objective of their *metaphysica specialis* is to prove God's existence. In contrast, Plato's *metaphysica specialis* is intended not as a demonstrative theology but as his rhetorical art of *kalâm*. Far from providing a demonstrative ground for politics, this theology merely serves as a rhetorical defense of law.

Plato's inquiry into politics is actually a phenomenological analysis of the needs of the human soul as they manifest themselves in politics, or a political psychology. This psychology is not metaphysical in at least two senses. First, Plato does not argue, as some modern thinkers do, that the human mind is the ground of the natural whole. Second, Plato does not assume the existence of human *nature* when he inquires into politics. For instance, he does not assume that human beings possess principles of practical reason by nature. Rather, he treats politics phenomenologically. He interrogates the commonly accepted opinions about the divine origins of law. Through such an interrogation he is led to wonder whether what makes law divine is, on the one hand, that it is permanently inscribed in the divine order underlying the whole or, on the other hand, that it promotes some opinions about what is just and what is noble as if they were divine or from on high. Although the shame-filled human being lives in fear of these opinions and the indignant human being honors them, Alfarabi's Plato nowhere argues that these opinions are natural or permanent. (True, the *kalâm* or rhetorical defense of these opinions may require that one argue as if they are natural.) On the contrary, both the shame-filled life and the indignant life proved self-contradictory and "unnatural" at every turn. The defectiveness of these ways of life was most evident in their inability to inquire into the truth of the opinions the law promotes. Ultimately, nature only uncovers itself here at the limit of the opinions inculcated by the law. The truly natural way of life proves to be the life of inquiry into the truth of these opinions.

Whereas metaphysical dogmatists attempt to replace the popular myths about the order of the divine and natural order with a demonstrative metaphysics, Alfarabi's Plato recognizes the futility of this objective. Plato, like Socrates, possesses knowledge of his ignorance above all about the order of the whole.[1] Although he lacks this knowledge, through an analysis of the needs of the human soul he becomes aware of the defectiveness of the popular myths. They fail to meet the human needs they promise to meet. Consequently, the theology in bk. 10 is intended not as an equally dogmatic replacement for the popular myths but merely as a corrective for their defects from the political or human point of view. The achievement of a demonstrative theology is not only futile but also unnecessary because of the heterogeneity of human nature and the nature of the whole.

Plato arrives at the conclusion that human nature exists as the consequence of a phenomenological analysis of the needs of the human soul. He does not assume the existence of such a nature. Human nature merely proves to be the most accessible part of the order underlying the whole. Indeed, the (natural) human desire to know the order of the whole is the foremost evidence of the existence of such an order. Of course, it is possible to reduce this human desire to a choice to project order, as does Nietzsche, if not Heidegger. That it is possible does not make it true. The only way to determine which interpretation is true is to begin (without assumptions) by inquiring into the political things as they present themselves. The inquirer has no more right to begin by assuming the nonexistence of human nature or the natural whole than by assuming their existence.[2]

Those who begin by assuming their nonexistence believe that rational human inquiry is little more than a decision to impose order dressed up as a desire. Thus, philosophy is merely the most spiritual form of a kind of religious impulse to find order where none exists. Perhaps Plato is more capable of grasping the religious impulse to project an order on the whole than are those who reduce philosophy to this same impulse. Human beings project an order on the whole because their unfulfilled desire to know the whole gives rise to anger (*thumos*). (The decision, choice, or will to impose order whether spiritual or not is barely distinguishable, if at all, from *thumos*.) In order to continue to inquire rather than to project, the philosopher must renounce such anger. Such health of the soul is made possible only by means of a thorough inquiry into the soul.

NOTES

Preface

1. Reiner Schurmann, *Heidegger on Being and Acting: From Principles to Anarchy*, trans. Christine-Marie Gros and Reiner Schurmann (Bloomington: Indiana University Press, 1990), introduction.

2. See, for example, Martin Heidegger, "Time and Being," in *On Time and Being*, trans. Joan Stambaugh (New York: Harper and Row, 1972), 1–24, esp. 21.

3. Martin Heidegger, *Being and Time*, trans. John Macquarrie and Edward Robinson (Oxford: Basil Blackwell, 1973), 34.

4. See Martin Heidegger, *The Question of Being*, trans. William Kluback and Jean T. Wilde (New Haven, Conn.: College and University Press, 1958), esp. foreword.

5. For an early reference to the difference between Being and beings or the ontological difference, see Martin Heidegger, *The Basic Problems of Phenomenology*, trans. Albert Hofstadter (Bloomington: Indiana University Press, 1975), 17.

6. Martin Heidegger, *Kant and the Problem of Metaphysics*, 4th ed., enlarged, trans. Richard Taft (Bloomington and Indianapolis: Indiana University Press, 1990), 4–8.

In spite of his Scholastic prejudice in favor of *metaphysica specialis*, Kant presaged Heidegger's own return to the question of Being. He did so by engaging in the most intense inquiry into what makes knowledge possible. Kant recognized that it was not enough to ask how *metaphysica specialis*, the highest form of "ontic knowledge," was possible; it was necessary to ask how *metaphysica generalis*, the "ontological knowledge" that makes such ontic knowledge possible, was itself possible.

7. Heidegger, *Being and Time*, intro. 1, sec. 4, or pp. 32–35.

8. Heidegger would be uneasy with the claim that he focuses on human action, because he tries to eschew the traditional distinction between theory and practice, rest-

ing as it does on the view that theory concerns the contemplation of permanent essences. When I use *action* in what follows, I refer to human activity prior to any distinction between theory and practice.

9. Heidegger, *Being and Time*, pt. 1, div. 1, chap. 3, secs. B and C, or pp. 122–49.

10. Ibid., 98.

11. As I have already implied above, Heidegger does not begin his inquiry into Being by applying a phenomenological analysis to theoretical understanding, because to do so would be to privilege the permanent and unchanging over the changing. By contrast, Kant's analysis of the forms of intuition as Newtonian space and eternal time begins by privileging unchanging theoretical constructs over mere changeable human action. Similarly to Heidegger, Alfarabi's Plato and Plato's Athenian Stranger (and Socrates) do not begin their analysis of human being with theoretical constructs about immortal gods or God but with commonly accepted opinions about the divine and the role of such opinions in the establishment of law. Now, Heidegger's beginning with the changing realm of human action should not preclude the possibility that there might be a permanent hierarchy of potential human ends, among which philosophy or theoretical inquiry might be included. If by beginning with Being that is not a being—and thus, among other things, not an *eternal* God—Heidegger precludes the possibility that anything might prove to be permanent, then his inquiry into Being must be viewed as dogmatic and insufficiently phenomenological. For how can human beings know before they have even begun to inquire into Being that everything is by definition impermanent? Heidegger's rejoinder that human finitude dictates this seems dubious to me. Why it seems so, I cannot explain here.

12. For evidence that our politics is not as free of belief as one might suppose, it is worth considering tolerance. (See the end of Rousseau's *Social Contract* for his provocative identification of tolerance as the sole negative dogma he requires of his citizens.) The surest sign that tolerance is not strictly rational is that even the tolerant, like the "intolerant" traditional religious believers, exclude those who do not share their views. Tolerant citizens will not admit into their community traditional (intolerant) believers if the latter take their beliefs so seriously as to require that their neighbors share them (lest their souls be consumed by hellfire, etc.) Similarly yet differently, tolerant individuals demand a certain shallowness of religious belief of their neighbors. Unlike the tolerant or the intolerant, Alfarabi's Plato can live with any and all neighbors because he, like Socrates, requires nothing of his neighbors' souls; he only desires to learn about human needs from every human type he confronts.

13. Even when Heidegger discusses less humble practical matters such as "guilt" and "conscience" in *Being and Time*, he approaches them as social phenomena (pt. 1, div. 1, chap. 2 or pp. 312–48). I do not mean to suggest by this that Heidegger's analysis is "anthropological" in a sense he repeatedly denied. I merely mean to suggest that "guilt" and "conscience" in the Christian sense that Heidegger understands them do not concern the public or political realm directly. This is due in no small part to the depth of the distinction between the ecclesiastical and political realms in the Christianity after Luther (as well as the post-Enlightenment Europe) that Heidegger was analyzing. Even though Heidegger was a German Catholic, questions of guilt and conscience—in other words, of the state of one's soul—had for him, as for all Europeans, become a highly interior matter, of concern primarily to oneself and one's priest.

Introduction

1. Muhsin Mahdi, "The *Editio Princeps* of Fârâbî's *Compendium Legum Platonis*," *Journal of Near Eastern Studies* 20, no. 1 (January 1961): 1-2.

2. See *Compendium Timaei Platonis*, ed. P. Kraus and R. Walzer, Corpus Platonicum Medii Aevi, no. 1 (London: Warburg Institute, 1951), 39 (in Arabic part). Dimitri Gutas attempts to use this fragment cited from Maimonides' *Commentary on the Aphorisms of Hippocrates* as proof that the *Summary* is an imitation of Galen's "Synopsis of the *Laws*," an assertion that I will discuss later in this introduction. (See Dimitri Gutas, "Galen's Synopsis of Plato's *Laws* in Arabic," unpublished article to be published by G. Fiaccadori, supplied to me by the author in 1991.)

In this fragment, Maimonides mentions that he had thought that Galen was long-winded in his compendia until he read a particular passage of his *Compendium of Plato's "Laws"* in which he criticizes another author for his long-windedness in commenting on a saying of Hippocrates. Gutas infers from this that Maimonides considered Galen's *Compendium* (which Gutas refers to as his "Synopsis of the *Laws*") to be briefer than his other commentaries on Plato's dialogues. Furthermore, he infers that the brevity of the "Synopsis" is strong evidence that Alfarabi's *Summary*, which is often quite brief in summarizing the *Laws*, is little more than Alfarabi's slavish reproduction of Galen's "Synopsis." I cannot agree that Maimonides' remarks are evidence that he considered Galen's "Synopsis" to be unusually brief: One can criticize another for being long-winded while being long-winded oneself. Maimonides' remarks seem to constitute an ironic attack on Galen.

3. Cicero reproduces in the general prelude to his own laws the religious content of the religious prelude to the laws in Plato's dialogue (cf. Plato's *Laws* 715e7-16a3 with Cicero's *Laws* 2. 7). In contrast, Alfarabi suppresses the religious content of this prelude (see *Summary*, disc. 4.9). In the next two chapters, I will argue that this suppression is in fact the correct interpretation of Plato's intention.

4. Mahdi, "*Editio Princeps*," 11 n. 43, citing al-Bîrûnî, *Taḥqîq ma li-l-Hind min maqûlah* (Alberuni's India), ed. Edward Sachau (London: n.p., 1887), 55:9-20, 59:17-19, 193:11-15.

5. É. des Places, "La tradition indirecte des *Lois* de Platon (livres 1-6)," in *Mélanges J. Saunier*, ed. P. Gardette, P. Gallay, and J. Molager (Lyon: Bibliothèque de la Faculté Catholique des Lettres de Lyon, 1944), 27.

6. Avicenna, *On the Division of the Rational Sciences*, selections translated by Muhsin Mahdi, in *Medieval Political Philosophy*, ed. Ralph Lerner and Muhsin Mahdi (Glencoe, Ill.: The Free Press, 1963), 97.

Avicenna literally says that this treatment is given by both Plato and Aristotle in their respective "books on the laws." He also says that both Plato and Aristotle presented their treatments of kingship in their respective books on the regime, namely, the *Republic* and the *Politics*. In the modern edition of the *Politics*, Aristotle criticizes Plato for discussing in the *Laws* the laws rather than the regime of the second-best city. He seems to imply that Plato should have done in the *Laws* what he did in the *Politics*. Not only is there no evidence that Aristotle wrote a book on laws, but Aristotle criticizes Plato for writing such a book. Of course, there is no evidence that Avicenna had access to Aristotle's *Politics*. In view of Avicenna's probable ignorance of the *Politics*, his assertion about a hypothetical Aristotelian *Laws* is comprehensible. Nevertheless, this does not give a sufficient account as to why Avicenna would have made such a speculation.

7. Alfarabi, *Compendium Legum Platonis* (*Talkhīṣ nawâmīs Aflâṭûn*), Arabic text and Latin translation by Francesco Gabrieli (London: Warburg Institute, 1952).

8. W. Montgomery Watt, review of *Compendium Legum Platonis*, by Alfarabi, *Journal of the Royal Asiatic Society* 3-4 (1953): 160.

9. S. M. Stern, review of *Legum*, by Alfarabi, *Bulletin of the School of Oriental and African Studies (University of London)* 17 (1955): 398.

10. Because my purpose is to draw what inferences I can about how Alfarabi interprets Plato from the analogy he draws between the ascetic and Plato, I cannot fully explore the meaning of this analogy here. Alfarabi hints in it at something that will become clearer later when I discuss his interpretation of the first two books of the *Laws*. All of the monotheistic communities are characterized to a lesser or greater extent by asceticism. The asceticism of Alfarabi's community, like the asceticism of the communities that the Athenian's two interlocutors come from, Crete and Sparta, is symbolized by its laws against wine drinking. One of the leading tasks of Plato's Athenian Stranger in the first two books of the *Laws* is to persuade his interlocutors that their laws should permit wine drinking. His object in doing so is to enable them to join with him in inquiring into the goodness of their own laws as well as to weaken their resistance to changing their laws. Asceticism is perhaps the strongest ally any law can have against those who might see any reason for changing it. As I will explain in chapter 7, it is ultimately contrary to the best interests of the law to resist all change. Plato and, perhaps more strikingly, Alfarabi oppose asceticism not only by advocating wine drinking but also by adopting a more consistent approach to the truth than is adopted by Alfarabi's ascetic.

11. Of course, Alfarabi's use of an unmethodical method—or better yet, his eschewal of method—as a means of limiting access to the sciences stands in stark contrast to the Enlightenment faith in method as a means of providing everyone, or nearly everyone, access to the sciences.

12. See previous note.

13. Alexis de Tocqueville, *Democracy in America*, vol. 2, pt. 1, chap. 20.

14. On the latter point in particular, see Muhsin Mahdi, "Orientalism and the Study of Islamic Philosophy," *Journal of Islamic Studies* 1 (1990): 73-98.

15. As I will show in the next section, the former is the view of Dimitri Gutas. The latter is the view of Watt in his review, cited above.

16. For discussions of the quality of Arabic translations of Greek texts via Syriac in general and the tradition of producing especially accurate translations initiated by Ḥunayn b. Isḥâq in particular, see Majid Fakhry, *A History of Islamic Philosophy*, 2d ed. (London: Longman, 1983).

17. Mahdi, "*Editio*," 6.

18. See Max Meyerhoff's description of the renowned Bait al-ḥikmah (House of Wisdom), the school of translation of which Ḥunayn was the most well-respected member: "During the first half of this 3rd/9th century translations were primarily made into Syriac, then, in the second half, more and more into Arabic, and the older translations were studiously revised." In "From Alexandria to Baghdad," an unpublished translation by Anton Heinen supplied to me by Muhsin Mahdi in 1992, p. 20. "Von Alexandrien nach

Baghdad," *Sitzungsberichte der Preussischen Akademie der Wissenschaften*, 23 (1930): 403.

19. As Majid Fakhry explains in his *History*, al-Ma'mûn was so zealous in his pursuit of the sciences that he sent emissaries to Byzantium in the ninth century to collect Greek texts for translation into Syriac and Arabic.

On Ḥunayn b. Isḥâq's persistence in the search for the best texts available, also see Raymond Klibansky's *Continuity of the Platonic Tradition during the Middle Ages* (New York: n.p., 1982), 15.

20. See É. des Places, *Platon oeuvres complètes* (Paris: Société d'édition "Les belles lettres," 1976), tm. 11, 1re partie, p. ccvii, and L. A. Post, *The Vatican Plato and Its Relations*, Philological Monographs, no. 4 (Middletown, Conn.: American Philological Association, 1934), 6, 9.

21. See Muhsin Mahdi, "Al-Fârâbî," in *Dictionary of Scientific Biography*, ed. C. C. Gillispie, vol. 4 (New York: Charles Scribner's Sons, 1971), 523.

22. See Meyerhoff, "From Alexandria," 23-29 and "Von Alexandrien," 405-09.

23. See Michel Tardieu, "Ṣâbiens coraniques et 'Ṣâbiens' de Ḥarrân," *Journal Asiatique* 273, nos. 1-2 (1985): 21-26.

24. Interestingly, Alexandre Kojève, in the recently published Strauss-Kojève correspondence, indicates that he believes that Alfarabi was probably indebted with respect to his political Platonism to a line of heterodox Neoplatonists, among whom he numbers Julian the Apostate, Sallustius, and Damascius. Kojève makes this claim for three primary reasons: (1) These authors appear to be atheists who look with disdain on Plotinian Neoplatonism; (2) they appear to possess an art of esoteric writing; (3) when the Platonic Academy was exiled first from Athens and then from Antioch by Justinian, Damascius led it to Persia. See Leo Strauss, *On Tyranny*, revised and expanded version, ed. Victor Gourevitch and Michael S. Roth (New York: Free Press, 1991), 269-76, 294-99, 301.

All of the evidence in Tardieu's article (evidence which shows no sign of having been inspired by Kojève's speculation–see the previous note) lends credence to Kojève's speculation about possible links between Alfarabi and Damascius et al. (see especially Tardieu's note that the Emperor Julian prayed in Ḥarrân at the temple of the moon before his final military defeat: "Ṣâbiens coraniques," 1). Nonetheless, I cannot agree on the basis of the texts cited by Kojève (as well as on the basis of his article on the Emperor Julian, "The Emperor Julian and His Art of Writing," chap. 6 of *Ancients and Moderns*, ed. Joseph Cropsey [New York: Basic Books, 1964], 95-113) that the Emperor Julian, Sallustius, or Damascius possessed more than the smallest hint of a political philosophy of the sort one finds in Alfarabi and in Plato. (See Emperor Julian, *The Works of Emperor Julian*, Loeb Classical Library edition, [esp. vol. 1] [London: William Heinemann, 1913]; Sallustius, *Concerning the Gods and the Universe*, ed. and trans. Arthur Darby Nock [Cambridge: Cambridge University Press, 1926]; and Damascius, *La vie d'Isidore*, trans. A.-Ed. Chaignet in Proclus, *Commentaire sur le Parménide*, tm. 3 [Paris: Ernest Leroux, 1903].) Why, if these thinkers possessed a political philosophy, did they not present it openly? Of course, one cannot suggest that they possessed an esoteric or oral tradition concerning the Platonic political philosophy, because, as Strauss often indicates, Platonic political philosophy is the exoteric face of Platonic philosophy.

25. Alfarabi, *Compendium Legum Platonis.*

26. Mahdi, "*Editio.*"

27. For Druart's bases for inferring that the Escurial MS must predate 1277–78, see Alfarabi, *Le Sommaire du livre des "Lois" de Platon*, in a critical Arabic edition and with an introduction by Thérèse-Anne Druart forthcoming in *Bulletin d' Etudes Orientales* (Damascus) 47 (1985), intro., sec. 2 (b). As you will see below, Gutas appears to have been unaware of many of the facts Druart adduces about the chronological relation between the Leiden and Escurial MSS.

28. Dimitri Gutas, "Galen's Synopsis of Plato's *Laws* in Arabic," unpublished article to be published by G. Fiaccadori; supplied by the author in 1991.

29. Thérèse-Anne Druart, "Un sommaire du sommaire Farabien des *Lois* de Platon," *Bulletin de philosophie médiévale* 19 (1977): 43–45. Druart reasonably infers from the fact that the manuscript in which the Escurial MS is included is all written in the same hand, apparently by the eleventh-century doctor-philosopher-theologian Abû 'l-Faraj b. al-Ṭayyib, that the Escurial MS was an abridgement by Ibn al-Ṭayyib (pp. 44–45). Gutas tries to demonstrate that Ibn al-Ṭayyib could not have been the author of the Escurial MS. In order to understand why Gutas attempts this questionable demonstration, see my explanation of Gutas's misreading of Druart's 1977 article. For the "demonstration," see Gutas, "Galen's Synopsis," 3, 7, 8.

30. See Gutas, "Galen's Synopsis," 2. Note also that Gutas refers to *L* in all three of the tables in section 1 of his article as if it were Alfarabi's original.

31. I did not feel the need to include in the body of my text an in-depth analysis of Gutas's three arguments (in sections 1–3 of his article) "proving" that the third text is non-Alfarabian, because they do not represent the divergence from the interpretation of Druart that Gutas implies they do. His arguments are in brief the following: (1) *E* preserves readings of the *Laws* found in the Greek not found in "Farabi's exposition" (Gutas, "Galen's Synopsis," 2) (that is, in *L*). (2) *E* contains material not found in "the long version" (ibid., 4) (that is, in *L*). (3) *E* contains a textual variation from "Farabi's text" (ibid., 8) (that is, *L*) that no mere abridger of a text would make. Druart has included arguments akin to (1) and (2) in the introduction to her forthcoming critical edition of the *Summary* in order to justify *her* interpretation of the textual tradition. Gutas's third argument is of little use other than to show how low an estimate Gutas has of the abridger who compiled *E*. Does one really need a "conscious and demonstrable editorial policy" (ibid., 8) to account for an abridger's replacing *bal wa-* with *lâkin*? As we will see shortly, Gutas's estimate of Alfarabi is only slightly higher than his estimate of the abridger of the *Summary* who compiled *E*.

32. Posidonius faults Plato for wasting time with preludes. Alfarabi's attitude toward Plato's innovative introduction of preludes, however, is altogether positive: Alfarabi does not merely summarize but elaborates upon Plato's treatment of preludes—see *Summary*, discourse 4.16. (For further discussions of preludes, see chapters 1 and 10.) He favors the addition of preludes to the laws because he, like Plato, is concerned with divine law rather than mere law or law proper. Divine law, unlike mere law, is concerned with opinions and with the soul as well as with the body. Cf. *Summary*, discourse 5.6–9 with the silence in the *Crito* about the soul. Opinions and the soul are affected directly by preludes rather than by the law proper.

Finally, as will become clear in chapter 1, Alfarabi's procedure of summarizing is the reverse of the procedure one would expect a follower of Posidonius to follow. In view of Posidonius's loathing of Plato's preludes, one would expect Posidonius's follower to devote a great deal of time to reproducing the legal code in the *Laws*, set out primarily in bks. 9-12. Alfarabi breaks off his *Summary* precisely at the point in bk. 9 where the Athenian begins laying down the legal code in earnest.

33. See Mahdi, "*Editio*," 6 and in particular the sentence with n. 21 citing G. Bergsträsser, *Ḥunain Ibn Isḥâq: Über die syrischen und arabischen Galen-Übersetzungen* ["Abhandlungen für die Kunde des Morgenlandes" 12. Band, no. 2] (Leipzig: n.p., 1925), Arabic text, 50 and see Gutas (following Mahdi's lead) "Galen's Synopsis," 11 and n. 24.

34. See Mahdi's argument against the same approach to Alfarabi elsewhere. Mahdi, "Al-Fârâbî's Imperfect State," review of *Alfarabi's Perfect State*, by Richard Walzer, *Journal of the American Oriental Society*, 110, no. 4 (1990): 698.

35. Stern says the following in his review: "I would agree . . . with the suggestion of the editor [Gabrieli] himself that it is based on a Greek compendium of Plato's *Laws* (we know that there existed a certain number of Greek compendia of Plato's works)." But Stern goes on to show that he has a higher estimate of Alfarabi than does Gutas: "But then the attribution to Farabi can hardly be maintained, for it is difficult to see why Farabi should have made a compendium of a compendium." Stern, review of *Legum*, by Alfarabi, *Bulletin of the School of Oriental and African Studies* 17 (1955):398.

36. For the rare cases of the latter usage, see discourses 3.6; 5.3 and 5.15; and 7.2.

37. For the latter "hint," see Leo Strauss, *What is Political Philosophy?* (Glencoe, Ill.: Free Press, 1959; Chicago: University of Chicago Press, 1988), 134 and Mahdi "*Editio*," 6 n. 20.

38 Alfarabi, *Le Sommaire du livre des "Lois" de Platon*, Arabic edition by Druart, intro., sec. 3. Because the later evidence uncovered concerning the true title of Alfarabi's work on the *Laws* is so inconclusive, I believe it is still useful to read Mahdi's discussion of the title of the *Laws* ("*Editio*," 1 n.1). This discussion would probably justify the use of either the term "Compendium" or "Synopsis" as an abbreviated form of the title. I have chosen to use the title *Summary* both for the sake of a greater convenience of distinction between Galen's lost "Synopsis" and the *Summary* and because of the precedent set by Strauss of calling it this in *What is Political Philosohy?*

39. Gutas misleadingly cites Pines's article on the Arabic translation of Aristotle's *Politics* (S. Pines, "Aristotle's *Politics* in Arabic Philosophy," *Israel Oriental Studies* 5 [1975]: 150-60, esp. 154-56) as proof that "Greek political texts seem to have reached Arabic in an abridged form," n. 26 to p. 11 of "Galen's Synopsis." The neglect of Aristotle's political philosophy by the medieval Muslim (and in turn Jewish) philosophers is widely recognized. This neglect is also widely recognized to have been supplemented by an avid interest in Plato's political philosophy. It is unlikely that the neglect of Aristotle's *Politics* was simply the result of an absence of adequate translations. It is far more likely that it was the result of Aristotle's relative lack of interest in the problem of divine law or in law simply. See Muhsin Mahdi, "Philosophy and Political Thought: Reflections and Comparisons," *Arabic Sciences and Philosophy* 1 (1991): 15-20.

40. I will be making use of Druart's critical edition of the *Summary* based on the assumption that the two less complete manuscripts, *K* and *E*, can be used to correct the readings of the manuscript that is both in the best condition and the most complete, namely, *L*. For detailed information on the guiding principles of Druart's method of edit-

ing, see in *Le Sommaire du livre des "Lois" de Platon* the introduction, esp. section 6, "Les principes d'édition."

Direct quotations of the *Summary* are taken from Mahdi's translation of Druart's edition. Sometimes, however, I supply an alternative translation that I prefer along with the Arabic transliteration.

Chapter 1. The Roots of the Laws

1. Cf. Ernest Barker, *Greek Political Theory,* 5th ed. (Strand, U.K.: Methuen, 1960), 339. Despite his extraordinarily high estimation of the legislative sections of the *Laws,* Barker never really discusses the legislation.

2. Plato, *The Laws of Plato,* ed. E. B. England, 2 vols. (Manchester: Manchester University Press, 1921), 1:1.

3. Alfarabi, *Enumeration of the Sciences,* trans. Muhsin Mahdi, in *Medieval Political Philosophy,* ed. Ralph Lerner and Muhsin Mahdi (Glencoe, Ill.: Free Press, 1963), 27 and *Iḥṣâ' al-'ulûm,* Osman Amine, 2d ed. (Cairo: Dâr al-Fikr al-'Arabî, 1949), 107.

4. Leo Strauss, *What is Political Philosophy?* (Glencoe, Ill.: Free Press, 1959), 164.

5. Alfarabi, *Enumeration,* in Lerner and Mahdi, 28–29 and in Amine, (1949), 109–11.

6. Muhsin Mahdi, "Science, Philosophy, and Religion in Alfarabi's *Enumeration of the Sciences,*" in *The Cultural Context of Medieval Learning,* ed. J. E. Murdoch and E. D. Sylla, Boston Studies in the Philosophy of Science, no. 26 (Dordrecht Holland: D. Reidel, 1975), 113, citing *Enumeration* in Amine, 43 (lines 4–6).

This popular art of *kalâm* is usually referred to in English as "dialectical theology." The translation alludes to the dialectical style in which practitioners of *kalâm* present their theology. Although Alfarabi recognizes the need to present a theology in defense of the law, his *kalâm* shares little in common with traditional dialectical theology. Consequently, I have chosen not to use the English phrase to render *kalâm* in order to avoid misleading the reader into confusing the less popular art of *kalâm* developed by Alfarabi with the popular or traditional art of dialectical theology. For an extensive discussion of the popular art, see Richard M. Frank, "The Science of *Kalâm,*" *Arabic Sciences and Philosophy,* 2 (1992): 7–37.

7. See Maimonides' assertion in *Guide of the Perplexed,* 1:71 in edition by S. Munk, *Le Guide des Égarés,* 3 vols. (Paris: n.p., 1856–66), 98a, that the art of *kalâm* he offers to replace that of the popular art of *kalâm* will not contradict "the nature of existence [or contend] against sense-perception." (All page numbers such as "98a" referring to the Munk edition henceforth will be in brackets.)

8. See Strauss's assertion that the rhetoric used in the preludes in the *Laws* should not be confused with the truly philosophic rhetoric described in the *Phaedrus.* Leo Strauss, review of *Man in his Pride,* by David Grene, in *What is Political Philosophy?,* 301.

9. Maimonides, *Guide,* 1:71 [94b]. Also see Alfarabi, *Book of Letters,* in an unpublished translation by Muhsin Mahdi supplied by Mahdi in 1991, paras. 149–50, and in *Kitâb al-ḥurûf,* ed. Muhsin Mahdi (Beirut: Dâr al-Machreq, 1969), paras. 154–55.

10. Maimonides, *Guide*, 1:31 [34b].

11. See Leo Strauss, *What is Political Philosophy?*, 139.

12. See Maimonides' statement above and chapter 10 below.

13. Alfarabi, *Enumeration*, in Lerner and Mahdi, 27 and in Amine (1949), 107.

14. This elevated understanding of *kalâm* as an aspect of the legislative art–indeed, the highest–should be distinguished from another presentation of what could be called a philosophic art of *kalâm* in Alfarabi's *Book of Letters*, trans. Muhsin Mahdi, para. 145 and pp. 2:21 and 22 and in *Kitâb al-ḥurûf*, ed. Muhsin Mahdi, 152. In the *Book of Letters*, the philosophic art of *kalâm* is clearly subordinated to the philosophic legislative art. It appears to be limited in scope to the use of rhetoric. In contrast, in the *Summary* the philosophic *mutakallim* employs both rhetoric and dialectic. (He practices the latter, however, as a student of political science! The truly philosophic *mutakallim* needs to know the truth about what he is defending in order to defend it most effectively.)

Cf. the *Enumeration*, where *kalâm* also seems to be subordinated to political science. Note, however, that political science is purely analytic in the *Enumeration*: it analyzes political phenomena; it does not legislate. This reflects the fact that the *Enumeration* is descriptive of Alfarabi's own community, in which the law was not legislated by a political philosopher. (Perhaps philosophic *kalâm* shares a rank in the *Book of Letters*–a commentary on Aristotle's *Metaphysics*–similar to popular *kalâm* in the *Enumeration* because Aristotle presents an understanding of the arts and the sciences that is closer than Plato's to the everyday or popular understanding presented in the *Enumeration*.) For other accounts–such as the *Book of Letters*, where political science or political philosophy is not merely descriptive–see, for instance, *Attainment of Happiness*, in *Philosophy of Plato and Aristotle*, paras. 57-58, pp. 46-47, where the (political) philosopher is identified with the (philosophic) legislator.

The only other discussion that comes close to the *Summary*'s elevated understanding of *kalâm* is the discussion of the supreme virtuous ruler's art of dialectic–which is actually an art of rhetoric and dialectic–in the *Book of Religion*, in unpublished translation by Charles Butterworth supplied by Mahdi in 1991, para. 6, pp. 7-8 and in *Kitâb al-millah wa-nuṣûṣ ukhrâ*, ed. Muhsin Mahdi, 47-48.

15. Mahdi, "Science, Philosophy, and Religion," 140.

16. I have chosen not to mention Rhadamanthus here, though Kleinias mentions him in close connection with the Athenian's mention of Minos, because his role in legislating for Crete is vague even according to Kleinias's own account. According to Pangle, Kleinias says that Rhadamanthus "regulated judicial affairs correctly," which may or may not mean that he participated in the act of legislation. Another possible reading of the Greek is that Rhadamanthus "distributed judicial penalties correctly" (*dianemein ta peri tas dikas orthôs*), which makes it sound as if Rhadamanthus did not participate in legislating. For another Platonic reference to Rhadamanthus that supports this interpretation, see *Minos*, 318d-20d.

17. Avicenna, *On the Divisions of the Rational Sciences*, trans. Muhsin Mahdi, in Lerner and Mahdi, 97.

18. Cf. Alfarabi, *Virtuous City*, in *Alfarabi on the Perfect State*, ed. and trans. Richard Walzer (Oxford: Clarendon Press, 1985), chap. 15, para. 10 (pp. 244-45); and *Book of Religion*, trans. Butterworth, para. 1, p. 2 and *Kitâb al-millah*, ed. Mahdi, 44.

19. See, for instance, Leo Strauss, *What is Political Philosophy?* 160.

20. Thomas Pangle, "The Political Psychology of Religion in Plato's *Laws*," *American Political Science Review* 70, no. 4 (1976): 1077.

Also see Strauss's suggestion that "the wisdom of the Platonic Socrates is . . . [that] the true knowledge of the souls, and hence of the soul, is the core of the cosmology (of the knowledge of the things aloft)" in *Socrates and Aristophanes* (Chicago: University of Chicago Press, 1966), 314.

21. Alfarabi, *Maqâlah fī aghrâḍ mâ ba'da al-ṭabī'ah* [On the purposes of Aristotle's *Metaphysics*], in *Tis' rasâ'il, risâlah* 2 (Hyderabad: n.p., 1926), 3. And see Mahdi, "Science, Philosophy, and Religion in Alfarabi's *Enumeration of the Sciences*," 130.

Contrast this characterization of the subject matter of *Metaphysics, Lambda* as *kalâm* with Alfarabi's inclusion of the same subject matter within "metaphysics" (*mâ ba-'da al-ṭabī'ah*) in his account of the "generally known" sciences in the *Enumeration*, end of chapter 4, in *Iḥṣâ' al-'ûlûm*, ed. Osman Amine, 3d ed. (Cairo: Anglo-Egyptian Library, 1968), 120–23. It seems that this subject matter is "generally" mistaken for metaphysics. (The role played by *Metaphysics, Lambda* in Aristotle's arrangement of the sciences is already taken up by the popular art of *kalâm* in the *Enumeration*.)

22. See Alfarabi, *Kitâb al-ḥurûf* [Book of letters], ed. Muhsin Mahdi (Beirut: Dâr al-Machreq, 1969), editor's (English) preface, xi.

23. Ibid. Also see *Attainment*, in Alfarabi, *Philosophy of Plato and Aristotle*, para. 55 (pp. 44–46).

24. Mahdi, "Alfarabi on Philosophy and Religion," *Philosophical Forum* 4, no. 1 (1973): 1-25, esp. 12–15 and 19. The claim that philosophy precedes religion may in at least two senses be true and in one sense false (or mythical): Philosophy precedes religion insofar as demonstrative philosophy precedes philosophically revised religion, and false philosophies (which are not truly philosophy) precede popular religion. Philosophy actually follows religion insofar as demonstrative philosophy follows popular religion.

25. Alfarabi, *Book of Letters*, para. 149 in Mahdi trans., 2:24 and in Mahdi ed., 153–54.

26. Leo Strauss, *What is Political Philosophy?*, 148.

27. Ibid.

28. What may be less salutary about modern political beliefs is that they do not appear to be beliefs at all. As I mentioned in the preface, Rousseau reminds us that in spite of its negative character tolerance is itself merely a belief.

29. See Ernest Gellner, *Reason and Culture* (Oxford: Basil Blackwell, 1992), 42.

Chapter 2. Alfarabi's Platonism

1. Leo Strauss, "How Farabi Read Plato's *Laws*," in *What is Political Philosophy?* Muhsin Mahdi's "*Editio Princeps* of Alfarabi's *Compendium Legum Platonis*" also deals in brief with the substance of the *Summary*.

2. To begin with, note that Augustine, following the usage of the Neoplatonists themselves, refers to them as "Platonists." See *City of God*, bk. 8, chap. 12. By "Platonists," Augustine means above all Plotinus and Porphyry. For the role of these two thinkers in Augustine's thought, see the chapter entitled "The Platonists" in Peter

Brown, *Augustine of Hippo: A Biography* (London: Faber & Faber, 1969), 88–100 and L. Grandgeorge, *Saint Augustin et le neo-platonisme*, vol. 8 in *Sciences réligieuses* (Paris: Bibliothèque de l'école des hautes études, 1896), 35 and 48; reprinted, Frankfurt: Unveränderter Nachdruck; 1967.

For the kinship between Christianity and Neoplatonism, see Augustine, *Confessions*, bk. 7, chap. 9 and *City of God*, bk. 8, chaps. 9–11.

3. For Augustine's praise of the "Platonists," see *Confessions*, bk. 7, chap. 20; bk. 8, chap. 2 and *City of God*, bk. 8, chaps. 4–8.

4. Of course, this view is usually derived from Socrates' use of the Ideas. From this it is inferred that Plato divides what is into a world of appearances and the true world of the Ideas. As I noted in the preface, far from accepting such a dichotomy as a Platonic doctrine, Alfarabi is silent about the Ideas in his account of Plato's philosophy. In contrast, the Neoplatonists made a quasi-religious doctrine out of this dichotomy. For evidence that Augustine viewed Plato, and not only the "Platonists," as promoting this doctrine, see *City of God*, 8.11 end. Furthermore, Augustine shares the belief in this dichotomy and mirroring (See A. H. Armstrong, "St Augustine and Christian Platonism," in *Augustine: A Collection of Critical Essays*, ed. R. A. Markus [New York: Anchor Books, 1972], 3–17, esp. 11–12)—although he places greater emphasis on the impediments to bridging the gap between this world of appearances and the ideal otherworld than the "Platonists."

I am not alone in arguing that Augustine confuses Plato with the Neoplatonists. See L. Grandgeorge, *Saint Augustin et le neo-platonisme*, 52–54.

5. See, for instance, *Virtuous City*, in *Alfarabi's Perfect State*, ed. Walzer, chap. 2, para. 2, pp. 94–97 and the *Political Regime*, in an unpublished English translation by Miriam Galston, 1 and in ed. Fauzi Najjar (Beirut: al-Maṭba'ah al-kâthûlîkiyyah, 1964), 31-32.

In a lecture on Alfarabi (delivered in October 1991), Muhsin Mahdi noted that although Alfarabi uses the Neoplatonic theory of emanation, in taking it over he modifies it in one crucial respect: The Neoplatonic God is beyond being and thus beyond the comprehension of the intellect; Alfarabi's God or First Cause is in all cases the highest intellect. Thus, Alfarabi's Neoplatonism is a "decapitated Neoplatonism" or Neoplatonism without the characteristically mystical God. Of course, it is the mysticism of the Neoplatonists proper that is at the root of their disdain for political things.

It could be argued that the Christian tradition, especially Augustine, does not share this view of God with the Neoplatonists. Indeed, Augustine's God is the highest being, rather than beyond being (see *City of God*, bk. 12, chap. 2). More importantly, however, his God, like the One—and unlike Alfarabi's highest intellect—is mysterious (see *Confessions*, bk. 1, chap. 4).

6. For example, Majid Fakhry, "Al-Fârâbî," in the chapter entitled "The Further Development of Islamic Neo-Platonism" in his *A History of Islamic Philosophy*, 2d ed. (London: Longman, 1983), 107–28, esp. 116–18; B. Carra de Vaux, "Al-Fârâbî," in the *Encyclopaedia of Islam*, 1st ed., vol. 2 (Leyden: E.J. Brill Ltd, 1927), 53–55, esp. 54; Abdurraḥmân Badawî, "Al-Fârâbî," in *Histoire de la philosophie en Islam* (Paris: Libraire Philosophique J. Vrin, 1972), 478–575, esp. 538; and most recently, Thérèse-Anne Druart, "Al-Farabi and Emanationism," in *Studies in Medieval Philosophy*, ed. John F. Wippel (Washington, D.C.: Catholic University of America Press, 1987), 23–43. For additional

examples from other authors see Miriam Galston's, "A Re-examination of al-Fârâbî's Neoplatonism," *Journal of the History of Philosophy* 15, no. 1 (January1977): 14.

For the notable exceptions to this consensus, whose lead I am following in this chapter, see Paul Kraus, "Plotin chez les Arabes. Remarques sur un nouveau fragment de la paraphrase des *Ennéades*," *Bulletin de l'Institut d'Egypte* 23 (1941): 269–71; Muhsin Mahdi's "introduction, 1962 Edition" to his translation of *Alfarabi's Philosophy of Plato and Aristotle*, rev. ed. (Ithaca: Cornell University Press, 1969), esp. 3–4 (note Mahdi's striking reminder that one of the philosophers' greatest opponents, al-Ghazâlî, recognized the inauthenticity of Alfarabi's supposed Neoplatonism); and Galston's "Re-examination."

7. Contrast the *Book of Letters*, perhaps his most metaphysical work, in which he presents neither his nor Aristotle's *metaphysica specialis*.

8. Fakhry, *History*, 117.

9. As I will explain in chapter 4, there may be some basis for the speculation that Alfarabi wrote a commentary on the *Republic* that has not come down to us. There is not, however, any basis for such speculation about the *Timaeus*–the traditional vehicle for the Neoplatonic appropriation of Plato.

10. For the view that these passages present a (revised) religion rather than Alfarabi's metaphysics, see *Kitâb al-millah wa-nuṣûṣ ukhrâ*, ed. Mahdi (Arabic introduction), 12–13 cited in Miriam Galston, *Politics and Excellence: The Political Philosophy of Alfarabi* (Princeton: Princeton University Press, 1990), 201 n. 43, and *Alfarabi's Philosophy of Plato and Aristotle*, trans. Mahdi, "introduction, 1962 Edition," 4.

11. See, for instance, *Political Regime* in ed. Lerner and Mahdi, 33–34 and in ed. Najjar, 72–73. Alfarabi treats the voluntary or volition, as Aristotle does, as desire guided by intellect. Cf. Thomas Aquinas's view of volition as something more than the equivalent of the Aristotelian desire for ends (*Summa Theologiae*, la2ae. 8, 2). More importantly, his view of volition or will is influenced profoundly by Christian tradition. Indeed, will is determined not only by knowledge but also by original sin (*Summa Theologiae*, la2ae. 83, 1 and 3). Although original sin is a Christian doctrine, its existence depends upon the view shared by all of the monotheistic traditions that human beings, being made in the image of God, possess a radical freedom of the will with respect to sin akin to God's freedom in creating the world out of nothing.

12. A further irony worth noting is the similarity, in spite of the more obvious opposition, between the conviction of the medieval natural law theorist, Thomas, that *both nature and politics* are teleological and the conviction of modern natural law theorists (such as Hobbes) that *both nature and politics* are nonteleological.

13. Richard Walzer, "Al-Fârâbî," in *Encyclopaedia of Islam*, new ed., vol. 2, pt. 2 (Leiden: E. J. Brill, 1965), 779–80.

14. Walzer, "Al-Fârâbî," 779 and *Alfarabi's Perfect State*, 420.

15. Walzer, "Al-Fârâbî," 779 and *Perfect State*, 424–26.

16. See Ralph Lerner, "Beating the Neoplatonic Bushes," review of *Alfarabi's Perfect State*, by R. Walzer, *Journal of Religion* 67 (October 1987): 510–17, esp. 517. Also see Mahdi's "Al-Fârâbî's Imperfect State," review of *Alfarabi's Perfect State*, by R. Walzer, *Journal of the American Oriental Society* 110, no. 4 (1990): 696–705.

Cf. Walzer's view with my discussion in the introduction of Kojève's proposal that Alfarabi's predecessors in political philosophy were Damascius, Sallustius, and the Emperor Julian rather than Plato.

The most extensive contemporary treatment of the Middle Platonic tradition with which Alfarabi could have had contact–that is, the Greek rather than the Latin thread of the Middle Platonic tradition–is John M. Dillon's *Middle Platonists* (London: Duckworth, 1977). The most extensive treatment of the Latin tradition of Middle Platonism is Stephen Gersh's *Middle Platonism and Neoplatonism: The Latin Tradition,* 2 vols. (Notre Dame, Ind.: University of Notre Dame Press, 1986).

I found no hint of a developed political philosophy among the authors discussed by Dillon other than Cicero (who, of course, is part of the Latin tradition of Middle Platonism). This is not surprising in light of Dillon's concern in his book with "a type of Platonism, heavily influenced by Pythagorean transcendentalism and number mysticism, which, rather than the Stoicizing materialism of Antiochus, is the foundation of Middle Platonism, in the sense in which that term is understood in this book" (*Middle Platonists,* 182–83). The political philosophy of Plato and of Alfarabi is, if anything, a response to or rejection of the madness of Pythagorean metaphysics (see Leo Strauss, *What is Political Philosophy?,* 186 n. 23).

17. See Walzer, "Al-Fârâbî," 779.

18. Alfarabi, *Harmonization,* 1 in an unpublished translation by Fauzi Najjar supplied by Charles Butterworth in 1986.

19. See, for instance, B. Carra de Vaux, "Al-Fârâbî," in *Encyclopaedia of Islam,* 1st ed., 2: 54.

20. Galston, "Re-examination," 15. Oddly enough, Druart in "Al-Farabi and Emanationism," 26 follows Galston in affirming Alfarabi's awareness that the *Theology* is not an authentic Aristotelian work, but, contrary to Galston, maintains that Alfarabi viewed it as supplying a necessary supplement to Aristotelian "metaphysics." To justify such an interpretation, Druart must (1) deny that other texts in which Alfarabi uses such Neoplatonic imagery, such as the *Virtuous City* and *Political Regime,* are fundamentally political writings (and affirm that they are metaphysical writings) (esp., pp. 26 and 38) and (2) affirm that the *Harmonization* is as much a philosophic book as, for instance, the *Book of Letters* (p. 24). The former, I have already argued, is implausible, and the latter, I will argue, is implausible.

21. Galston, "Re-examination," 17.

22. *Alfarabi's Philosophy of Plato and Aristotle,* translated (and introduced by) Mahdi, "introduction, 1962 Edition," 4. Contrast Druart, who seems to think that although Alfarabi's emanationism is not Aristotelian, he intends it to be a replacement for Aristotelian metaphysics ("Emanationism," 24).

23. Note that the Plato treated in the *Summary* is referred to by Alfarabi as "the wise" Plato (disc. 5.18[c] and conclusion). The scribe for the Leiden manuscript has mistakenly referred to Plato in his colophon to the *Summary* as the "divine Plato"–see *Compendium Legum Platonis,* ed. F. Gabrieli, p. 43, line 14 and in unpublished translation by Mahdi, 45.

24. Galston, "Re-examination," 15.

25. Indeed, as a result of the above inquiry into the *Book of Letters* and in particular into what it reveals about Aristotle's purposes in writing his *Metaphysics,* I am inclined to acknowledge agreement between Plato and Aristotle on the crucial question of the possibility of metaphysical knowledge. Contrast Leo Strauss, *On Tyranny,* revised and expanded edition with Strauss-Kojève correspondence (New York: Free Press, 1991), 277.

I cannot, however, rule out the possibility that Alfarabi merely makes it *appear* that Aristotle agrees with Plato on the question of the possibility of metaphysical knowledge because the belief that metaphysical knowledge is possible is somehow inimical to Alfarabi's own (Platonic) political philosophy.

26. Galston, "Re-examination," 31.

27. Alfarabi, *Harmonization*, trans. Najjar, 39. Contrast Maimonides, *Guide*, 2:15 [34a].

28. Druart, "Emanationism," 28–29, 36–37.

29. Muhsin Mahdi, "Alfarabi against Philoponus," *Journal of Near Eastern Studies* 26, no. 4 (October 1967): 236–37 n. 9.

30. For additional, although by no means exhaustive, thoughts on Galston's account of Alfarabi, see my review essay on *Politics and Excellence* (as well as books by Stephen Torraco and Marvin Fox) in Joshua Parens, "Theory and Practice in Medieval Aristotelianism," *Polity* 26 no. 2 (1993): 317–30. As the reference to Aristotle in the title of this essay implies, I take a different approach to her book in that essay from the one I take here.

31. All page numbers in this section refer to the pages of Miriam Galston's *Politics and Excellence: The Political Philosophy of Alfarabi* (Princeton: Princeton University Press, 1990).

32. On this point in particular, compare my review of Galston's book in Parens, "Theory and Practice," 319–22.

33. Alfarabi is reported to have written such a commentary, but it has not survived. The report that we have about this commentary from Ibn Ṭufayl in *Hayy Ibn Yaqzan* is, morally speaking, quite shocking. See Ibn Ṭufayl, *Hayy Ibn Yaqzan*, selections translated by George Atiyeh, in Lerner and Mahdi ed., 140 and *Ḥayy Ben Yaqdhân*, ed. Léon Gauthier, 2d ed. (Beirut: n.p., 1936), 13–14.

34. I believe that I have shown in my discussion of the introduction to the *Summary* that Alfarabi acknowledges the necessity of, and therefore is willing to follow the example of, Plato's esotericism. See the introduction to the present book.

Galston gives some weight to the political purpose of Plato's and Alfarabi's esotericism and even reports Alfarabi's treatment of that purpose in the introduction (pp. 37–38). By making this purpose secondary, however, she enables herself to neglect its role in favor of what she considers to be the far more important pedagogical purpose, i.e., enabling students to discover the truth on their own (p. 52).

35. The tendency to reject the distinction between more and less exoteric works is particularly striking in an author who did such a fine job in her "Re-examination" of revealing the exoteric, that is to say, purely political, import of the *Harmonization*.

Chapter 3. Natural Right versus Natural Law

1. Just how far Plato's view diverges from natural law theory is indicated by what Alfarabi describes as Plato's recourse to "religion" and consequently to an art of *kalâm* even in the best city. Even in the best city, reason is not able to rule in a thoroughgoing manner.

2. For such references to the *Sophist,* see the opening lines of *Being and Time.* For such references to the *Republic* and *Phaedrus,* see Martin Heidegger, *Nietzsche,* vol. 1, *The Will to Power as Art,* trans. David Farrell Krell (San Francisco: HarperCollins, 1991), chaps. 19-24, esp. 22 and 23. And on Heidegger's view that Plato, not merely Nietzsche's "Platonism," attributes a doctrinal role to the distinction between ideal and appearance in Plato, see ibid., pp. 149-51. One reason why Heidegger falls prey to this misinterpretation of Plato is that he fails to recognize that Socrates' initial recourse to the "doctrine of Ideas" did not have a metaphysical but rather a moral or political motivation—he has initial recourse to the Ideas in order to account for the noble or beautiful and the good. See *Parmenides* 130b and *Phaedo* 100b–c.

Similarly, in *Disseminations* (trans. Barbara Johnson [Chicago: University of Chicago Press, 1981), Derrida's book on the *Phaedrus,* he is interested above all in what he deems to be Plato's primary action as the founder of the Western history of *metaphysics,* namely, the promotion of "logocentrism." According to Derrida, Socrates originated the quintessential logocentric (or metaphysical) argument that speech is superior to writing. Derrida's leading argument is that speaking does not present a more accurate account of the way things are than does writing. On the contrary, just as the reader of texts is in fact herself or himself a writer of said texts, so all speaking, including speaking about nontexts, is a rewriting of the text of "reality." In other words, all speech and all writing are both, in a sense, creative writing.

3. See the preface, n. 1.

4. For a similar but far briefer elaboration of this same argument, see Joseph P. Maguire, "Plato's Theory of Natural Law," in *Yale Classical Studies,* ed. Alfred Bellinger (New Haven: Yale University Press, 1942), 10: 153 and 175. Also see John Wild, *Plato's Modern Enemies and the Theory of Natural Law* (Chicago: University of Chicago Press, 1953), esp. 139.

At the 1991 Midwest Political Science Association meetings in Chicago, Robert W. Hall of the University of Vermont (Department of Philosophy) presented a paper entitled "Plato's Theory of Natural Law Revisited," in which he defended the interpretation of Solmsen and Maguire. In his paper, Hall presented his defense as a response to Gisela Striker's argument in favor of the traditional view that the Stoics offered the first theory of natural law (Gisela Striker, "Origins of the Concept of Natural Law," in *Proceedings of the Boston Area Colloquium in Ancient Philosophy,* ed. J. G. Cleary [London: n.p., 1987], 2: 79-94).

5. Although it has traditionally been argued that natural law made its first appearance with the Stoics, Strauss shows that the natural law teaching of the Stoics and of Thomas Aquinas have only a name in common. Only the confluence of the Stoic natural law teaching or of the "Ciceronian natural-law teaching" with revealed religion produces the mature form of the natural law teaching, i.e., Thomas's natural law teaching (see Strauss, *Natural Right and History* [Chicago: University of Chicago Press, 1953], 153). Cf. Striker's presentation of Strauss's view (in Striker, "Origins," p. 80). Striker conflates the mature form of the natural law teaching with its Stoic form, much as Robert Hall (like Solmsen before him) conflates it with the Platonic natural right teaching.

6. Friedrich Solmsen, *Plato's Theology* (Ithaca: Cornell University Press, 1942), 170.

7. Ibid., 156 and 167, and similarly Eric Voegelin, *Order and History*, vol. 3, *Aristotle and Plato* (Baton Rouge: Louisiana State University Press, 1957), 227.

8. Solmsen, *Plato's Theology*, 133.

9. Of course, the fact of human disobedience to these universal ethical principles raised a problem for the far more profound thinker, Thomas Aquinas, who solved the problem by acknowledging a divergence between the existence of the principles and the diversity of conclusions drawn from these principles. See Leo Strauss, "On Natural Law," in *Studies in Platonic Political Philosophy* (Chicago: University of Chicago Press, 1983), 142.

10. Solmsen, *Plato's Theology*, 167 bottom.

11. Jerome Hall, "Plato's Legal Philosophy," *Indiana Law Journal* 31, no. 2 (Winter 1956): 183. Contrast Alfarabi's statement that "the idea of the Philosopher, Supreme Ruler, Prince, Legislator, and Imam is but a single idea" in the *Attainment of Happiness*, in *Philosophy of Plato and Aristotle*, para. 58, p. 79. According to Alfarabi, the "philosopher-legislator" and not the written (or even "natural") law embodies what Hall calls "perfect knowledge." See chapter 4.

12. Ibid., 192 and esp. n. 72.

13. Ibid., 204.

14. Hall is not alone in making this argument. For example, see Werner Jaeger, "Praise of Law," in *Interpretations of Modern Legal Philosophies*, ed. Paul Sayre (New York: n.p., 1947), 365 and Glenn R. Morrow, "Plato and the Law of Nature," in *Essays in Political Theory Presented to George H. Sabine*, ed. Konvitz and Murphy (Ithaca: Cornell University Press, 1948), 24–33.

15. Werner Jaeger, "Praise of Law," 352–75.

16. Ibid., 371 and Huntington Cairns, *Legal Philosophy from Plato to Hegel* (Baltimore: Johns Hopkins University Press, 1949), contrast the first accurate paraphrase on p. 35 with the second inaccurate paraphrase on p. 36.

17. Esp. see ibid., 29.

18. Frequently, the legalists turn away from the *Laws* to the *Republic* and its so-called "theory of Ideas" to justify such an interpretation: Hall, "Plato's Legal Philosophy," 205; Jaeger, "Praise of Law," 366–67 and 372; and Cairns, *Legal Philosophy*, 35. Ultimately Solmsen, who exemplifies the ethical interpreter of the *Laws*, acknowledges the greater debt of Christian natural law to the "theory of Ideas" than to bk. 10 of the *Laws* (Solmsen, *Plato's Theology*, 191–92).

Chapter 4. Is the Best City Ruled by Law?

1. Mahdi, "Science, Philosophy, and Religion in Alfarabi's *Enumeration of the Sciences*," 144.

2. *Alfarabi's Philosophy of Plato and Aristotle*, trans. Mahdi, 66 and *De Platonis Philosophia*, ed. F. Rosenthal and R. Walzer (London: Warburg Institute, 1943), 21.

3. *Timaeus* 17c and 26c8.

4. Leo Strauss, "Farabi's Plato," in *Louis Ginzberg Jubilee Volume*, ed. Saul Lieberman, Shalom Spiegel, Solomon Zeitlin, and Alexander Marx (New York: American Academy for Jewish Research, 1945), 380 n. 55.

5. Strauss did not limit this view of Alfarabi's (as well as of Maimonides') understanding of Plato to the article under discussion. See Strauss, *Philosophy and Law,* trans. Fred Baumann (Philadelphia: Jewish Publication Society, 1987), 103 and 109–10. And see Galston's recapitulation of this as Strauss's interpretation in *Politics and Excellence,* 147 n. 5 and Joel Kraemer's affirmation of this interpretation in "The *Jihâd* of the *Falâsifa,*" *Jerusalem Studies in Arabic and Islam* 10 (1987): 292, 316.

In this passage, Strauss seems to have confused Cicero's plan for his own *Republic* and *Laws* with Cicero's interpretation of the relation between Plato's *Republic* and *Laws.* As I explained in the introduction, Cicero's *Republic* presents his understanding of the regime of the best *politically possible* city (a city of the kind found in Plato's *Laws*) rather than his understanding of the regime of the best or virtuous city (a city of the kind found in Plato's *Republic*). At this time, Strauss seems to have mistakenly identified Cicero's teachings with the Stoic natural law teaching he places in the mouth of one of his characters. Contrast Strauss, *Natural Right and History* (Chicago: University of Chicago Press, 1953), 153–56.

6. *Politics* 1265a10 and contrast Galston, *Politics and Excellence,* 146–47 n.3.

7. Strauss, "Plato," in Leo Strauss and Joseph Cropsey, eds., *History of Political Philosophy,* 3d ed. (Chicago: University of Chicago Press, 1987), 87, citing *Politics* 1265a1-4.

8. Thomas Pangle, "Interpretive Essay" in *Laws of Plato,* trans. Pangle (Chicago: University of Chicago Press, 1988 reprinted by permission of Basic Books, 1980), 504.

9. See Leo Strauss, *The Argument and the Action of Plato's Laws* (Chicago: University of Chicago Press, 1975), 185–86.

10. Thus, this ruler and his successors all form a "single soul."

11. Alfarabi, *Political Regime* in Lerner and Mahdi, 37 and in Najjar, 81.

12. See *Republic* 423d8–26a4, esp. 425b6–8.

13. That the *Laws* and consequently the *Summary* concern the second-best city is borne out by the unusual frequency with which Alfarabi uses the term "tradition" (*sunnah*), especially in discourses 2 and 3. Of course, tradition is that which is good by virtue of its being old, i.e., unchanged for a long time.

14. Also see Alfarabi's treatment of the "rule of tradition" in *Book of Religion,* paras. 9 and 14b in Butterworth, trans. 10 and 18 and Mahdi, ed. 50 and 56. And cf. its rough equivalent in *Virtuous City* in Walzer, ed. chapter 15, para. 13, pp. 248–53. According to Walzer's translation, one of the characteristics of this "second ruler" (*ra'īs thanī*) is that he be a "philosopher." The Arabic term that he renders as "philosopher" is *ḥakīm.* This term should be rendered as "wise man" because (1) there is an Arabic term for "philosopher," namely, *faylasûf,* which Alfarabi uses with great frequency and because (2) this term is used to refer to the "first ruler" (*ra'īs awwal*) described in para. 12, who is the counterpart of Plato's philosopher-king.

15. See *Statesman* 297d5.

16. All the following quotes in this paragraph are from pp. 152–54 in *What is Political Philosophy?* (Glencoe, Ill.: Free Press, 1959).

17. Although Strauss suggests in *What is Political Philosophy?* that Socrates does not appear in the *Laws,* he also notes in the preface to his commentary on the *Laws, The Argument and the Action of Plato's "Laws,"* that Aristotle considered the Athenian Stranger to be Socrates and that Plato gives hints in the *Crito* to the same effect. But in

the *Argument* Strauss also reminds us that the Socrates about whom Plato drops hints in the *Crito* is the fictitious Socrates of the Platonic dialogues. In the *Crito*, the Platonic Socrates acts as the spokesman of the Athenian laws. And in the *Minos*, he discusses the question, What is law?

Plato's Socrates seems to have been more willing to talk about law, as opposed to the virtuous ways of life, than was Xenophon's Socrates. As Strauss himself has indicated, Xenophon's Socrates is probably truer to life than is Plato's (*Xenophon's Socratic Discourse* [Ithaca: Cornell University Press, 1970], 83). This more Socratic Socrates could not be persuaded to discuss the question of what law is. Alcibiades had to turn to Pericles for that (Strauss, "On the Minos," in *Liberalism, Ancient and Modern*, [Ithaca: Cornell University Press, 1989], 65). Perhaps Plato chose to call the Athenian Stranger by that name, rather than by the name Socrates, because he is the most Platonic Socrates, or the incarnation of Socrates which is furthest from the flesh-and-blood Socrates he had known.

18. *The Laws of Plato*, ed. E. B. England, 1:202. See below.

19. Cf. Young Socrates' willingness to deem any regime as "outstandingly right," whether it is ruled by law or not in *Statesman* 293d5-e10.

20. I prefer the term "tyrannizes" here just as I prefer "tyranny" to "despotism" in order to render the cognate *taghallub* (in disc. 4.4-5 and 5.12 which are summaries of passages from the *Laws*–709e and 735d3, respectively–in which the parallel term *turannis* is rendered "tyranny" in Pangle's translation).

21. This use of *ṣawâb* as "rightness" or "correctness" should be compared to the use of *orthos* to describe the virtuous city ruled tyrannically by philosophy at *Statesman* 293c7.

22. On the potentially positive meaning of "tyranny," cf. Seth Benardete's similar treatment of statesmanship unconstrained by law in his commentary to his translation of the *Statesman* in *The Being of the Beautiful: Plato's Theaetetus, Sophist, and Statesman* (Chicago: University of Chicago Press, 1984) , 3.129.

23. See Strauss, *Argument*, 56.

24. See ibid., 71-72.

25. Cf. the relative silence about the ruled in the *Republic*.

26. Bk. 5 is the only monological book in the *Laws*. Although the Athenian orchestrates the silence of his interlocutors, Kleinias, not to mention Megillus, easily accepts his silent role.

27. For Nestor's leading defect, his lack of "effectiveness," see Pangle's n. 9 to bk. 4.

28. A contrast between one of the leading tasks of Socrates in the *Republic* and one of the leading tasks of the Athenian Stranger in the *Laws* is worth noting here. It appears likely from Xenophon's account of Socrates' discussion with Glaucon, Plato's brother (*Memorabilia* 3. 6), that one of Socrates' tasks in the *Republic* is to dissuade Glaucon from pursuing his tyrannical aspirations. Consequently, the philosopher-king is presented as the antithesis of the tyrant in Socrates' account of the kinds of regimes and souls (bks. 8-9, beginning). In contrast, one of the Athenian Stranger's tasks in the *Laws* is to persuade Kleinias, an old man, that he possesses certain tyrannical longings that he should tap as a future ruler-legislator for Magnesia, no matter how un-Cretan that might

be. Consequently, the Athenian Stranger emphatically identifies the most desirable ruler of Magnesia as a young tyrant.

29. I thank Nathan Tarcov for this insight. He mentioned it during a graduate seminar he taught with Ralph Lerner and Hillel Fradkin on the *Laws* and the *Summary* at the University of Chicago in 1990–91.

30. That even this is unlikely in the long run is implied by 740e3 ff.

31. And according to Strauss as well. See Strauss, *Argument*, 82.

32. I thank Nathan Tarcov for this insight about the disobedient character of founders.

33. This fact about the colonists may be a contributing factor in Alfarabi's decision to loosen the Athenian's prohibitions against citizens' participating in trade. I will discuss this decision in chapter 5.

34. It will become fully apparent only in the next chapter why I believe Alfarabi is alluding here and throughout the *Summary* to Islam in particular among the revealed religions.

35. It is worth noting in passing that in Alfarabi's reference to "provisions and nourishment" he says nothing about making such provisions of food "moderate," as the Athenian implies should be the case (737d3). Once again, Alfarabi signals that his regime is not to be as austere as is the Athenian's.

36. *Aṣḥâb* and *ṣaḥâbah* are different plural forms of the same triliteral root *ṣ-ḥ-b*.

37. No doubt Alfarabi's attempts to downplay the difference between the best and the second-best city are in large part responsible for Strauss's suggestion in his earlier interpretation of the *Plato* that Alfarabi's understanding of the relation between the city in the *Laws* and the city in the *Republic* was akin to Cicero's (that is, with the Stoic natural law teaching).

As I mentioned in section 1 above, Alfarabi does not downplay the difference between these two cities in the *Political Regime* and the *Virtuous City* to nearly the same extent that he does in the *Summary* and the *Plato*. Alfarabi's boldness in the *Political Regime* and the *Virtuous City* is made evident when one compares them with Maimonides' even greater reticence about the inferiority of the rule of written law as compared with the rule of living intellect. See Leo Strauss, *What is Political Philosophy?*, 163–64.

38. For an explanation of this metaphor, see *Laws*, ed. England, 1:513.

39. Mahdi rightly reserves the word "regime" to render *siyâsah*; however, I supply "regime" as an alternative for rendering *ri'âsah* because Alfarabi seems to mean what I have been calling the "regime proper," the ruling offices. Alfarabi's distinction between "rulers and rule" seems to be a rendering in reverse order of the Athenian's distinction between "ruling offices and officeholders" rather than his distinction between the ruling offices (and officeholders) and the laws.

40. Although Alfarabi's city in the *Summary* is not one of the ignorant cities, which Alfarabi describes as opposite to the virtuous city (see *Political Regime* in Lerner and Mahdi, 41–42 and in Najjar, 87), it is also not the city ruled by philosophers or "supreme rulers without qualification" (see my discussion of the "supreme ruler without qualification" and the "prince of the tradition" above, as well as *Political Regime* in Lerner and Mahdi, 36–37 and in Najjar, 79–81).

Chapter 5. Plato's City and Alfarabi's Regime

1. *Virtuous City* in *Alfarabi's Perfect State,* trans. and ed. Walzer, chap. 15, para. 2 (pp. 228–31). Cf. *Political Regime* in Lerner and Mahdi, 32 and in Najjar, 69 where the largest political grouping is more vaguely said to be an association of "many nations" (*umam kathîrah*) rather than "the inhabited world." It is reasonable for Alfarabi to present a less optimistic account of the "small, medium, and large" political associations in the *Political Regime,* because its primary focus is not the "virtuous city" but the "regime"–including the vicious regimes–more broadly speaking. (Note that Alfarabi goes into far greater depth about the vicious regimes in the *Political Regime* than he does in the *Virtuous City.* Cf. *Virtuous City* in Walzer, *Alfarabi's Perfect State,* chap. 15, paras. 15–20 [pp. 252–59] with *Political Regime* in Lerner and Mahdi, 42–53 and in Najjar, 87–103.)

2. Muhsin Mahdi, "Alfarabi," in Leo Strauss and Joseph Cropsey, eds., *The History of Political Philosophy,* 3d ed. (Chicago: University of Chicago Press, 1987), 223. Cf. Galston, *Politics and Excellence,* 151–53. Although she cites this same passage, she neglects or considers unimportant an implication of Mahdi's interpretation that is important for this chapter: The virtuous nation and virtuous association of the inhabited world derive their virtue from that of the best city.

3. See, for instance, the *Attainment of Happiness* in *Philosophy of Plato and Aristotle,* paras. 45–46, (pp. 39–40).

4. For the definition of a nation as an association of cities, see the *Political Regime* in Lerner and Mahdi, 32 and in Najjar, 69.

In the *Summary* Alfarabi never uses the term *ummah,* usually rendered as "nation" in translations of his other works, not to mention the phrase *ijtimâ' . . . al-ma'mûrah* (association of the inhabited world). (Cf. *Virtuous City* in Walzer, chap. 15, para. 2 [pp. 228–29].) On the contrary, he refers to the regime under discussion in the *Summary* only as "the city" (*al-madînah*). If he were also to refer to it as a nation, we would expect it to have more than one legislator. When he mentions a multiplicity of cities–which are never said to be in association with one another–he indicates that they have different legislators (see disc. 7.11, 7.13, and 7.14). In connection with the one city that is his main concern, he mentions only one legislator (disc. 2.13).

Alfarabi, however, does use the term *bilad* once, which Mahdi renders as "country" (disc. 8.8). In this passage Alfarabi appears to imply that his "city," unlike the Athenian's, might be composed of more than one "country." (See chapter 7, section 1 for a further discussion of this passage.) Generally speaking, *bilad* refers to a smaller geographical area than does *ummah* (nation). More importantly, although *ummah* carries the connotation of "religious community," *bilad* does not. Thus, Alfarabi cannot be said to imply that his "city" contains a multiplicity of religions (or nations) as does the association of the inhabited world discussed in the *Virtuous City.* Perhaps when Alfarabi appears to imply that his city is composed of a multiplicity of "countries," he has in mind the kind of diversity within the Islamic *ummah* exemplified by adherence to one of the four juridical schools, rather than by adherence to a diversity of religions. Indeed, over the centuries these juridical schools have become associated with specific countries within the Islamic community.

5. See Strauss, *What is Political Philosophy?*, 147.

6. Of course, water—or the lack thereof—during extensive travels can be assumed to have been a problem not only during the original Islamic emigration (*hijrah*) from Mecca to Medina, alluded to in the previous chapter, but also and more importantly during the yearly pilgrimage (*ḥajj*) to Mecca, another one of the pillars of Islam.

To my knowledge, the Athenian never mentions, as does Alfarabi, providing "travel facilities" (*asbâb sabîliyyah*) to the needy (cf. 763d with disc. 6.16). Plato's city is, of course, not large enough to require such facilities. And as we will see in the course of this chapter, his city has far more tightly controlled borders than does Alfarabi's.

7. I am assuming that Alfarabi did not envision the kind of innovations in government envisioned by modern political theorists (which make great size compatible with a kind of democratric and republican regime). For Alfarabi as for Plato, the larger the city, the less conducive it is to a democratic (or republican) regime. Contrast *The Federalist*, nos. 10 and 51.

8. Cf. Zeus's "monarchy" with the rule of Kronos, which, in depriving human beings of participation in their own government (713d), resembles the contemporary more closely than the ancient Persian monarchy.

9. The Athenian does this by never explicitly stating which equality is monarchic and which is democratic. Although which is which becomes clear by the end of this later passage, it is apparent that the Athenian delays clarification to represent dramatically the city's inevitable tendency to blur this distinction (757d8).

10. Using wealth to determine how to distribute honors is only an indirect concession to democracy, because, as we will see in the next section, wealth is the title to rule of the few wealthy rather than the many poor. Because the physical strength of the many poor (democracy) is so much more powerful than intellect (true monarchy), it needs to be counterbalanced by the monetary strength or power of the wealthy. As will be confirmed in the next section, from the point of view of the second-best city's compromise between intellect and physical strength, wealth inclines the city toward intellect and away from physical strength; however, from the point of view of the best city's rule of intellect, recourse to wealth is a concession to the antiphilosophic democratic claims of strength.

11. Note the reversed order of the terms "freedom and friendship," as well as the initial silence about prudence—cf. the reference to "perfect intellect" in discourse 3.15.

12. At least one reason for Alfarabi's favoring of the monarchic element or tyranny is that he is describing the kind of power the legislator should have in establishing the laws at the founding of the city rather than the kind that should be given to the ruling offices that are to administer the laws after the founding (cf. 693b3).

13. See Ibn Bâjjah, *Governance of the Solitary*, trans. Lawrence Berman, in Lerner and Mahdi, *Medievel Political Philosophy*, 127–28 and *Tadbîr al-mutawaḥḥid*, ed. Miguel Asín Palacios (Madrid-Granada: n.p., 1946), 11; for Averroës' indirect reference, see his *Commentary on the "Republic"* (*Averroës on Plato's "Republic,"* trans. Ralph Lerner [Ithaca: Cornell University Press, 1974], 102; see n. to 79.1–8 and 79.7, 8) and for a direct reference, see his "middle or longer" *Commentary on the "Rhetoric"* (*Talkhîṣ al-khaṭâbah*, ed. Muḥammad Salîm Sâlim [Cairo: n.p., 1967], 136 ff.). (For the description of this commentary as a "middle or longer" commentary, see Charles E. Butterworth, "Rhetoric and Islamic Political Philosophy," *International Journal of Middle East Studies* 3 [1972]: 187–98, esp. 188.)

14. Averroës, *Talkhîṣ al-khaṭâbah*, ed. Muḥammad Salîm Sâlim, 138.

15. Alfarabi may also be silent about enslavement to the law in discourse 6.12 if one interprets discourse 6.12 as a summary of 762e2–9 rather than of 770b3–71a6.

16. See Maimonides, *Guide*, 1:31 [34b].

17. See Strauss, *Argument*, 38.

18. See ibid., 46.

19. For the privileged access this eventually offers the wealthy, see ibid., 85.

20. That both intellect and prudence come later than strength is evident from the Athenian's description of the virtues found in the first of the four regimes, dynasty (679c7)—in his account of the genesis of regime types in human history (opening of bk. 3).

The confusion of the older with the more natural is inevitable in any prephilosophic community. The Athenian's interlocutors, coming from Sparta and Crete as they do, make this confusion. See Strauss, *Argument*, 8. Also see Leo Strauss, *Studies in Platonic Political Philosophy* (Chicago: University of Chicago Press, 1983), 195.

21. To gain our bearings in this context, we need only note the use of "a virtuous city" to describe the colony at discourse 5.13 and the use of "the virtuous city" at discourse 6.1.

22. Alfarabi's uses the following terms in the *Summary* for political offices: "ministers [*wuzarâ'*], people with [or men of] experience [*ahl al-tajârib*], advisors [literally, 'those possessing opinions,' *aṣḥâb al-ra'i*], and administrators [*tadbîr*]" (disc. 6.6 and also see disc. 6.10). Cf. these, especially the penultimate term, with his usage in the *Aphorisms* of the term "advisors on great matters" (literally, those possessing opinions on great matters, *dhawû al-ârâ' fî-l-umûr al-'iẓâm*) (*Fuṣûl muntaza'ah*, ed. Fauzi Najjar [Beirut: Dâr al-Machreq, 1971], no. 57 [p. 65]).

23. The possible but unlikely exception is in discourse 6.12 where Alfarabi mentions that Plato commanded "selecting [or electing, *yantakhib*] for important and urgent matters those legislators and also rulers who are men with some experience in freedom." Considering the extraordinary importance of selecting legislators, it seems highly unlikely that Alfarabi would leave this matter to election.

24. Note that Druart in her critical Arabic edition indicates she has not detected any parallel between discourse 6.6 and the *Laws* in this general vicinity.

25. See *Republic* 419a ff. As we will see shortly, Alfarabi, unlike the Athenian, includes artisans as a part, even if a lowly part, of the citizen body. The inclusion of artisans in the citizen body is compatible with the payment of warriors: paid warriors are, in a sense, artisans of war.

26. There is one passage in which Alfarabi *might* refer to establishing borders in discourse 6.3. In this paragraph, he is summarizing a Platonic passage in which, however, the Athenian makes no reference to establishing the city's borders (the passage being summarized could be anywhere between 753e and 755a5, probably either 754a11 or 755a2). Mahdi translates the passage in question (p. 30, line 21 of Gabrieli's edition), "He spoke at length about this, mentioning such things as how a city's *borders are drawn* [*tuḥaddadu*] when it is established." The Leiden MS has *tattaḥidu* (the eighth form of the root *w-ḥ-d*, meaning "to be united"). Gabrieli found this reading problematic: He added diacritical points to the second and third letters of the roots, making it *tuttakhadhu* = *tu'takhadhu* (the passive of the eighth form of *'a-kh-dh*, meaning "to be taken or be occupied"). As cited above, Mahdi offers the most substantial modification by suggesting that

the original *t* be dropped and an additional *d* be added to the end, thus *tuḥaddadu* (the passive of the second form of the root *ḥ-d-d*, meaning "to be delimited"). Although Gabrieli appears not to have been aware of the Kabul MS, it contains his conjectured reading. This could mean that Gabrieli happened upon the correct reading by conjecture. I am inclined to believe that it means that both Gabrieli and the scribe who copied the Kabul MS happened upon the same conjecture. I prefer to follow Druart in keeping the more dependable reading of the Leiden MS: "He spoke at length about this, mentioning such things as how a city *is united* [*tattaḥidu*] when it is established." This passage could refer to the task of uniting the purpose of Knossos with the new Magnesian regime as parents are united with their children (745b–d). If *L*'s reading of this passage is retained, then I am correct that Alfarabi never refers explicitly to the borders of the city.

27. This omission also corroborates my view that Alfarabi attempts to conceal the difference between the colony (second-best city) and the best city.

28. As we will see, Alfarabi eventually treats this subject in a manner not wholly unlike the Athenian's here (in disc. 8.8 and cf. the related and possibly contradictory treatment of this same subject earlier at disc. 2.1[c]).

29. But cf. discourse 8.1.

30. Of course, only strangers are artisans in the Athenian's city (846d).

31. Cf. Alfarabi's narrower use of the phrase "free person or man" (*ḥurr*) in discourse 9.2.

32. See the previous paragraph, discourse 8.10, and compare it with the passage it summarizes, 846d–47e2, esp. 846d–47b2: Whereas the Athenian suggests merely that citizens are artisans in an extended or metaphorical sense, Alfarabi suggests this as well as that artisans are citizens. In a large regime that is ruled monarchically, as compared with a smaller democratic (or republican) city, the meaning of citizenship undergoes a dilution. Once again, Alfarabi's tendency to incline the city toward monarchy draws it closer to the extreme monarchy of contemporary Persia rather than to the monarchy (or aristocracy) of ancient Persia, not to mention the monarchy (or aristocracy) in the *Republic*. Of course, Plato is even more resistant to the inclusion of artisans as a proper part of the best city in the *Republic* than he is to their inclusion as a proper part of the second-best city in the *Laws*.

33. Strangers serve as an indispensable economic (not to mention intellectual) link between the small Greek polis and its neighbors. Because of its greater size, Alfarabi's regime acquires a degree of self-sufficiency that makes such a link dispensable.

34. In the preceding paragraph, discourse 6.8, Alfarabi summarizes the Athenian's discussion of "monarchic and democratic equality" or, as Aristotle calls them, "distributive" and "arithmetic" justice. Aristotle places his discussion of the character traits bearing on the handling of money, treated by Alfarabi in 6.9, immediately before his discussion of the two forms of justice. Alfarabi has reversed the position of these two subjects but has also juxtaposed them. I can only venture the guess that he intends by this imitation and modification of the *Ethics* to criticize Aristotle's choice to treat these character traits concerning money first. Aristotle's procedure in this work seems to be to analyze first that which is more indispensable for political life. Perhaps Alfarabi is criticizing Aristotle's view that ethical traits regarding money are more primary than questions of justice in political life—which could have something to do with Aristotle's silence on the problem of divine law.

35. As a Spartan, Megillus is intensely interested in learning why Sparta has failed to achieve its most ambitious imperial aspirations. The very intensity of those aspirations led Sparta to oppress their so-called allies, Argos and Messene. Because he is aware of Megillus's sensitivity to the accusation that Sparta was guilty of imperialism in its dealings with its allies (see Strauss, *Argument,* 44), the Athenian reserves his harshest criticism of imperialism for the league as a whole rather than for Sparta alone.

36. One might expect Alfarabi to use the Arabic term for divine law here, namely, *sharî'ah.* Perhaps this would have been too bold. Yet he encourages us to think of Islam by using the term *nâmûsîyan* (revelation) in this same sentence.

37. The impression that Alfarabi has a politically practicable theory of a "world state" may derive from a confusion between his best and second-best (or politically practicable) city. Cf. Kraemer, "The *Jihâd* of the *Falâsifa,*" 292 and 316–19 and Galston, *Politics and Excellence,* 151–53. Alfarabi may be capable of conceiving of a world regime ruled by intellect without viewing it as a viable practical aspiration. Indeed, like Plato in the *Republic,* perhaps he envisions such a regime to clarify the limits of politics.

38. See 831c4 and cf. Alfarabi's summary of this passage in discourse 8.3. Note that, despite Alfarabi's inclusion of artisans within the citizen body, he consistently reveals his understanding as to why Plato excludes artisans. The necessary implication of this is that he is fully self-conscious in this deviation from Plato.

Chapter 6. War as a Purpose of the Second-Best Regime

1. Socrates expresses the hope that the virtuous city will live in the midst of a Greek nation in which the cities will not ravage one another as they do in his time (466e–472e5). Nevertheless, Plato makes it apparent that any city such as Socrates' moderate city, ruled by a philosopher-king, would be sorely tested by its less moderate neighbors (see 422a4–23b).

2. Of course, this is not to deny that intellect as something less than itself, namely, as cleverness, is especially useful in war.

3. The Athenian attacks Kleinias's theory of the war of all against all within the early pages of bk. 1 at the same time that he identifies prudence with intellect, and he begins to rehabilitate war in bk. 3 at the same time that he identifies prudence with good breeding. See chapter 8 below for an account of the identification of prudence first with intellect and later with good breeding.

4. Alfarabi appears to view the Athenian's mention of the election of military rulers at so early a stage in his discussion of the election of the ruling offices in general as an indicator of the importance Plato ascribes to war (755c–56b).

Note that I have chosen not to follow Mahdi in translating *asbâb* as "concerns." *Asbâb* is the plural of the term *sabab,* which is sometimes used in a clearly technical fashion to refer to the efficient "cause." See, for instance, discourse 1.1. I believe Alfarabi is also using it in this technical sense in discourse 6.4. Cf. the use of *asbâb* in discourse 6.14 (in Gabrieli ed., p. 33 line 3) and in discourse 6.9 (p. 32 line 8) where it is translated by Mahdi as "concerns."

5. In his *Political Regime* in Lerner and Mahdi, 44 and 46 and in Najjar, 89–90

and 94, Alfarabi characterizes the two "ignorant regimes" that are closest to the virtuous city in terms of their "love of domination" (or tyranny, *maḥabbat al-ghalabah*). The ignorant regime most like the best city, the "timocratic [*karâmiyyah*] city or association," contains citizens who have a moderate love of tyranny. In contrast, the "despotic [or tyrannic, *taghallub*] city or association" contains citizens who have an excessive love of tyranny.

6. To get an idea of how a young tyrant might have responded to this suggestion, see Glaucon's reaction to Socrates' city of necessity in the *Republic*, 372c–74a.

7. Nathan Tarcov and Ralph Lerner drew my attention to the dubiousness of this example.

8. The reader should see not only the passage cited (*Odyssey* 9.112–15) in its context, but also Odysseus's explanation of his decision to investigate whether the Cyclopes are "savage" (*agrioi*) toward strangers (9.175) and his description of their savagery (9.287).

9. According to Muhsin Mahdi in his authoritative work, *Ibn Khaldun's Philosophy of History* (London: George Allen and Unwin, 1957), 263 n. 1, Ibn Khaldûn's use of *'aṣabiyyah* differs from Alfarabi's. The former views *'aṣabiyyah* both as a source of division *and* as a source of unity; the latter views it merely as a source of division. Thus, Mahdi translates *'aṣabiyyah* in his book on Ibn Khaldûn as "social solidarity" rather than as "clannishness."

But perhaps Ibn Khaldûn has not departed from Alfarabi in the respect Mahdi suggests. For Alfarabi, although *'aṣabiyyah* is a source of division between different clans, it is certainly a source of unity within the clan (or *dunasteia*). The common purpose of fighting common enemies unites the members of the clan. Once the law has unified clans into a city, the city's common fighting purpose still derives from the *'aṣabiyyah* of its citizens, especially of its leading clan. Is *'aṣabiyyah* really a greater source of unity than this in the *Muqaddimah*? As Mahdi himself notes, Ibn Khaldûn never identifies what he calls the "natural rule or governance *(mulk ṭabī'ī)*" in which one clan rules a group of other clans by virtue of its superior *'aṣabiyyah* without the assistance of a law (divine or "rational") as a "regime" (ibid., 264–65). The reason why he does not refer to it as a regime is obvious: The result of this kind of rule is not the minimum of internal peace necessary for political life but "constant war [i.e., civil war] and confusion" (ibid., 265).

For Mahdi's two discussions of the role of *'aṣabiyyah* in the *Muqaddimah*, see ibid., 193–204 and 253–70. For all of his citations of the *Summary* (referred to in ibid. as *Nawâmîs*), see the footnotes on pp. 236, 256, 260, 262–65, 268, 274, 282, and 284.

Chapter 7. Legal Innovation: Law as an Imitation of Intellect

1. See Thomas Aquinas, *Summa Theologiae*, la2ae.99, 2. Thomas, however, allows for the lawfulness of killing in self-defense (in contrast to Augustine) and the righteousness of waging just war (ibid., 2a2ae.40, 1 and 64, 6).

2. Contrary to what one might expect, Thomas identifies "conscience" as a "habit" and "act" rather than a "power" (or "faculty") (ibid., la.79, 13).

3. See Strauss, *Argument*, 100–101.

4. This desire for knowledge is more fundamental than the desire for mastery, because the latter is a reaction to the original failure to grasp the whole through one's

primitive awareness of it. In contrast, the former is merely a more developed form of the original awareness of the whole.

5. In the next chapter, I will explain that in the *Laws* the two political cures are the morality of shame and the morality of indignation. Neither of these cures exists at present in its distinct ancient form, but some mean between them constitutes the morality of practically all human beings in the United States.

6. In the *Political Regime,* Alfarabi attributes *national* differences in large part to climate. Differences in climate give rise to national differences by virtue of three things: "natural makeup" (*khilaq ṭabî'iyyah*), "natural character" (*shiyam ṭabî'iyyah*), and language. According to Alfarabi, language is not merely of conventional origin but "is composite (it is conventional but has a basis in natural things)." *Political Regime* in Lerner and Mahdi, 32 and in Najjar, 40.

7. The verb rendered here "to control" has the root form, *gh-l-b,* from which the various terms referring to conquering, despotism, and, above all, tyranny throughout the *Summary* are derived.

8. See 788b, which Alfarabi never summarizes in discourse 7, and 797a ff., which he does summarize.

9. With the qualification "or most" Alfarabi reminds the reader that even this supreme ruler may not rule all nations.

10. Another difference between the *Summary* and the *Attainment* that should be kept in mind is that the prince in the *Attainment* rules over a multiplicity of *nations* all of which seem to be afforded the leeway to pursue their own religion or their own version of the law given by the prince. As we saw in chapter 5, the legislator in the *Summary* is never said to rule over more than a city, let alone a multiplicity of nations.

For Alfarabi's discussion of the prince's rule of "all or most nations," see the *Attainment of Happiness* in *Philosophy of Plato and Aristotle,* paras. 44–46 (pp. 38–40).

11. *Ṭâ'ifah* is the reading of the Escurial MS. Retention of the reading of the Leiden MS ("person" [*wâḥid*]) would make the point even more emphatically. In either case, Alfarabi speaks of the need to administer carefully not merely each "region" (*buq'ah*) but, at a minimum, each "group" in a region.

12. Alfarabi does use the term "country" to refer to the area that one governor might rule. As I have already indicated in the introduction to chapter 5, the term rendered "country," *bilad,* does not refer generally speaking to an area as large as a "nation" (*ummah*). Above all, *bilad* does not carry the connotation of circumscribing a religious community, as does *ummah.* Indeed, the Islamic *ummah* is composed of a number of countries. Furthermore, as noted earlier, *bilad* could be used to refer to different countries (and even different climatic regions), such as now belong to different juridical schools within Islam.

The two terms Alfarabi uses that Mahdi renders as "group" are *qawm,* pl. *aqwâm* and *ṭâ'ifah.* He usually uses the latter term in the phrase *ṭâ'ifah min al-nâs,* literally "group of people," and it is even more indeterminate in meaning than *aqwâm,* which usually refers to groups of a size smaller than a city. This is evident in Alfarabi's usage, especially in discourse 5.18 and 6. 3, where he uses the term to refer to a part of the city. There is, however, one instance in which he uses *qawm* to refer to all of the people in the city (disc. 3.4). According to Druart's second appendix, he uses the term *qawm* (or its plural form) in the following passages: discourse 1.5, 7 (twice), 13, 15; 2.1 (twice) and

2 (twice); 3.2 and 4 (twice); 5.7, 9 (twice), 18; 6.3; and 8.4 and 8. Although I have not made an exhaustive search through all of his uses of *ṭâ'ifah*, and Druart does not provide a listing of the instances in which the term is used, it is worth comparing his use of it in discourse 2.1(c) and (e) with his use of it in discourse 8.7-8.

13. Cf. this analogy with the only vaguely related passage in the *Laws* at 843e.

14. The only people who are truly free under the rule of written law are those who are capable of doing without its guidance. See discourse 9.7.

15. See Strauss, *What is Political Philosophy?*, 146.

16. Alfarabi already set a precedent of neglecting the Athenian's discussions of family and private matters in discourse 6. More specifically, he omits a summary of marriage (771e-776b5); of the effect of marriage on common meals (779e-81d7); of the desires for food, drink, and sex and sacrificial rituals (781e-83b2); and of procreation (783b3-85b10).

17. See Maimonides, *Guide*, 1.31 [34b].

18. And contrast Alfarabi's description of Zeus as "the father of mankind" (disc. 1.1).

19. The model of the Egyptians reappears in the discussion of conservation and innovation in bk. 7 (799a).

20. Indeed, the roles both of chanting prayers and singing the call to prayer were not a source of shame in Alfarabi's community.

21. Alfarabi's (expansion of the Platonic) argument concerning innovation is not to be confused with any of the modern schools of historicism, which all rest on the assumption that there is not a hierarchy of human ends. Rather, if ends are permanent but the character of members of a community changes over time, then law must be altered to continue to aim for the same mark.

22. It is useful to recall that in discourse 6.2-3 Alfarabi describes the need for the legislator to somehow "contrive" (*ḥîlah*) the acceptance of "those regimes and that order [*tartîb*]."

23. See above, chapter 4.

24. For a discussion of the Athenian's play on words here—the term *nomoi* refers both to laws and to a kind of sung poetry—see Pangle's n. 21 to bk. 7 (and its reference in turn to n. 26 of bk. 4).

25. I prefer this rendering of *kalâm* to Mahdi's rendering of it as "statements," because it is more consistent with its rendering elsewhere. Furthermore, it draws our attention to a kinship between the *mutakallim* and the poet that I will discuss later.

26. In chapter 9, I will discuss only the first part of this "digression" (800b5-803e4), which is summarized in discourse 7.7-8.

27. As I have suggested above, the Athenian's discussion of legal innovation appears primarily as a discussion of innovation in games, music, and "laws." The Athenian is so successful in concealing the implications of his discussion for law proper that Druart has suggested that discourse 7 summarizes not bk. 7 of the *Laws* but the discussion on innovation in bk. 6 at 769a8 ff., which is a far more explicit discussion of *legal* innovation than the present passage in bk. 7.

28. See Leo Strauss, *Persecution and the Art of Writing* (Glencoe, Ill.: The Free Press, 1952; reprint, Chicago: University of Chicago Press, 1980), 128-31. And contrast Alfarabi's usage here of "natural tradition" with, for instance, Thomas Aquinas's view that all human beings possess a knowledge of certain principles of practical intellect.

Chapter 8. The Rule of Law and Good Breeding

1. Note that Alfarabi is silent about this enslavement to the laws and the gods or God (disc. 3.14 and 15). This could mean one or more of three things: (1) Alfarabi understands Plato's view on the enslavement to the laws, etc. to be negative despite the Athenian's praise of it, (2) he is reducing the role of the gods even more than Plato does because he is a more rationalistic thinker than is Plato, or (3) he sees no need to emphasize the virtues of enslavement to the laws, etc., because his community as a monotheistic community needs no encouragement to subordinate itself more to God (cf. Maimonides, *Guide*, 1.31 [34b]). I am inclined to believe that only the first and third interpretations are likely in light of my general working assumption that one should first try to understand deviations in the *Summary* from the *Laws* as adjustments by Alfarabi of Plato's teaching to his own time and place.

2. Strauss, *What is Political Philosophy?*, 149.

3. Alfarabi, *Kitâb al-ḥurûf*, ed. Mahdi, para. 63, (p. 98, line 19).

4. Here I mean "legislation" in the broader sense that includes both the laws and their preludes. As I will show, "good breeding" is the product of the preludes rather than of the laws proper.

5. See Strauss, *What is Political Philosophy?*, 148–49.

6. See Strauss, *Argument*, 22–23.

7. This definition of the education of the perfect human being should also be compared with the definition of the education of the perfect citizen at 643e6. This latter definition will be discussed in chapter 10.

8. For the possible alternate reading of *ḥilm* as *ḥukm* with *L*, see Druart's n. 4 to discourse 2.1.

9. *Ta'dîb* should be rendered "discipline" to be consistent with the translation used in discourse 5. For example, see discourse 5.4.

10. Strauss has identified this "relativist" opinion as the opinion that ultimately displaces what he calls the "Dorian law of laws" that allows for bad laws to be inspected and revised by the old (Strauss, *Argument*, 10–11 and 31). The belief in this opinion is what makes the ruling citizens, especially such as Megillus, resistant to altering the laws.

11. The awkwardness of "knowledges" (as opposed to "opinions") to the ear of the English reader, I believe, is not an accident. The existence of an opinion on a subject implies the existence of other opinions on the same subject in the same respect, whereas knowledge on a subject does not imply the existence of other "knowledges" of the same subject in the same respect.

12. Alfarabi seems to be alluding by the term *ijtimâ'* to what is frequently rendered as "consensus" in English, *ijmâ'*, which is the consensus of opinion among those learned in the religious sciences (*'ulamâ'*).

13. It is useful to note here that in the *Summary* Alfarabi never uses the term *ta'aqqul*, the term he uses as the equivalent of *phronêsis*, for instance, in the *Aphorisms*—where he seems to mean by it what Aristotle means by *phronêsis*. See Galston, *Politics and Excellence*, 77.

14. The notion that there is more than one understanding of the virtues in the *Laws* is perhaps most obvious in the suggestion that the rulers and the ruled have dif-

ferent virtues, which is implicit in the Athenian's list of worthy titles to rule and be ruled and Alfarabi's two lists of titles to rule and titles to be ruled. Thomas Pangle has probably been most straightforward in asserting the existence of a multiplicity of versions of the virtues in the *Laws*. See his "Interpretive Essay" in his translation, p. 426.

15. The Muslim reader of the *Summary* is likely to think of the Islamic usage of the term "tradition" (*sunnah*) to refer to the accounts of the life of the Prophet, Muhammad, which are said to have been received from his Companions. "Tradition" even in this specifically Islamic sense does not merely mean the exemplary behavior of the Prophet. It means exemplary behavior that can be used as a legal guideline. A "tradition" once recorded as a *ḥadīth* and accepted as authoritative in one of the schools of jurisprudence becomes a part of the sources of *fiqh*, jurisprudence.

It appears that Alfarabi has a broader understanding of "tradition" in mind. He first uses "traditions" in discourse 2.1(b) to refer to those things that had been sustained by the unchanging ancient Egyptian musical forms. Perhaps the most revealing usage of "tradition" is in discourse 3.2(c). There Alfarabi uses "traditions" to refer to those prelegal customs possessed by the members of the patriarchally ruled *dunasteiai*. The Athenian refers to as (1) "ancestral laws" (*patrioi nomoi*) (680a7), (2) "customs" (*ethê*) (681b), and finally, as viewed against the background of the overarching law that combines the best of the customs of the various *dunasteiai*, (3) "customs" (*nomima*) (681c5). Cf. the usage of "ancient traditions" (*sunan qadīmah*) in discourse 3.16 and 9.7. Here "tradition" seems to include music as an aspect of custom indistinguishable from what one might call, with the potential of being misleading, the legal aspect of custom.

Also see chapter 4, section 1, where the so-called "king of the tradition" is discussed. There the traditional is linked with the written, viz., the unchanging.

16. See 700c5–8.

17. For a discussion of Alfarabi's eventual abandonment of the distinction between citizen and stranger, especially in discourses 7 and 8, see above chapter 5.

18. See 850b.

19. The motivation of the spirited man's anger is his conviction that all things are self-moved and thus responsible for their own actions. Socrates' view that human beings act unjustly involuntarily reflects his view that human beings are drawn "erotically" toward what they believe to be good. This conflict between the spirited and erotic views of human existence is writ large or theologically in bk. 10. Of course, Alfarabi is silent about this. In a passage I am unable to cover in this study, however, he addresses in strictly human terms the spirited man's attribution of responsibility—in a discussion of the voluntary and involuntary in discourse 9.8–10.

20. The Athenian's shift from spirited "man" (while discussing punishment of others) to spirited "human being" (while discussing self-punishment or restraint) may be intended to suggest that although men and women are equally capable of experiencing spiritedness, men are better suited, if only by virtue of physical strength, to acting as the executors of punishment.

21. Indeed, the Athenian merely makes two obscure references to the personal daimon of the spirited person (732c4 and c6) and one reference to "the god" (*ton theon*) (732d) rather than the gods.

22. Also see 688b7–c2: The human being who lacks "intelligence" should not pray. Note that in this passage "intelligence," as I have shown earlier in this chapter, is

indistinguishable from the consonance between the "opinion" about what pleasures and pains are just and the decent human being's experience of pleasure and pain, and thus from "good breeding."

Chapter 9. Pleasure and Indignation

1. In this chapter, I will use the term "Dorian" at times rather loosely to refer not only to the Spartan community but also to the Cretan. (At other times, for instance when discussing Megillus, I sometimes use it to refer only to his Spartan community.) Of course, Cretans were not Dorians. There is, however, significant common ground between the Spartans and Cretans. Above all, Spartan law was modeled after the Cretan law. Consequently, citizens of the two communities share many customs in common, relative abstinence from wine drinking and promotion of homosexual relations among men. I use the term "Dorian" for the lack of another term that refers accurately to both Spartans and Cretans.

A good indicator of how much the Cretan and Lacedaemonian regimes have in common is the fact that when the Athenian offers a thumbnail sketch of Kleinias's own Cretan city, Knossos, it could just as well be a sketch of Megillus's Sparta (666e–67a7).

2. The basis of Megillus's disgust is that the kind of behavior that accompanies wine drinking at festivals is punishable by Spartan law. Cf. Kleinias's condemnation of wine drinking as the cause of "complete degradation" (*apasan phauloteta*) (646b7). Kleinias's condemnation is based less on a fear of punishment than on disdain. As we saw in the previous chapter, the fear of punishment is characteristic of the morality of shame rather than the morality of indignation.

3. Cf. discourse 4.18(c) where the "divine" is the orderly or regular, if not the strictly limited.

4. Note that "this education" is of the perfect human being rather than citizen. For the latter education, see the previous chapter.

5. Cf. the explicit exclusion of all "other" forms of tragedy than the one presented in the *Laws* in a passage Alfarabi does not summarize (817a4–d8).

6. See Cephalus's deeds and speeches in the opening pages of the *Republic.*

7. The *Laws of Plato*, translated with notes and interpretive essay by Thomas L. Pangle (Chicago: University of Chicago Press, 1988, reprinted by permission of Basic Books), 482.

8. For an example of the contrast between "citizen" and "ruler" as equivalent to the distinction between "ruler" and "ruled" in Alfarabi's, as opposed to Plato's, parlance, see discourse 8.3.

9. Alfarabi does not summarize the Athenian's description of the war games at 829e9–31b10, although he briefly summarizes the description of gymnastic at 832e–33e in discourse 8.4.

10. Which virtues Alfarabi has in mind is somewhat ambiguous. The passage refers to "the virtues through or accompanying combat" (*al-faḍâ'il bi-l-jihâd*). One could translate *bi* either as rendering combat the instrument of the virtues, as Mahdi does, or perhaps in the least derivative sense as "with" in the sense of "accompanying." However

one translates *bi*, it is likely that Alfarabi has, above all, courage in mind, but especially in light of his use of the plural one cannot exclude the possibility that he has other virtues in mind as well. Of course, combat would also contribute to the cultivation of bodily strength, one of the excellences Alfarabi describes as a "human virtue" in discourse 1.7.

11. Strauss, *Argument*, 120.

12. Contrast in the *Symposium* Socrates' sobriety in spite of having drunk a great deal (215e) with Alcibiades' drunkenness (212d).

13. Pangle appears to have introduced the term "ordinances" in the absence of an obvious antecedent for *duoin* (841d).

14. Thus, the Athenian acknowledges that wine can loosen constraints on anger (645d7, 649b6). In other words, wine has an affect on anger similar to the affect it has on desires: it intensifies them. But, of course, the effects of wine are opposed in the two cases.

15. Leo Strauss, "Plato," in L. Strauss and J. Cropsey, eds., *History of Political Philosophy*, 3d ed. (Chicago: University of Chicago Press, 1987), 87.

Chapter 10. Poetry and Inquiry into Law

1. As I noted in chapter 1, "dialectic" appears to coincide with the dialectical inquiry into the purpose of the law's roots or political science. "Discussion" is, of course, *kalâm*. Note that even dialectic here appears to be somewhat lacking in probity.

2. Alfarabi frequently uses certain other terms and phrases to open his paragraphs with great frequency. I should note that Mahdi also renders *'amad* (disc. 1.4; 7. 10 and 12) and *qaṣad* (disc. 1.17, within the body of the paragraph) as "to turn."

3. Cf. the identification of songs as "characteristic of men" (*arrenôpon*) when they incline to "courage" (*andreian*) and "characteristic of women" (*thêlugenesteron*) when they incline to the "orderly" (*kosmion*) (802e12–803a).

4. Cf. *Laws*, 719d7 and my discussion of it later, especially in n.5.

5. It may be worth noting that the Athenian in his general prelude prescribed the "most moderate" (*hê sôphronestatê kallistê* [717d8]) rather than the medium-sized funeral. It is not self-evident that the Athenian meant "medium-sized" when he spoke of the "most moderate" funeral. Perhaps Kleinias, as the courageous man's proponent, interprets the Athenian's reference to "most moderate" to mean one thing in all settings, "the medium size."

6. For example, the sacrificial laws of the Bible acknowledge that poor people should be expected only to sacrifice smaller, cheaper animals.

7. Note that here the Athenian does not entertain the even more problematic difference between different (psychological) types of people, such as the different kinds of artisans whose pleasures conflict. Nevertheless, his reference to gender differences alludes to the problem posed by the law's aiming ultimately in all things, even in the laws concerning women, at the promotion of the courageous man's way of life.

8. On the use of "we" to refer to Alfarabi as opposed to Plato, see *What is Political Philosophy?*, 143.

9. Whether as a result of the influence of an Alexandrian classification of the sciences or not, Alfarabi, unlike Aristotle, includes "poetics" and "rhetoric" in the *Organon.* (See the questions and answers appended to Mahdi, "Science, Philosophy, and Religion in Alfarabi's *Enumeration of the Sciences.*") By including these arts among the logical arts or sciences, Alfarabi seems to imply that these arts are intimately bound up with science in a way that, for instance, the law's command, which is subrhetorical and subpoetic, is not.

10. The classic example of the poet's confusion of philosophic indifference to certain pleasures with asceticism is Aristophanes' *Clouds.* Two noteworthy nonpoets who have also subscribed to this view are Muḥammad b. Zakariyyah al-Râzi and Nietzsche (see Leo Strauss's *Socrates and Aristophanes,* introduction and conclusion).

Strauss's description of the relation between the poet's way of life and the philosopher's way of life (cited earlier in part) is worth citing (in full): "Accordingly the wisdom of the Platonic Socrates is superior to the wisdom of the poets: The truth discerned by the poets must be integrated into the all-comprehensive truth with which the philosopher is concerned; or the true knowledge of the souls, and hence of the soul, is the core of the cosmology (of the knowledge of the things aloft)." Leo Strauss, *Socrates and Aristophanes,* 314.

Conclusion

1. *Apology* 19a–e.

2. Of course, Heidegger's denial of the existence of human nature is not unprecedented. Nevertheless, one wonders whether his particular denial goes hand in hand with his focus on the more-humble forms of human action and his neglect of politics. Perhaps this focus cuts off his access to philosophy as the natural way of life. By focusing on the more-humble forms of action, he fails to detect the existence of a natural hierarchy among the ways of life—ranging from the more-humble forms of action through political action to philosophic activity. Of course, providing evidence of this conjecture is beyond the purview of this study.

BIBLIOGRAPHY

Primary Sources by Plato and Alfarabi

Alfarabi. *Alfarabi's Philosophy of Plato and Aristotle.* (*Attainment of Happiness*, the *Philosophy of Plato*, and the *Philosophy of Aristotle.*) Translated with an introduction by Muhsin Mahdi. New York: The Free Press of Glencoe, 1962; revised edition, Ithaca: Cornell Paperbacks, 1969. *Taḥṣîl al-sa'âdah.* Hyderabad: n.p., A.H. 1345 *De Platonis Philosophia.* Edited by F. Rosenthal and R. Walzer. London: Warburg Institute, 1943.

——. *Aphorisms of the Statesman.* Edited and translated by D. M. Dunlop. Cambridge: Cambridge University Press, 1961. *Fuṣûl muntaza'ah.* [Selected Aphorisms.] (More complete Arabic version) edited by Fauzi Najjar. Beirut: Dâr al-Machreq, 1971.

——. *Book of Letters.* In an unpublished translation by Muhsin Mahdi supplied by Muhsin Mahdi in 1991. *Kitâb al-ḥurûf.* Edited by Muhsin Mahdi. Beirut: Dâr al-Machreq, 1969.

——. *Book of Religion.* In an unpublished translation by Charles Butterworth supplied by Muhsin Mahdi in 1991. *Kitâb al-millah wa-nuṣûṣ ukhrâ.* Edited by Muhsin Mahdi. Beirut: Dâr al-Machreq, 1968.

——. *Enumeration of the Sciences.* Chapter 5. Translated by Mushin Mahdi. In *Medieval Political Philosophy*, ed. Ralph Lerner and Muhsin Mahdi, 22–30. Glencoe, Ill.: The Free Press, 1963. *Iḥṣâ' al-'ulûm.* Edited by Osman Amine. 2d ed. Cairo: Dâr al-Fikr al-Arabî, 1949. And 3d ed. Cairo: The Anglo-Egyptian Library, 1968.

——. *The Harmonization of the Opinions of the Two Sages: Plato, the Divine, and Aristotle.* In an unpublished translation by Fauzi M. Najjar supplied by Charles Butterworth in 1986.

——. *Maqâlah fî aghrâḍ mâ ba'da al-ṭabî'ah.* [On the purposes of Aristotle's *Metaphysics*]. In *Tis' rasâ'il,* risâlah 2. Hyderabad: n.p., 1926.

——. *Political Regime.* The first half is in an unpublished translation by Miriam Galston supplied by Charles Butterworth in 1986. The second half is translated by Fauzi M. Najjar. In *Medieval Political Philosophy,* ed. Ralph Lerner and Muhsin Mahdi, 31-57. Glencoe, Ill.: The Free Press, 1963. *Al-Siyâsât al-madaniyyah.* Edited by Fauzi M. Najjar. Beirut: al-Maṭba'ah al-kâthûlîkiyyah, 1964.

——. *Alfarabi's Perfect State* (literally, *The Principles of the Opinions of the Citizens of the Virtuous City*). (*Mabâdi' ârâ' ahl al-madinah al-fâḍilah.*) Arabic text edited and English translation by Richard Walzer. Oxford: The Clarendon Press, 1985.

——. *Summary of the Laws.* In an unpublished translation by Muhsin Mahdi supplied by Muhsin Mahdi in 1991. *Le Sommaire du livre des "Lois" de Platon.* (*Jawâmi' kitâb al-nawâmîs li-Aflâṭûn.*) In a critical Arabic edition and with an introduction by Thérèse-Anne Druart forthcoming in *Bulletin d'Études Orientales* (Damascus), 47 (1995). Earlier edition: *Compendium Legum Platonis.* (*Talkhîṣ nawâmîs Aflâṭûn.*) Arabic text and Latin translation by Francesco Gabrieli. London: Warburg Institute, 1952.

Plato. *Apology.* Translated by Thomas G. West and Grace Starry West. In *Four Texts on Socrates: Plato's "Euthyphro," "Apology," and "Crito" and Aristophanes' "Clouds."* Ithaca: Cornell University Press, 1984.

——. *The Laws of Plato.* Translated with notes and an interpretive essay by Thomas L. Pangle. Chicago: University of Chicago Press, 1988 reprinted by permission of Basic Books (1980). (Greek text.) *Platon oeuvres complètes.* Edited by É. des Places. Vols. 11-12, *Les Lois.* Paris: Société d'édition "Les belles lettres," 1976. (Philological commentary.) *The Laws of Plato.* Edited and with commentary by E. B. England. 2 vols. Manchester: Manchester University Press, 1921.

——. *Minos.* Translated by Thomas L. Pangle. In *The Roots of Political Philosophy: Ten Forgotten Socratic Dialogues,* edited by Thomas Pangle. Ithaca: Cornell University Press, 1987. *Minos.* Loeb Classical Library edition. Vol. 12. Cambridge, Mass.: Harvard University Press, 1937; reprinted 1979.

——. *Parmenides.* Translated by R. E. Allen. Minneapolis: University of Minnesota Press, 1983.

——. *Republic.* Translated by Allan Bloom. New York: Basic Books, 1968.

Republic. Loeb Classical Library edition. Vols. 5 and 6. Cambridge: Harvard University Press, 1930; revised edition 1938; reprinted 1978.

——. *Statesman*. Translated and with commentary by Seth Benardete. In *The Being of the Beautiful: Plato's Theaetetus, Sophist, and Statesman*. Chicago: University of Chicago Press, 1984. *Politicus*. Loeb Classical Library edition. Vol. 8. Cambridge: Harvard University Press, 1925; reprinted 1975.

——. *Timaeus*. Loeb Classical Library edition. Vol. 9. Cambridge: Harvard University Press, 1929; reprinted 1981.

Other Primary Sources

Aquinas, Thomas. *Summa Theologiae*. 60 vols. Translated by the Blackfriars. New York: McGraw-Hill, 1968.

Aristotle. *Metaphysics*. Loeb Classical Library edition. 2 vols. Translated by Hugh Tredennick. London: William Heinemann, 1933.

——. *Politics*. Loeb Classical Library edition. Translated by H. Rackham. London: William Heinemann, 1932.

——. *Rhetoric*. Loeb Classical Library edition. Translated by John Henry Reese. Cambridge: Harvard University Press, 1926; reprinted 1957.

Augustine. *City of God*. Translated by Marcus Dods. New York: Modern Library, 1950.

——. *Confessions*. Translated by R. S. Pine-Coffin. New York: Penguin Books, 1961.

Averroës. *Averroës on Plato's "Republic." (Commentary on the "Republic.")* Translated by Ralph Lerner. Ithaca: Cornell University Press, 1974

——. *Talkhîs al-khaṭâbah*. [Commentary on the *Rhetoric*.] Edited by Muḥammad Salîm Sâlim. Cairo: n.p., 1967.

Avicenna. *On the Division of the Rational Sciences*. Selections translated by Muhsin Mahdi. In *Medieval Political Philosophy*, ed. Ralph Lerner and Muhsin Mahdi, 95–97. Glencoe, Ill.: The Free Press, 1963.

Cicero. *De Res Publica* and *De Legibus*. Loeb Classical Library edition. Vol. 16. Cambridge: Harvard University Press, 1928; reprinted 1988.

Damascius. *La vie d'Isidore*. Translated by A.-Ed. Chaignet. In *Proclus, Commentaire sur la Parménide*, vol. 3. Paris: Ernest Leroux, 1903.

Derrida, Jacques. *Disseminations*. Translated by Barbara Johnson. Chicago: University of Chicago Press, 1981.

de Tocqueville, Alexis. *Democracy in America*. 2 volumes. Translated by Henry Reeve, revised by Francis Bowen. New York: Vintage Books, 1945.

Galen. *Compendium Timaei Platonis.* Edited by P. Kraus and R. Walzer. Corpus Platonicum Medii Aevi, no. 1. London: Warburg Institute, 1951.

Heidegger, Martin. *The Basic Problems of Phenomenology.* Translated by Albert Hofstadter. Bloomington: Indiana University Press, 1975.

——. *Being and Time.* Translated by John Macquarrie and Edward Robinson. Oxford: Basil Blackwell, 1973.

——. *Kant and the Problem of Metaphysics.* 4th ed., enlarged. Translated by Richard Taft. Bloomington and Indianapolis: Indiana University Press, 1990.

——. *Nietzsche.* Vol. 1, *The Will to Power as Art.* Translated by David Farrell Krell. San Francisco: HarperCollins, 1991.

——. *The Question of Being.* Translated by William Kluback and Jean T. Wilde. New Haven: College and University Press, 1958.

——. "Time and Being." Translated by Joan Stambaugh. In *On Time and Being.* New York: Harper and Row, 1972.

Ibn Bâjjah. *Governance of the Solitary.* Selected passages translated by Lawrence Berman. In *Medieval Political Philosophy,* ed. Ralph Lerner and Muhsin Mahdi, 122–33. Glencoe, Ill.: The Free Press, 1963. *Tadbîr al-mutawaḥḥid.* Edited by Miguel Asín Palacios. Madrid-Granada: n.p., 1946.

Ibn Ṭufayl. *Hayy Ibn Yaqzan.* Selected passages translated by George N. Atiyeh. In *Medieval Political Philosophy,* ed. Ralph Lerner and Muhsin Mahdi, 134–62. Glencoe, Ill.: The Free Press, 1963. *Ḥayy ben Yaqdhân.* Edited by Léon Gauthier. 2d edition. Beirut: n.p., 1936.

Julian, The Emperor. *The Works of Emperor Julian.* Loeb Classical Library edition. 2 vols. London: William Heinemann, 1913.

Maimonides. Fragment of the *Commentary on the Aphorisms of Hippocrates.* In an appendix to *Compendium Timaei Platonis,* 39. Edited by P. Kraus and R. Walzer. Corpus Platonicum Medii Aevi, no. 1. London: Warburg Institute, 1951.

——. *Le Guide des Égarés.* (*Dalâlat al-ḥâ'irîn*). [Guide of the perplexed.] Edited by S. Munk. 3 vols. Paris: Chez A. Franck, Libraire, 1856.

——. *Treatise on the Art of Logic.* Selections translated by Charles Butterworth in *Ethical Writings of Maimonides,* edited by Raymond L. Weiss with Charles Butterworth. New York: Dover Publications, 1975. *Al-Maqâlah fî ṣinâ'at al-manṭiq.* In "Maimonides' Arabic Treatise on Logic," in *Proceedings of the American Academy for Jewish Research,* vol. 34 (1966).

Sallustius. *Concerning the Gods and the Universe.* Translated by Arthur Darby Nock. Cambridge: Cambridge University Press, 1926.

Xenophon. *Memorabilia*. Loeb Classical Library edition. Vol. 4. Cambridge: Harvard University Press, 1923; reprinted 1979.

Secondary Sources

Armstrong, A. H. "St Augustine and Christian Platonism." In *Augustine: A Collection of Critical Essays*, ed. R. A. Markus, 3-37. New York: Anchor Books, 1972.

Badawî, 'Abdurraḥmân. "Al-Fârâbî." In *Histoire de la philosophie en Islam*, 478-575. Paris: Libraire Philosophique J. Vrin, 1972.

Barker, Ernest. *Greek Political Theory*. 5th edition. Strand, U.K.: Methuen, 1960.

Brown, Peter. *Augustine of Hippo: A Biography*. London: Faber & Faber, 1969.

Butterworth, Charles E. "Rhetoric and Islamic Political Philosophy." *International Journal of Middle East Studies* 3 (1972): 187-98.

Cairns, Huntington. *Legal Philosophies from Plato to Hegel*. Baltimore: Johns Hopkins University Press, 1949.

De Vaux, B. Carra. "Al-Fârâbî." In *Encyclopaedia of Islam*, 1st edition, 2:54. Leyden: E. J. Brill, 1927.

des Places, Édouard. "La tradition indirecte des *Lois* de Platon (livres I-VI)." In *Mélanges J. Saunier*, ed. P. Gardette, P. Gallay, and J. Molager, 27-40. Lyon: Bibiliothèque de la Faculté Catholique des Lettres de Lyon, 1944.

Dillon, John M. *The Middle Platonists*. London: Duckworth, 1977.

Druart, Thérèse-Anne. "Al-Farabi and Emanationism." In *Studies in Medieval Philosophy*, ed. John F. Wippel, 23-43. Studies in Philosophy and the History of Philosophy, no. 17. Washington, D.C.: Catholic University of America Press, 1987.

——. "Un sommaire du sommaire Farabien des *Lois* de Platon." *Bulletin de philosophie médiévale* 19 (1977): 43-45.

Fakhry, Majid. *A History of Islamic Philosophy*. 2d ed. London: Longman, 1983.

Frank, Richard M. "The Science of *Kalâm*." *Arabic Sciences and Philosophy* 2 (1992): 7-37.

Galston, Miriam. *Politics and Excellence: The Political Philosophy of Alfarabi*. Princeton: Princeton University Press, 1990.

——. "A Re-examination of al-Fârâbî's Neoplatonism." *Journal of the History of Philosophy* 15, no. 1 (January, 1977): 13-32.

Gellner, Ernest. *Reason and Culture*. Oxford: Basil Blackwell, 1992.

Gersh, Stephen. *Middle Platonism and Neoplatonism: The Latin Tradition*. 2 vols. Notre Dame, Ind.: University of Notre Dame Press, 1986.

Grandgeorge, L. *Saint Augustin et le neo-platonisme*. Vol. 8 in *Sciences réligieuses*. Paris: Bibliothèque de l'école des hautes études, 1896. Reprint, Frankfurt a.M.: Unveränderter Nachdruck, 1967.

Gutas, Dimitri. "Galen's Synopsis of Plato's *Laws* in Arabic." An unpublished article to be published by G. Fiaccadori supplied to me by the author on 21 March 1991.

Hall, Jerome. "Plato's Legal Philosophy." *Indiana Law Journal* 31, no. 2 (Winter 1956): 171-206.

Hall, Robert W. "Plato's Theory of Natural Law Revisited." An unpublished paper presented at the 1991 Midwest Political Science Association meetings, Chicago.

Jaeger, Werner. "Praise of Law." In *Interpretations of Modern Legal Philosophies*, ed. Paul Sayre, 352-75. New York: n.p., 1947.

Klibansky, Raymond. *The Continuity of the Platonic Tradition during the Middle Ages*. New York: n.p., 1982.

Kojève, Alexandre. "The Emperor Julian and His Art of Writing." In *Ancients and Moderns*, ed. Joseph Cropsey, 95-113. New York: Basic Books, 1964.

Kraemer, Joel. "The *Jihâd* of the *Falâsifa*." *Jerusalem Studies in Arabic and Islam* 10 (1987): 287-324.

Kraus, Paul. "Plotin chez les Arabes. Remarques sur un nouveau fragment de la paraphrase des *Ennéades*." *Bulletin de l'Institut d'Egypte* 23 (1941): 267-95.

Lerner, Ralph. "Beating the Neoplatonic Bushes." Review of *Alfarabi's Perfect State*, by Richard Walzer. *Journal of Religion* 67 (October 1987): 510-17.

Maguire, Joseph P. "Plato's Theory of Natural Law." In *Yale Classical Studies*, ed. Alfred Bellinger, 10: 151-78. New Haven: Yale University Press, 1942.

Mahdi, Muhsin. "Al-Fârâbî." In *Dictionary of Scientific Bibliography*, edited by C. C. Gillispie, 4:523-26. New York: Charles Scribners' Sons, 1971.

——. "Alfarabi against Philoponus." *Journal of Near Eastern Studies* 26, no. 4 (October, 1967): 233-59.

——. "Alfarabi on Philosophy and Religion." *Philosophical Forum* 4, no. 1 (1973): 1-25.

——. "Al-Fârâbî's Imperfect State." Review of *Alfarabi's Perfect State*, by Richard Walzer. *Journal of the American Oriental Society* 110, no. 4 (1990): 691-726.

——. "The *Editio Princeps* of Fârâbî's *Compendium Legum Platonis.*" *Journal of Near Eastern Studies* 20, no. 1 (January 1961): 1-24.

——. *Ibn Khaldun's Philosophy of History*. London: George Allen and Unwin, 1957.

——. "Orientalism and the Study of Islamic Philosophy." *Journal of Islamic Studies* 1 (1990): 73-98.

——. "Philosophy and Political Thought: Reflections and Comparisons." *Arabic Sciences and Philosophy* 1 (1991): 9-29.

——. "Science, Philosophy, and Religion in Alfarabi's *Enumeration of the Sciences.*" In *The Cultural Context of Medieval Learning*, ed. J. E. Murdoch and E. D. Sylla, 113-46. Boston Studies in the Philosophy of Science, no. 26. Dordrecht, Holland: D. Reidel, 1975.

Meyerhoff, Max. "From Alexandria to Baghdad." In an unpublished translation by Anton Heinen supplied by Muhsin Mahdi in 1992. "Von Alexandrien nach Baghdad." *Sitzungsberichte der Preussischen Akademie der Wissenschaften* 23 (1930): 389-429.

Morrow, Glenn R. "Plato and the Law of Nature." In *Essays in Political Theory Presented to George H. Sabine*, ed. Milton R. Konvitz and Arthur E. Murphy, 17-44. Ithaca: Cornell University Press, 1948.

Pangle, Thomas L. "The Political Psychology of Religion in Plato's *Laws.*" *American Political Science Review* 70, no. 4 (1976): 1059-77.

Parens, Joshua. "Theory and Practice in Medieval Aristotelianism." *Polity* 26, no. 2 (1993): 317-30.

Post, L. A. *The Vatican Plato and Its Relations*. Philological Monographs, no. 4. Middletown, Conn.: American Philological Association, 1934.

Schurmann, Reiner. *Heidegger on Being and Acting: From Principles to Anarchy*. Translated by Christine Marie Gros and Reiner Schurmann. Bloomington: Indiana University Press, 1990.

Solmsen, Friedrich. *Plato's Theology*. Ithaca: Cornell University Press, 1942.

Stern, S. M. Review of *Compendium Legum Platonis*, by Alfarabi. *Bulletin of the School of Oriental and African Studies, University of London* 17 (1955): 398.

Strauss, Leo. *The Argument and the Action of Plato's "Laws."* Chicago: University of Chicago Press, 1975.

——. "Farabi's Plato." In *Louis Ginzberg Jubilee Volume*, ed. Saul Lieberman, Shalom Spiegel, Solomon Zeitlin, and Alexander Marx, 357-93. New York: American Academy for Jewish Research, 1945.

——. *Liberalism, Ancient and Modern*. Ithaca: Cornell University Press, 1989.

——. *Natural Right and History*. Chicago: University of Chicago Press, 1953.

——. *Persecution and the Art of Writing.* New York: The Free Press, 1952; reprint, Chicago: University of Chicago Press, 1980.

——. *Philosophy and Law.* Translated by Fred Baumann. Philadelphia: Jewish Publication Society, 1987.

——. *Rebirth of Classical Political Rationalism.* Selected and introduced by Thomas Pangle. Chicago: University of Chicago Press, 1989.

——. *Socrates and Aristophanes.* Chicago: University of Chicago Press, 1966; Chicago: University of Chicago Press (Midway reprint), 1980.

——. *Studies in Platonic Political Philosophy.* Chicago: University of Chicago Press, 1983.

——. *Thoughts on Machiavelli.* Glencoe, Ill.: The Free Press, 1958.

——. *On Tyranny.* Revised and expanded edition by Victor Gourevitch and Michael S. Roth. New York: The Free Press, 1991.

——. *What is Political Philosophy?* Glencoe, Ill.: The Free Press, 1959; reprint, Chicago: University of Chicago Press, 1988.

Strauss, Leo, and Joseph Cropsey, eds. *The History of Political Philosophy.* 3d edition. Chicago: University of Chicago Press, 1987.

Striker, Gisela. "Origins of the Concept of Natural Law." Vol. 2 of *Proceedings of the Boston Area Colloquium in Ancient Philosophy,* ed. J. G. Cleary, 79-94. London: n.p., 1987.

Tardieu, Michel. "Ṣâbiens coraniques et 'Ṣâbiens' de Ḥarrân." *Journal Asiatique* 273, nos. 1-2 (1985): 1-44.

Voegelin, Eric. *Order and History.* Vol. 3 of *Aristotle and Plato.* Baton Rouge: Louisiana State University Press, 1957.

Walzer, Richard. "Al-Fârâbî." In *Encyclopaedia of Islam,* new edition, vol. 2, pt. 2, 779-81. Leiden: E. J. Brill, 1965.

Watt, W. Montgomery. Review of *Compendium Legum Platonis,* by Alfarabi. *Journal of the Royal Asiatic Society* 3-4 (1953): 160.

Wild, John. *Plato's Modern Enemies and the Theory of Natural Law.* Chicago: University of Chicago Press, 1953.

INDEX